009551049

D0121442

CONVERGENCE, COHESION AND INTEGRATION IN THE EUROPEAN UNION

Also by Robert Leonardi

ITALIAN CHRISTIAN DEMOCRACY:
The Politics of Dominance (*with Douglas A. Wertman*)

REGIONAL DEVELOPMENT IN AN INTEGRATING
EUROPEAN MARKET: The Case of Tuscany

THE GOVERNMENT AND POLITICS OF ITALY

THE INSTITUTIONALIZATION OF REGIONAL
GOVERNMENTS IN ITALY
(*with R. D. Putnam and R. Y. Nanetti*)

THE REGIONS AND THE EUROPEAN COMMUNITY: The
Impact of the Single Market on the Underdeveloped Areas

THE REGIONS AND EUROPEAN INTEGRATION:
The Case of Emilia Romagna

YEARBOOK OF ITALIAN POLITICS

Convergence, Cohesion and Integration in the European Union

Robert Leonardi

Jean Monnet Lecturer in European Union Politics and Policy, and
Director of the Economic and Social Cohesion
Laboratory of the European Institute
London School of Economics and Political Science

St. Martin's Press

First published in Great Britain 1995 by
MACMILLAN PRESS LTD
Houndmills, Basingstoke, Hampshire RG21 2XS
and London
Companies and representatives
throughout the world

A catalogue record for this book is available
from the British Library.

ISBN 0–333–62788–1

10   9   8   7   6   5   4   3   2   1
04   03   02   01   00   99   98   97   96   95

Printed and bound in Great Britain by
Ipswich Book Co. Ltd
Ipswich, Suffolk

———————————————————————————

First published in the United States of America 1995 by
Scholarly and Reference Division,
ST. MARTIN'S PRESS, INC.,
175 Fifth Avenue,
New York, N.Y. 10010

ISBN 0–312–12384–1

Library of Congress Cataloging-in-Publication Data
Leonardi, Robert, 1945–
Convergence, cohesion and integration in the European Union /
Robert Leonardi.
p.   cm.
Includes index.
ISBN 0–312–12384–1
1. Europe—Economic integration.   2. European federation.
I. Title.
HC241.L42   1995
337.1'4—dc20   94–31779
                                                  CIP

To Marcello and the challenge of the future

Contents

1 Cohesion in the European Union

INTRODUCTION

During the 1980s the goal of economic and social cohesion became an important part of the debate on economic convergence and political integration in the European Union (EU). The three concepts – convergence, cohesion and integration – have in the past been used in separate disciplines to study specific aspects of economic and political developments in Europe.[1] Now the three concepts can and must be used together to understand the underlying changes taking place in the structure of European society and political institutions. The discussion will focus on cohesion because that is the goal that has achieved prominence in the European debate and has been forcefully emphasised in the changes to the Rome Treaty following the Single European Act and the Maastricht Treaty.

In the latter, cohesion is mentioned as a central concern in achieving economic convergence and monetary union among the member states and regions of the EU. That concern has intensified as difficulties have mounted in maintaining exchange-rate stability in the European currency markets and in meeting the criteria for countries to become active participants in monetary union. Cohesion is defined in the 1985 Single European Act as 'reducing disparities between the various regions and the backwardness of the least-favoured regions' (Article 130a). Article 130c discusses the role of the European Regional Development Fund in helping to 'redress the principal regional imbalances in the Community through participating in the development and structural adjustment of regions whose development is lagging behind'.

The 1991 Maastricht Treaty reaffirmed the EU's commitment to cohesion, and the Delors II budget proposal, agreed in December 1992 at the Edinburgh Summit, carried with it a strong commitment to increase spending in the less developed member states by doubling the Structural Funds (Regional Fund, Social Fund and Agricultural Guidance Fund) and

1

creating a new Cohesion Fund to operate over the next six years. At Edinburgh the EU agreed to set aside 156 billion ECU at 1992 prices to promote socioeconomic cohesion and spur the development of the less favoured areas and countries.[2] The bulk of that amount, 141 billion ECU, is earmarked for the Structural Funds and the second round of Community Support Frameworks (CSFs),[3] while 15 billion ECU are destined for the new Cohesion Fund to promote European-wide transport networks and environmental projects.[4]

The rationale for EU spending on cohesion is provided by a variety of philosophical and practical considerations. In fact the most important reason for including cohesion as a primary EU goal is to achieve European integration – that is, treating the EU as the embryo of a greater European political union.[5] Cohesion in the context of European integration implies commitment on the part of the member states to the principle of mutual solidarity and the belief that collective action through a partnership between the EU and national/regional/local governments can play an important part in improving economic and social conditions. Cohesion is thus dependent on a belief in the possibility that European economies can converge – that is, move toward similar levels of development and social well-being. To achieve these goals, the EU needs to undertake a serious programme to promote factor mobility so that capital, technology and skills will flow to the less developed areas, helping them eventually to achieve self-sustaining growth.

Cohesion would be a less compelling goal if the EU were to be conceived only as a free-market area where economic forces alone determine the flow of investments, the structure of production, the distribution of purchasing power and the level of consumption, and where no higher political goals are posited.[6] Instead, for the EU the pursuit of cohesion represents a clear and strong commitment to the principle of solidarity, or a 'community of interests', on the part of the more developed states in favour of the poorer and peripheral areas (Taylor, 1983, p.167). Low levels of development imply greater difficulty in locally providing the funding sources to finance the growth programmes needed to reduce the gap between the most-and least-favoured areas in the EU.

Given that less developed areas are generally characterised

by a scarcity of skilled labour and inedequate capital supplies and infrastructure (roads, railways, airports, communications, energy supplies and so on), since the early 1980s the more developed EU countries have been willing to commit extensive resources, through EU institutions and programmes, to help finance development projects designed to increase the ability of poorer areas to engage in endogenous and self-sustaining forms of economic development. For example, in 1990 the most developed area in the EU (Hamburg) had five times the level of development of the poorest area (Alentejo in Portugal). Without substantial help from the EU it is difficult to imagine how Alentejo could ever develop itself and reduce the gap between the real and potential development prospects that separate its economic future from that of Hamburg.

Commitment to the goal of cohesion negates the view that regional development aid from the EU to member states and underdeveloped regions constitutes a 'side-payment', as argued by Marks (1992, pp. 194–204), to mollify the divergent interests of the less developed states vis-à-vis the interests of the developed ones. As will be argued below, the empirical prospects for cohesion are posited on economic convergence taking place. Underdevelopment is thus conceived by the EU as a temporary rather than a permanent economic condition afflicting the less developed regions and states. According to this perspective the Structural Funds policy represents an *economic policy*, designed to spur economic development, and not a *social policy* that will raise levels of consumption without changing the basic structural characteristics of peripheral and depressed economies.[7]

Among the drafters of the 1957 Rome Treaty, the expectation was that the problem of economic underdevelopment would be solved by the trickle-down effect of overall development of the Common Market, making it unnecessary to adopt proactive policies.[8] As a consequence, the Rome Treaty foresaw the creation of the Social Fund to spur labour migration and training, and the European Investment Bank to help finance infrastructure projects in the less developed parts of the Common Market.

Belief that substantial convergence of regional and national economies could be achieved in the short to medium term began quickly to erode in the 1960s (Barzanti, 1965), and by the 1970s confidence in a purely market solution to the problem of regional development and economic and social convergence gave way to a more active role on the part of European institutions (Pinder, 1983). In 1974 the European Regional Development Fund was set up to provide support for national development programmes. During the first half of the 1980s the EC initiated a series of experiments in Naples and Belfast in an attempt to define a more dynamic and effective socio-economic development policy through the principles of planning (that is, EC development aid must be part of an overall development plan) and coordination, requiring coordination of the activities of the three Structural Funds when operating in the same geographic area.[9] The results from these experiments were subsequently introduced into the formulation and implementation of the Integrated Mediterranean Programmes (1987–92) and the first round of the Community Support Frameworks (1989–93). Following the publication of the Thomson (1973) and MacDougall (1977) reports (CEC, 1973 and 1977), it became clear that the success of development policies and attempts at regional planning were strongly linked to the size of allocated financial resources as well as to their efficient use in mobilising endogenous resources and self-sustaining forms of local development.

The goal of cohesion also concerns the more practical problems facing member states and regions in the periphery of the EU in participating in economic and monetary integration (Mitsos, 1993). Past efforts by the EC with regard to regional policy and aid to structural change in the less developed regions involved an attempt to achieve a better allocation of resources, ensure the spread of welfare gains throughout the Community, and equalise the conditions needed for the production of goods and services through a sustained convergence dynamic. Key to the latter was reducing production-factor differences between core and less developed regions through an equalisation of their physical (infrastructure, communication links, transportation facilities) and human (education and skills of workforce) capital attributes. Thus the EC clearly rejected the conception of regional policy as a social policy based on the transfer of wealth from rich to poor areas to subsidise personal incomes and offset existing inequalities in levels of consumption.

An integral part of the creation of the Single Market and the move toward European monetary integration is that integration should be beneficial to all. As expressed by Doyle (1989, p. 79), the stronger economies in the EU should not be permitted to pick and choose those elements of economic and monetary integration that they like 'and disregard the rest'. At the same time it is recognised by many observers that, during the process of economic convergence and monetary integration, the peripheral economies of Europe will be faced with the more serious structural adjustments. The EU must be ready to provide underdeveloped areas with increasing financial resources to enable them to tackle both existing problems and the economic dislocation that will manifest itself as the EU moves toward an increasingly integrated market.[10]

The weaker national economies will have to make two types of adjustment in preparing for eventual economic and monetary integration. The first involves changes in macroeconomic policies to meet the criteria contained in the Maastricht Treaty concerning the convergence of European economies in preparation for European Monetary Union (EMU). The 1991 Treaty stipulates that, to participate as a full partner in the final stages of EMU, national economies must meet convergence criteria involving the size of budget deficits (at levels of 60 per cent of GDP) and levels of inflation and interest rates (a maximum of, respectively, 1.5 per cent and 2 per cent above the 'three best performing member-states in terms of price stability' – House of Commons, 1992, p. 112).

If member states do not meet these criteria they will have to reduce their budgetary deficits through reductions in government spending and social provision. In practical terms this means that EMU will have a second major impact on the meso (regional) economic policy of member states – budgetary contraints will force national governments to reduce their funding of extensive investment projects at the national, regional and local level.[11] Thus, in the run-up to EMU the less-developed states in the EU are faced with a contradictory situation. On the one hand, they have to reduce national spending and the size of the public deficit to meet EMU convergence criteria. On the other hand, they are expected and encouraged to converge toward the stronger European economies – if they want to reap the full benefits arising from the creation of a common European currency and a central bank system – in the absence of substantial investment programmes and without being allowed to manipulate of exchange rates to encourage exports.[12]

An additional factor in the creation of an active EU regional policy is provided by the expectation that economic integration will produce more positive benefits for the stronger central economies of Europe than for the weaker peripheral ones. In 1989 the Delors Report on EMU stated that, without a proactive Community policy, the less developed countries may prove to be net losers from the integration process:

> Historical experience suggests . . . that in the absence of countervailing policies, the overall impact on peripheral regions could be negative. Transport costs and economies of scale would tend to favour a shift in economic activity away from less developed regions, especially if they were at the periphery of the Community, to the highly developed areas at its centre. The economic and monetary union would have to encourage and guide structural adjustment which would help poorer regions to catch up with the wealthier ones (CEC, 1989, p. 22).

Without access to additional EU resources to finance development projects, the poorer states will find themselves squeezed between the needs of budgetary discipline and spurring economic development, to the detriment of their future internal economic growth. As participants in monetary union, national governments will not be able to manipulate exchange rates, as was the case in the past, to influence international trade flows by encouraging the export of domestic products while limitating imports. To compensate for the lack of national adjustment measures in the Single Market and EMU convergence process, the EU has set aside ever-larger amounts to assist member states to reduce the gap between their level of development and that of the rest of the EU (European Parliament, 1991).

Apart from the political considerations of EU solidarity and the restrictions imposed on member states as part of the EMU convergence criteria, there remains the simple empirical question of whether convergence, translated into a future expectation of cohesion being achieved in regional and national economies, is in reality an abstract political principle designed to buy the consensus of poorer nation-states with respect to European economic integration, or whether it constitutes a real and practical goal that can be achieved in the medium to long term.[13] In both academic and policy-oriented literature on development the prospect of sustaining convergence and finally arriving at cohesion has never been evaluated or tested. Most surprisingly though, the EU has not carried out thorough and systematic evaluations of its regional-development expenditure programmes, despite the extensive resources that have been poured into development projects.[14] Single projects in individual countries have been evaluated, but the EU has not been able to come up with a uniform and comprehensive instrument to measure the socioeconomic impact of investment projects, nor has it empirically faced the question of whether its regional-development policy has spurred convergence since the 1970s.

The first round of the Community Support Frameworks (CSFs) were financed to the tune of 63 billion ECU (at 1988 prices) and the Integrated Mediterranean Programmes (IMPs) had a budget of 6.6 billion ECU (at 1986 prices) for projects in the Mediterranean areas of France, Italy and Greece (Bianchi, 1993; Papageorgiou and Verney, 1993). The latter projects were designed to ease market adjustments in response to the entry of Portugal and Spain into the EC, but it remains to be seen whether the IMPs did in fact aid structural adjustment in the agricultural sector and stimulate the development of alternative economic activities (Plaskovitis, 1993).

In the past the EC's evaluation exercises have been mainly focused on whether the money allocated has been spent as expected (that is, on the projects intended and during the timespan stipulated) rather than on evaluating the economic impact of the IMPs at the local level. The issue of whether the IMPs have in fact helped local economies to adjust their production strategies away from traditional products and toward new economic vistas has never been seriously addressed. A similar shortcoming is present in the unsystematic and uneven work carried out in evaluating the impact of the funds spent by the CSFs.[15] It remains to be seen whether the 6.6 billion ECU spent on IMPs and the 63 billion spent on CSFs have indeed improved the prospect of reducing regional and national socioeconomic disparities in the EU or whether the situation has been made even worse by inculcating a dependence mentality and stymieing endogenous and self-generated forms of development.[16]

Such considerations are important not just to academics concerned with the theoretical implications of publicly financed development efforts vis-à-vis private-market solutions; they also involve fundamental aspects of the EU integration process. Evaluations of the impact of EU regional and structural adjustment policies go to the heart of the concern about whether the EU can continue to retain the process of economic convergence and the goal of cohesion as fundamental aspects of the European decision-making process involving economic and social affairs. The dynamics of convergence and the prospects for cohesion also impact on the practical issue of whether government policies do produce positive economic outcomes or whether governments would achieve better results by not intervening in the distribution of economic factors.

The next round of increases in the funding of development projects has already been decided – the decision was made in Edinburgh and Copenhagen to double Structural Fund assistance (CEC, 1993b). However it is important for the EU as a whole to understand the positive or negative impact of past efforts on development in the poorer regions. What is at stake in the second CSF phase, to run from 1994 and 1999, is the credibility of the EU's regional development efforts, the continued commitment to the cohesion goals set out in the Single European Act and the Maastricht Treaty, the expenditure of increasingly large portions of the EU budget to reduce the gap between developed and underdeveloped parts of the EU, and the belief that the EU can tackle and resolve problems within the context of economic and political integration that have in the past eluded national governments.

The objective of this volume is to look in detail at the literature on economic and political integration and at data on economic convergence in EU member-states from 1950–91 in order to evaluate a series of crucial points concerning the prospect of economic convergence and its impact on political integration in Europe. These considerations involve:

– The historical record of development in Europe. Have national and regional economies converged in Europe during the postwar period or have differences increased?

– The future prospects for cohesion within nation-states. Can cohesion be achieved at both national and regional levels or do national and regional economic realities necessarily diverge?
– The convergence of policy sectors and productivity. Is Europe witnessing a convergence in national and subnational government policy approaches and outcomes?
– The evolving institutional architecture of the EU. Is the EU undergoing institutional and political change as a means of reinforcing economic convergence and as a spur to socio-economic cohesion?

To answer these questions a series of hypotheses have been formulated, based on the empirical record of convergence and divergence of national and regional-level economies in the postwar world. The conclusions from this analysis will then be used to (1) formulate an alternative model of European integration based on a more general thesis of political, economic and social convergence in Europe; (2) discuss in greater detail the consequences of integration; and (3) evaluate the prospect of achieving the cohesion goals set out in the Single European Act and the Maastricht Treaty and of using regional policy as a lever to advance the process of European integration. The volume concludes with an analysis of networking in the EU, a new approach to integration and state-building that is being implemented by EU institutions and a variety of public- and private-sector actors across Europe.

THE MOTIVATIONS BEHIND EUROPEAN INTEGRATION: NEOFUNCTIONALIST EXPLANATIONS AND THE MARKET

Since its inception in the 1951 Paris Treaty with the creation of the European Coal and Steel Community (ECSC), European integration has been oriented toward the creation of more than just a free-trade area (Lichtheim, 1963; Urwin, 1991). Political goals as well as economic ones were important in both the initial ECSC and the subsequent 1957 Rome Treaty, which created the European Common Market. The signatories of the Paris and Rome treaties had as one of their most significant goals the modification of the existing nation-state system in Europe. The reasons behind this orientation can be found in the shortcomings manifested by the nation-state system in Europe during the previous decades. Emphasis on the prerogatives of the nation-state had promoted instability in interstate relations to the point of bringing Europe to the edge of destruction during the First and Second World Wars, and the focus on the rights of nations and the uncompromising interpretation of national sovereignty had proven to be inadequate in protecting local interests in response to international economic competition. As a consequence, the nation-state system had the effect of reducing the role of European states to one of subordination to outside powers and weakening the role of Europe in the world economy. The only way of recapturing Europe's traditional role in world affairs was by uniting its forces through a process of economic and political integration.

Students of European integration have puzzled for a long time over why the European states have ceased to be wholly sovereign and 'why they voluntarily mingle, merge, and mix with their neighbors so as to lose the factual attributes of sovereignty while acquiring new techniques for resolving conflict between themselves' (Haas, 1971, p. 6).[17] The theoretical underpinnings of the neofunctionalist approach to European integration was focused on the attempt to understand, on the one hand, the political motivations and, on the other, the political impact of integration on nation-state systems. From the outset, neofunctionalists believed that European integration not only created supranational political institutions but also altered the functioning of existing national institutions. In this manner, the dynamic of integration was conceived as a longitudinal process that had to be studied over time by focusing on the creation of decision-making centres at the European level, while simultaneously looking at the changes taking place in the loci and at the methods used to resolve sector-specific policy issues.[18] Other approaches to European integration, such as functionalism and regime theory, have been less sensitive to the longitudinal change taking place at the two levels of national and supranational institutions.

INCREMENTALISM AND INTERGOVERNMENTALISM

From the late 1950s to the mid-1970s the objective of neofunctionalist theory was, firstly, to understand the motivation and process by which new political institutions were created at the European level, and secondly to map the convergence of existing, national decision-making systems (Lindberg, 1963). Working within the context of the provisions of the Rome Treaty on the Common Market, neofunctionalism emphasised process (incremental growth) rather than state-building in changing the structure and substance of decision making on economic and social policies.[19] The stress was on practical solutions to functional problems – that is, uncontroversial economic and social issues that could be more effectively resolved at an intergovernmental rather than a strictly national level. This provided the outputs to feed the process of integration and moved it from one functional area to another.[20] Institutional change was introduced into the system by a piecemeal process of shifts in power between national and supranational institutions. Increases in the power of the latter were brought about by the 'outcome of incremental accretions of authority, added to earlier commitments on the basis of needs as recognized in successive programmatic compromise decisions' (Haas, 1971, p. 14).

Intergovernmentalism, on the other hand, was the basis upon which decisions were made at the European level within the confines of common institutions and decision-making processes set out in the Rome Treaty. Fundamental to the functioning of the intergovernmental paradigm was the role of consensus – that is, that decisions could not be made unless all member-states were in agreement. Examples of the types of supranational decision-making centre where intergovernmentalism played an important role were the institutions created to prepare and make decisions: COREPER and the European Council. Outside the rulings of the European Court of Justice (ECJ), national governments were in a monopoly position to monitor and decide on all important matters coming up before the Common Market. And even in the area of EC law, the member-states always had a strong role in determining the pace at which the rulings of the ECJ were incorporated into national law and judicial behaviour.

The historical record shows that decision making under the Rome Treaty provisions was characterised by very limited forms of incrementalism in shifting policies from the national to the supranational level, and intergovernmentalism was clearly the dominant procedure by which decisions were made. Attempts by the Commission to introduce large doses of supranationalism into the activities of the Common Market ran into constant and systematic roadblocks that had been institutionalised by the Rome Treaty. With the initiation of France's June 1965 'empty chair' policy, the ability of the Commission to minimise the negative aspects of consensus voting and introduce a more dynamic element into intergovernmental negotiations was brought to a halt. The blocking of Council of Ministers deliberations effectively prevented incrementalism from further operating in the creation of new supranational institutions and in moving additional policy sectors from the national to the supranational level. In 1966 the Luxembourg Compromise stopped further European integration in its tracks. All attempts to increase the scope and pace of European integration (for example the Hague summit of 1969, the 1970 Werner Report on European monetary union, and the 1975 Tindemans Report on European Union) were halted by decision-making gridlock and a dysfunctional institutional structure. The Common Market had evolved to the limits achievable under 'negative integration' (that is, integration on the basis of eliminating internal barriers) by adopting an approach to decision making that was based on consensus, incrementalism and intergovernmentalism. On the basis of these three principles, the EC did not have sufficient momentum to continue toward 'positive integration', with the goal of building new institutions and allocating further powers and policy sectors to the supranational level through modification of the existing legal foundations.

Clear exceptions to this rule are the rulings of the European Court of Justice, whose impact on European integration has received surprisingly little attention from neofunctionalist writers. One of the more interesting and unexpected impacts of European integration has been the silent manner in which EC law has achieved ascendancy over national law and has come to influence national judicial procedures through a series of landmark court cases. Noteworthy here are the Van Gend en Loos (1963), Van Duyn (1974) and Francovich (1992) verdicts on the direct effect of EC regulations and directives. The pre-eminence of EC law was established with the Costa vs Enel (1964) and Simmenthal (1978) decisions, and the ECJ came to the defence of the rights and privileges of individual institutions in the EC with the Roquette Freres (1979) and Chernobyl (1990) rulings. Furthermore the ECJ laid the foundations for the future course of European economic integration with the Cassis de Dijon (1979) case, which established the principle of free movement of goods in the EC and mutual recognition of production standards across countries. In later rulings, such as in the Cowan case (1989), the ECJ established the right of people to move freely across national boundaries (Mancini, 1993).

Whether the activities of the ECJ can be said to have brought about 'incremental' rather than 'qualitative' changes to the rules governing the behaviour of the EU depends very much on the definition attributed to these concepts by students of European integration. Nevertheless ECJ decisions clearly lie outside the scope of intergovernmental decision making; no one has yet suggested that decisions of the ECJ are the product of intergovernmental bargaining. It is without doubt, though, that the activities of the ECJ continue to be part of an elite-oriented approach to institution building in the EU, being based on the forging of elite consensus on the exigencies and principles of European integration. Students of the ECJ are in agreement that decisions taken by the ECJ have built up over a number of years a body of Community law that has changed the functioning of national courts and legal procedures in a fundamental and decisive manner (Shapiro, 1992; Mancini, 1991; Smith, 1990; Cappelletti *et al.*, 1986).

Despite the importance of the rulings made by the ECJ during the 1960s and 1970s, informed public opinion and academic analyses continued to concentrate on the lack of change (defined at the time as 'Eurosclerosis') that characterized EC institutions and decision making. Closer scrutiny of the past, however, reveals that changes did start to seep into EC structures and procedures at the height of the concern over 'Eurosclerosis' and immediately thereafter.

During the last two decades institutional changes have significantly altered European-level decision-making patterns. There has been an increase in the scope of integration in decision making through the creation and institutionalisation of the European Council, and the direct election of a European-wide parliamentary body (the European Parliament) has raised the issue of the lack of democratic accountability of

European institutions. Subsequent changes introduced by the Single European Act and the Maastricht Treaty have moved integration along by introducing majority voting (SEA), begun massive shifts in policy areas to the European level (SEA and Maastricht), and made substantial modifications to the institutional structure through the introduction of codecision-making powers for the European Parliament and the creation of the Committee of Regions (Maastricht). After all these changes it is difficult to argue that decision making in the EU is still carried out on a strictly incremental basis founded on the model of intergovernmentalism in which the rule of unanimity still reigns supreme. Instead we have witnessed a very uneven line and form of development in European institutions. The introduction of reforms is due to a variety of factors and political forces outside the strict confines of nation-state structures. Private interests and associations have become active, and a greater role is being played by the mass media in organising public opinion and structuring the political agenda.

On this basis it is possible to describe the course of European integration during the last twenty-five years as having (1) manifested periodic leaps in the quality and content of institution building rather than being characterised by slow but constant incremental growth, and (2) become increasingly diffuse through the burgeoning number of actors involved in the process. Two of the initial qualitative leaps were made in 1974 and 1979 with the significant addition of two new institutions to the Community's structure. The first of these was the European Council, which at first sight, through the semesterisation of summits and the creation of a rotating presidency, seemed to reinforce the intergovernmentalist approach to decision making (Wessels, 1991). However in retrospect we can see that the European Council helped to institutionalise a high profile and an open, European-level process of political cooperation and compromise in decision making that had not existed before. The European Council has had an important role in raising public awareness of European issues and the decisions made by European leaders. In focusing the attention of the media during the European Summit and stressing the importance of a successful presidency, pressure was placed on governments to compromise and adopt a more flexible approach to decision making. The practical result of this combination of pressure and publicity was to do away with the principle of unanimity as a basis of decision making. The rotating presidency also added a clear political element to intergovernmental cooperation in the preparation and management of the EC agenda and a recurring measurement of a national government's European credentials.[21]

Contrary to what had initially been intended when creating the European Council, the intergovernmental decision-making process that had dominated deliberations at the administrative/ambassadorial/ministerial levels (with the activities of COREPER and the Council of Ministers) was undermined by exposing it to the outside world. In the past, both executive institutions had operated behind closed doors, and the principle of unanimity was easy to sustain by ministerial elites and ambassadors acting on instructions from their governments. However, when difficult decisions were postponed to negotiations taking place during summit meetings of the European Council, it was much more difficult to keep final decisions from the public arena and maintain rigid national positions.[22] Decisions taken by the Council immediately made national and international headlines. Participants in Council summit meetings had to pay close attention not only to what kind of decisions were made but also to how those decisions were interpreted by the media and the public. National leaders could no longer afford to paralyse European-level decisions; it became imperative for them to return from European summits as 'winners' and recognised leaders in the Community-building process. Thus the institutionalisation of the Council and the semesterisation of summit meetings substantially changed the role of intergovernmentalism and incrementalism in European decision making. Summits held in Milan (1985), Maastricht (1991) and Edinburgh (1992) were to demonstrate that, through the institutional procedures introduced with the European Council, it was more possible than ever before to introduce sudden, qualitative changes to the pace and goals of European integration than had been the case when all EU business was conducted behind closed doors.[23]

A similar qualitative leap in institution building, if not in policy decision making, took place in 1979 with the first direct elections of members to the European Parliament. Though the newly elected Euro-MPs represented a direct form of citizen representation in European affairs, the initial powers granted to the European Parliament were restricted to providing consultative rather than deliberative inputs into policy formulation (Jacobs, Corbett and Shackleton, 1992). Parliament had to wait until substantial modifications of the original Rome Treaty were introduced – through ratification of the Single European Act (SEA) and the Maastricht Treaty – before it was granted power over the budget (SEA) and a codecision-making role (Maastricht). In both cases the powers of the European Parliament were increased through a mix of compromise between maximalist and minimalist approaches to institutional reform and qualitative changes to the structure and relationships among EU organs.

The SEA represented a watershed in European affairs because it broke the institutional stalemate that had long blocked the shift of policy areas to the European level. The SEA achieved a breakthrough in European integration due to a number of important changes. First of all, it substantially did away with the principle of unanimity, which had already been weakened by the introduction of summits and the rotating presidency. While the SEA had officially introduced majority voting only for those decisions involving the realisation of the Single Market, the subsequent activities of the Council of Ministers and COREPER adopted the notion of majority voting in all areas directly and indirectly involving the Single Market. Attempts by some national governments to apply vetoes, based on declarations of 'vital national interest', were rejected by the other member states and eventually withdrawn. Such a change in decision-making rules was considered necessary to prevent governments from picking apart the implementation of the Single Market through individual exceptions for national products and interests, but it proved to have a wider political impact in fundamentally changing decision making at the EU level.

Secondly, the SEA and the subsequent Delors I budget proposal effectively transferred to the European level policy areas that had for years remained the exclusive prerogative of national governments. Among the most important of these were regional planning and development, rules governing competition and mergers, research and development, telecommunications, external economic relations and environmental standards.

Thirdly, the SEA placed the goal of the Single Market squarely on the political agenda and, as a consequence, mobilised the private sector behind economic convergence and European integration. The economic imperative of girding-up for world competition had changed the ability of national governments to control the direction and content of political and economic integration.

Finally, the SEA gave the EU a significant role in controlling the course and pace of European integration by projecting into the future a series of intergovernmental conferences designed to modify the legal bases of the Rome Treaty. The first intergovernmental conference on institutional change and monetary union produced the Maastricht Treaty, while another is foreseen for 1996 to undertake further modification of existing institutions and procedures in order to facilitate the realisation of full political and monetary union.

The cumulative impact of changes to EU law, institutional reforms and transfer of policy areas to the European level has served to modify the dynamic of European integration as described by neofunctionalists in their initial attempt to conceptualise the process. Today, not only has the EU changed its structures and procedures, but there has been a substantial change in the nature of Europe's economic structure and prospects. And these changes need to be taken into account in reformulating the theoretical implications of integration in Europe.

SPILLOVER AND THE ECONOMIC FOUNDATIONS OF NEOFUNCTIONALISM

The basic economic assumption underlying neofunctionalist theories is that area-wide common markets provide a better base for industrialisation and effective welfare policies than do national markets. In the case of Europe, the Common Market established a better distribution and sharing of scarce resources than was possible within an exclusively nation-state-oriented system. The move from national to multinational decision making and the integration of policy areas allowed for the realisation of economies of scale in policy making within an environment of opening up national markets to global competition. Functional spillover to a great extent symbolised in the political sphere what in economic terms is deemed the process of achieving economies of scale. However the process of spillover developed by the neofunctionalists suffered from two fundamental shortcomings. It did not consider the effects of integration on the public and private sectors, nor did it notice that during the initial period of integration the sectors chosen for supranational decision making were drawn from nationalised or highly subsidised industries. Thus the amount of spillover exercised in sectoral integration was significantly controlled by the nation-state. The private sector remained substantially outside the integration process and the state-building dynamic.

Neofunctionalist have argued that the goal of the European Coal and Steel Community (ECSC) was to bring greater efficiency to three economic activities (energy supply, mining, and steel production) that traditionally had been under tight governmental control in all the participating countries and basically operated in a non-market environment. These three economic activities were considered fundamental to the industrial development of the countries concerned, and therefore they remained tightly controlled by the national governments (Milward, 1984). Governmental control of these sectors was also considered vital as a means of guaranteeing and protecting the welfare of the country from potentially hostile foreign economic encroachments. Thus the argument of the neofunctionalists was that while economics may have served as the justification for integrating key economic sectors, the ultimate goals were still political in nature. The objectives in the case of the ECSC were:

1. To ensure national economic growth through all of the countries located along the Rhine sharing open access to resources and productive structures (that is, coal, iron ore, smelting and steel-rolling plants) that, taken as a whole, provided the basis for the reconstruction of Europe's traditional industrial heartland and helped to industrialise other parts of Europe.
2. To share labour resources by permitting a controlled transfer of workers from the mostly agricultural south of Europe to the industrialised north.

3. To put an end to the centuries-old dispute between France and Germany over the control of vital economic resources, which had resulted in a shifting of the French–German border on a number of occasions.

4. To make progress in European integration in the economic sphere while waiting for conditions to improve with respect to political integration and security policies (Haas, 1958; Spinelli, 1965).

Under the ECSC, joint management of energy resources and steel-production facilities was to be achieved by eliminating interstate trade barriers and encouraging 'competition' among enterprises, even though these enterprises were organised as national monopolies not subject to domestic competitive pressures. Thus the ECSC sought to open economic activity at the supranational level through collective management of the steel, iron-ore and coal sectors by a supranational authority.[24]

In a similar fashion, the initial evolution of the Common Market (EEC) also focused on a sector that had long been under strong government tutelage – agriculture (Milward, 1992). Rationalisation of both ECSC and EEC involved moving decision making from the national to the European level. Even though the Rome and Paris treaties had as their declared goals the elimination of tariffs and quantitative restrictions and the suppression of discrimination based on the national origin of products, progress on the reduction of impediments to trade proved to be very slow. Full internal liberalisation among the six member-countries was dependent on incremental political and institutional bargaining processes that took time to implement and had to be extensively negotiated by national political and administrative elites within the intergovernmental decision-making process. Accordingly a common external tariff (Customs Union) had to wait until 1969 to be realised. But the creation of a real common market did not become realistic until after the passage of the SEA, which undertook to modify the political procedures, institutional structures and economic policies envisioned by the original Treaty of Rome.

The economic conditions within which Europe was to operate in the 1980s required not only a change in institutions but also changing the entire conception of the conditions necessary to enable European companies to compete in the international arena. Foremost among these conditions was the ability of European companies to operate in an unhindered fashion throughout the EC (that is, in a market encompassing 340 million consumers), rather than in small, national markets, in order to realise economies of scale and rationalise management structures. The 1985 Treaty created a timetable for the implementation of the Single Market and authorised the Commission to assume responsibility for achieving compliance with Treaty provisions (Cameron, 1992).

Successfully achieving the Single Market was based on being able to mobilise the market and private economic concerns behind the European integration process and stimulating support for supranational institution building. Contrary to the experience during the previous two decades, an effective link was established between the structurally changed European market and European political institutions. In the past neofunctionalist theory had discussed the role of socioeconomic elites in European integration, but it had failed to recognise that private-sector elites had been substantially absent from the European integration process prior to the mid-1980s. Moreover, full integration of the private market would only be possible if nation-states in Europe abandoned their policies of closely monitoring internal economic activities through capital controls, state provisions and subsidies to protect domestic producers, and nationalisation strategies to stem company collapses or buy-outs by foreign competitors. A change in these policies meant that nation-states could no longer favour and protect 'national champions' in their competition with other firms operating in the European market.

The change from a state-managed to a more market-oriented industrial policy was made possible by two important national political developments. The first took place in France on the heels of the 1983 turnaround in French economic policy and the abandonment by Mitterrand of his 1981 policy of nationalisation and stimulation of internal demand (Ross, Hoffmann and Malzacher, 1987). The second was the deregulation programme pursued by Margaret Thatcher, first in the UK and later in Europe, as a means of conquering new markets for British industry and financial corporations (Hall, 1986). Taken together, these two developments opened the possibility and introduced the explicit need to reconfigure European industrial and competition policies at the supranational level by providing them with a much greater market component than had been the case in the past.

The passage of the SEA in 1985 represented an official re-cognition that past economic programmes oriented toward national economies and the role of national governments as ultimate guarantors and arbitrators of the market were no longer viable. The latter could now only be exercised, in a limited manner, by a supranational authority, but not before a larger European market was created. It was thought that the benefits of market deregulation and expansion needed to be realised before other changes to the institutions could be con-sidered. Thus the realisation of the Single Market preceded the holding of the intergovernmental conference to draft a Treaty of European Union.

During the late 1980s business treated the Single Market programme as a self-fulfilling prophecy, with companies chang-ing their tactics and market strategies in order to position themselves to meet the expected increase in European compe-tition and to take advantage of the opportunities that would be offered by the Single Market in 1993. One of the most visible consequences of the strategic decisions taken by the private sector was the series of mergers and acquisitions that began to roll through the European economy, along with a rush by non-EC companies to gain a place in the market before the 1992 deadline was reached.

The qualitative change in private-sector attitudes toward the European market, as well as the need to mount European-level lobbying efforts and gain recognition in Brussels, facil-itated the role of the Commission in influencing economic transactions. As part of the Single Market strategy and because of the added responsibilities conferred on it by the SEA, the Commission became more zealous in its application of the rules on competition, and undertook the monitoring of state subsi-dies and the promotion of a European-level R&D and indus-trial policy. An integral part of this approach was represented by the Commission's strategy of encouraging small and medium-sized firms to form networks to formulate and imple-ment European marketing and production strategies.

The recent economic (Single Market) and political (Maastricht) developments have placed into question the usefulness of neofunctionalist concepts such as incrementalism, intergovernmentalism and spillover in explaining aspects and the course of European integration and analysing national government behaviour. During the last decade the logic of economic integration in Europe has been decoupled from strict dependence on state control, but there is still a close link between economic and political integration. The market has now gained significant strength vis-à-vis the state in determining integration outcomes or solutions formulated by national governments. In addition, the relationship between nation-states (or intergovernmentalism) is no longer the exclusive or dominant factor in explaining nation-state, business, judicial or mass behaviour with respect to issues relating to European integration.

Robert Keohane and Stanley Hoffmann (1991) have suggested the need to use other hypotheses to explain the formulation of such historical documents as the Single European Act and the subsequent changes to the Treaty of Rome. One of these is the 'political economy' approach, which focuses on the need for European markets and business concerns to respond to the challenge posed by world-wide competitiveness; another is the 'preference-convergence' hypothesis, which stresses the convergence of policy preferences among domestic political elites in European countries. In both cases the suggested nexus between the nation-state apparatus and the private market becomes increasingly complex, and there are few guarantees that the nation-state will be able ultimately to control the flow of decisions taking place at the European level. There is, instead, growing evidence that an increasingly important role is being played by other institutional actors (Commission, European Parliament and European Court of Justice). Recent events have shown that market forces are no longer subject to significant control by national decision-making structures (businesses, financial institutions and even regional development agencies). World liquidity levels and the ability to transfer funds from one part of the world to another in a microsecond have reached such proportions that national currency fluctuations and the determination of exchange rates are no longer in the hands of state officials. The role of the media has also been enhanced in moulding public opinion on important decisions (referenda) and issues (for example a single currency) concerning economic and political affairs impacting on European integration.

The important point to remember here is that the last two modifications of the Treaty of Rome have reinforced economic integration while at the same time changing the institutions and procedures operating in the EU. Recent events have shown that the neofunctionalists were correct to argue that market convergence unaccompanied by the creation of supranational institutions to govern the market does not provide for a stable core of rules and regulations that are necessary for the predictable behaviour of market forces, nor does it automatically lead to some form of political integration. Haas wrote that 'economic integration unaccompanied by the growth of central institutions and policies does *not necessarily* lead to political community since no pressure for the reformulation of expectations is exercised. Free trade, therefore, cannot be automatically equated with political integration; nor can the interpenetration of national markets be so considered' (Haas, 1975, p. 9).

Instead, economic integration has to be accompanied by political integration if it is to become a lasting achievement. Otherwise a change in economic conditions or a national political climate might easily reverse the process and undo all the achievements and benefits gained from the initial stages of economic integration.[25] Political integration involves the formal transfer of power from national to supranational level over the economic areas that have been earmarked for integration, and the end-product of political and economic integration is the creation of a new political community superimposed on the preexisting nation-state system.

THE IMPACT OF SPILLOVER ON LEVELS OF GOVERNMENT

The 1985 and 1991 modifications of the Treaty of Rome highlight the limitations of the neofunctionalist approach in adequately conceptualising the dynamics of European integration. In addition to the shortcomings discussed above concerning the role of the state vis-à-vis the private sector in the early phases of European integration, a number of other failings of neofunctionalist theory in providing an adequate explanatory framework have become evident. A fundamental limitation of neofunctionalist theory has to do with its view of integration as a 'top-down process' and its inability to conceive of spillover effects in other than a sectoral perspective. Neofunctionalist theory rejects the possibility that the creation of the new European political community and economic market is a grass-roots phenomenon, pressure being directed from the bottom up to achieve higher levels of integration. Grass-root pressures are, instead, seen as incapable of overcoming the limitations of the nation-state. Integration, it is argued, is the result of a new set of rules by which centralised interest groups and national elites can operate to realise greater levels of efficiency in decision-making, policy implementation and economic outcomes. In fact, what was missing in the integration patterns of the 1960s and 1970s was spillover in the levels of action – that is, the involvement of subnational political and administrative elites and local actors in a Community-wide network of relations and decision-making processes. Neofunctionalists have argued that subnational-level elites can be involved in the integration process once the policy area is put under supranational control, but the subnational level is not seen as a key participant in the mobilisation of the integration dynamic. Thus regional policy is not considered a viable candidate for integration by neofunctionalists because regional development is deemed inimical to the logic of economies of scale.

As described by Leon Lindberg (1963), functional integration is posited on the logic of functional spillover and the commitment of interest-group leaders to their own self-interest. Crucial to the process is the interactive nature of socio-economic problems, which can, for analytical purposes, be separated into distinct entities but which in reality are closely interconnected. Once a specific action has been undertaken, the original goal can only be reached if further sectoral integration takes place. Functional spillover is seen as a dynamic that radiates out across institutions and processes at the national level and links this level to the formation of new policy-making structures above. Neofunctionalists have not conceived the process as a trickle-down effect mobilising forces and elites at other levels of the political system. Thus neofunctionalism does not provide a theoretical base to analyse the impact of integration on subnational elites and socioeconomic and political forces, as it leaves a void in trying to predict how the citizenry can become mobilised to participate in a bottom-up process of integration.

Economists have described in a similar fashion the creation of regional policies as the nation-state's response to the negative consequences of the interplay of the market and economies of scale on regional societies. In both neofunctionalist theory and economic theory stressing backwash effects,[26] the possibility of subnational elites and socioeconomic forces being active and constructive players in the European integration process is discounted. But the course of European integration after 1988 demonstrates that regional elites (and considerations of regional policy) are important actors and vigorous proponents of a new European institutional architecture in which EU organs are in direct contact with subnational elites (Leonardi, 1993c).

So how can the transition be made between, on the one hand, the expectations generated by neofunctionalist and economic theories and, on the other hand, the empirical reality emerging within the EU in the evolution of policy making and economic performance at the national and regional levels? To answer this and other questions relating to European integration and economic convergence we need to analyse the literature on regional disparities and centre–periphery relations, which have in the past informed the views of economists and political scientists in evaluating the dynamics of European economic integration, the evolution of disparities within the context of nation-states and the position of peripheral states within wider political unions.

NOTES

1. See the discussion of convergence in Cardoso, 1993; Quah, 1993; Nelson, 1991; Barro and Sala-i-Martin, 1991; Baumol, 1986; Sutherland, 1986. The concept of cohesion has been the primary focus of the Community's four Periodic Reports on Regional Disparities: CEC, 1981, 1984, 1987, 1991; Leonardi, 1993a. The literature on integration is extensive, but the two seminal works are Haas, 1958, and Lindberg, 1963.
2. See 'Conclusions of the Presidency – Edinburgh, December 12, 1992',

SN 456/92, press release, and 'Background Report, The Structural Funds for 1994–1999', ISEC/B16/93, 28 May 1993.

3. The Community Support Frameworks are development plans negotiated among the EU, national governments and regions/localities suggesting how the national governments and regions propose to spend contributions from the three Structural Funds. For a discussion of the CSFs see Nanetti, 1992.

4. The Cohesion Fund involves projects located in the EU's four poorest countries. Of the amount 52–58 per cent will go to Spain, 16–20 per cent to Greece and Portugal and 7–10 per cent to Ireland. Of the 141 billion ECU allocated by the Structural Funds, 96 billion ECU will go to the priority Objective 1 areas, which include the above four countries plus southern Italy, Corsica and the French DOM, Northern Ireland, Merseyside and the Scottish Highlands in the UK, Flevoland in the Netherlands and Hainaut in Belgium.

5. It should be remembered that the Maastricht Treaty is official known as 'The Treaty on European Union'. See Lodge, 1993, for a brief discussion of the implications of the concept of union.

6. See Molle, 1990, for a detailed discussion of the different assumptions and expected outcomes of the customs union, common market, and economic and monetary union.

7. E. T. Nevin (1990, p. 325) describes regional policy as an exercise designed 'to increase output and incomes, in absolute and/or relative terms, in areas believed to be operating below their true potential, or to reduce them in areas considered to be over-congested or in danger of becoming so'. For a thorough discussion of regional policy, see Armstrong and Taylor, 1993.

8. In the Preamble of the Rome Treaty a clear justification for regional policy was presented: 'Member states are anxious to strengthen the unity of their economies and to ensure their harmonious development by reducing the differences existing between the various regions and by mitigating the backwardness of the less favoured regions'.

9. For an interesting periodisation and conceptualisation of the different stages that have characterised the evolution of the EC's regional development policy, see Nanetti, 1990.

10. The EU is now starting to awaken to the fact that market integration may also have a negative impact on more developed areas, such as the old coalmining areas and those engaged in steelmaking and shipbuilding. Accordingly, the EU is currently committed to intervening more actively with regional development funds in peripheral, less developed areas as well as core, developed areas undergoing economic decline. This change in emphasis has been reflected in the increased size of the Objective 2 programme for the traditionally industrialised areas and in the appearance of new Objective 2 areas in previously 'developed' parts of the EU, such as metropolitan London.

11. EMU takes away from national governments their last instrument – manipulation of exchange rates – to help domestic producers vis-à-vis their European competition. The other instrument – tariffs – was given away as part of the accession process. Thus, with the loss of control of external tariffs and exchange rates regional policy becomes an

instrument designed to promote development through a restructuring of incentives targeted toward the improvement of the mobility of economic factors.

12. In 1993 the Spanish government published its 'Convergence Programme', in which it foresaw the reduction of national budgetary allocations through a 32 per cent reduction in infrastructure investments. See *El Pais*, 12 August 1993.

13. There has been considerable debate on this point in the EU. Hodges (1981: 1) cites Robert Marjolin who stated that the goal of the convergence of economic policies is just a 'pious wish' and not a concrete expectation. In the 1989 Delors Report the most widely shared view was that the weaker economies ran the risk of being net losers from integration. The question of cohesion has also been raised with regard to other large, integrated markets in economic convergence literature. See Barro, 1991; Barro and Sala-i-Martin, 1990; de la Dehesa and Krugman, 1992.

14. See CEC, 1993b, on the major evaluations of Structural Fund policies carried out to date by the EU. The ten models that have been experimented with are also briefly mentioned in CEC, 1992, pp. 113–14.

15. See Leonardi, 1993a, on the attempt to develop appropriate econometric models to evaluate the economic impact of small-scale investment projects at the local level.

16. In the analysis of attempts to spur economic development in Italy's Mezzogiorno, Riccardo Cappellin has concluded that past national development efforts through the Cassa per il Mezzogiorno most likely slowed down rather than spurred change in the regions of southern Italy. See Cappellin, 1993.

17. For a polemical criticism of neofunctionalism and the logic of spillover in relation to the ECSC and EEC, see Milward and Sorensen (1993).

18. Other approaches to the study of European integration, such as those emphasising the intergovernmental nature of decision making, are much more static in nature. They tend not to predict change over time and therefore downplay any emphasis on the prediction of dynamic change that can be used to test the validity of their hypotheses or assumptions. For a discussion of the various theoretical approaches to the study of European integration, see Taylor, 1983.

19. Of interest here is how Haas has described federalism in a manner that emphasises the role of subnational level considerations such as regional policy as a sign of federalism: 'Federalism, in short, seeks simultaneously to meet the need for more effective governmental action in some domains (through centralization) and the democratic postulate of local control and local autonomy (through decentralization)' (Haas, 1971, p. 20).

20. Haas has written that the 'style of bargaining is incremental, subdued, and unemotional and seeks reciprocity of benefits, unanimous agreement, and package deals among issue areas' (Haas, 1971, p. 14). Thus issues such as economic growth in peripheral areas is conceived as a technical issue of how to get growth started and then accelerated rather than as one of equity or solidarity.

21. Government leaders have many times had to conduct themselves in a much more pro-European manner than they may have desired in order not to expose themselves to both internal and external criticism. In November 1990 Margaret Thatcher paid the price of being isolated at a European summit. In this particular case, the crisis was triggered by the outcome of the October 1990 Rome summit, where the Italians outmanoeuvered the British prime minister, leaving her in a minority-of-one position. This isolation was judged by internal as well as external critics as leaving the UK government in a position from which it was not able to protect vital domestic-economy and other interests.

22. France's determined stance on the Blair House agreement remains the outstanding example of continued national rigidity. The results of the GATT negotiations illustrate how difficult it is for national governments in isolation to prevent major international agreements from being achieved.

23. Geoffrey Howe has written that the June 1989 Madrid summit, where the Delors EMU report was accepted by the member states, also produced a dramatic turnaround in the views of the British prime minister, who before the meeting gave no signs of having underwritten the implications of EMU or deciding to join the ERM. See *Financial Times*, 23 October 93.

24. The fate of the ECSC shows all of the limitations of a sectoral integration devoid of effective spillover into other sectors and the detachment of sectoral economic integration from political integration. Further integration of coal and steel were stymied in the 1960s and 1970s by the institutional gridlock that affected the wider EEC integration process. See Tsoukalis and Strauss, 1985; Howell *et al*, 1988; Hudson and Sadler, 1989.

25. Such a distinction is vital in considering the prospects of growth in newly proposed free trade areas, such as the North American Free Trade Area (NAFTA). In fact the NAFTA negotiators have recognised the need for a court of arbitration and an independent authority to manage the agreement, but have found it impossible to reach a mutually acceptable agreement on compromising national sovereignty in the pursuit of greater intra-area trade and economic growth.

26. For a discussion of this approach see Chapter 2.

REFERENCES

Armstrong, H. and J. Taylor (1993) *Regional Economics and Policy* (London: Harvester Press).

Barro, R. J. (1991) 'Economic Growth in a Cross Section of Countries', *Quarterly Journal of Economics*, vol. 106, pp. 407–43.

Barro, R. J. and X. Sala-i-Martin (1990) 'Economic Growth and Convergence across the United States', *Working Paper 3419* (Cambridge, MA: National Bureau of Economic Research).

Barro, R. J. and X. Sala-i-Martin (1991) 'Convergence across states and regions', *Brookings Papers on Economic Activity*, no. 1 (April).

Barzanti, S. (1965) *The Underdeveloped Areas Within the Common Market* (Princeton: Princeton University Press, 1965).

Baumol, W. J. (1986) 'Productivity growth, convergence and welfare: what the long run data show', *American Economic Review*, vol. 76, pp. 1072–85.

Bianchi, G. (1993) 'The IMPs: A Missed Opportunity?', in R. Leonardi (ed.), *The Regions and the European Community: The Response to the Single Market in the Underdeveloped Areas* (London: Frank Cass), pp. 47–70.

Cameron, D. R. (1992) 'The 1992 Initiative: Causes and Consequences', in A. Sbragia (ed.), *Euro-Politics: Institutions and Policymaking in the 'New' European Community* (Washington, DC: Brookings Institution), pp. 23–74.

Cappelletti, M. *et al.* (1986) *Integration Through Law*, vol. 1 (New York: De Gruyter).

Cappellin, R. (1993) 'Patterns and Policies of Regional Economic Development and Cohesion among the Regions of the European Community', in R. Leonardi, *The State of Economic and Social Cohesion in the Community Prior to the Creation of the Single Market: The View from the Bottom-Up* (Brussels: Commission of the European Communities), Chapter 3.

Cardoso, A. R. (1993) 'Regional inequalities in Europe – have they really been decreasing?', *Applied Economics*, vol. 25, pp. 1093–100.

CEC (1973) *Report on Regional Problems in the Enlarged Community* (Brussels: Commission of the European Communities).

CEC (1981) *Le Regioni d'Europa: Prima relazione periodica sulla situazione sociale ed economica nelle regioni della Comunità Europea* (Luxembourg: Office of Official Publications of the European Communities).

CEC (1984) *The Regions of Europe: Second Periodic Report on the Social and Economic Situation of the Regions of the Community, Together with a State of the Regional Policy Committee* (Luxembourg: Office of Official Publications of the European Communities).

CEC (1987) *The Regions in the Enlarged Community: Third Periodic Report on the Social and Economic Situation and Development of the Regions of the Community* (Luxembourg: Office of Official Publications of the European Communities).

CEC (1989) *Report on economic and monetary union in the European Community* (Luxembourg: Office of Official Publications of the European Communities).

CEC (1991) *The Regions in the 1990s: Fourth Periodic Report on the Social and Economic Situation and Development of the Regions of the Community* (Luxembourg: Office of Official Publications of the European Communities).

CEC (1992) *Second Annual Report on the Implementation of the Reform of the Structural Funds* (Luxembourg: Office of Official Publications of the European Communities).

CEC (1993a) 'Modeles economiques utilises pour l'evaluation del fonds structurels', mimeo, DGXVI.

CEC (1993b) *Community Structural Funds, 1994–1999* (Luxembourg: Office of Official Publications of the European Communities).

de la Dehesa, G. and P. Krugman (1992) *EMU and the Regions* (Washington, DC: Group of Thirty).

Doyle, M. F. (1989) 'Regional policy and European economic integration', in CEC *Report on economic and monetary union in the European Community*

(Luxembourg: Office of Official Publications of the European Communities), pp. 69–79.

European Parliament (1991) *A New Strategy for Social and Economic Cohesion After 1992* (Luxembourg: Office of Official Publications of the European Communities).

Getimis, P. and G. Kafkalas (eds) (1993) *Urban and Regional Development in the New Europe* (Athens: TOPOS).

Haas, E. B. (1958) *The Uniting of Europe* (London: Stevens and Son).

Haas, E. B. (1971) 'The Study of Regional Integration: Reflections on the Joy and Anguish of Pretheorizing', in L. Lindberg and S. Scheingold (eds), *Regional Integration: Theory and Research* (Cambridge, MA: Harvard University Press), pp. 3–42.

Haas, E. B. (1975) *The Obsolescence of Integration Theory*, (Berkeley: Institute of International Studies).

Hall, P. A. (1986) *Governing the Economy: The Politics of State Intervention in Britain and France* (Oxford: Oxford University Press).

Hodges, M. (1981) 'Liberty, Equality, Divergency: The Legacy of the Treaty of Rome?' in M. Hodges and W. Wallace (eds) *Economic Divergence in the European Community* (London: Allen & Unwin), pp. 1–15.

House of Commons (1992) *The Maastricht Treaty* (London: HMSO).

Howell, T. R. *et al.* (1988) *Steel and the State: Government Intervention and Steel's Structural Crisis* (London: Westview).

Hudson, R. and D. Sadler (1989) *The International Steel Industry: Restructuring, State Policies and Localities* (London: Routledge).

Jacobs, F., R. Corbett and M. Shackleton (1992) *The European Parliament*, second edition (London: Longman).

Keohane, R. O. and S. Hoffmann (1991) 'Institutional Change in Europe in the 1980s', in R. O. Keohane and S. Hoffmann (eds), *The New European Community: Decisionmaking and Institutional Change* (Oxford: Westview Press), pp. 1–39.

Leonardi, R. (1993a) 'Cohesion in the European Community: Illusion or Reality?', *West European Politics*, vol. 16, no. 4 (October), pp. 492–517.

Leonardi, R. (1993b) 'Feasibility study on the development of an econometric model for the analysis of the economic impact of cohesion fund projects' (London: London School of Economics, mimeo, December).

Leonardi, R. (ed.) (1993c) *The Regions and the European Community: The Response to the Single Market in the Underdeveloped Areas* (London: Frank Cass).

Lichtheim, G. (1963) *The New Europe* (New York: Praeger).

Lindberg, L. (1963) *The Political Dynamics of European Economic Integration* (London: Oxford University Press).

Lodge, J. (1993) 'Preface: the challenge of the future', in J. Lodge (ed.), *The European Community and the Challenge of the Future*, second edition (London: Pinter Publishers), pp. 1–36.

Mancini, F. (1991) 'The Making of a Constitution for Europe', in R. O. Keohane and S. Hoffmann (eds), *The New European Community: Decisionmaking and Institutional Change* (Oxford: Westview Press), pp. 177–94.

Mancini, F. (1993) '*Democracy and the European Court of Justice*', European Institute Working Papers (London: London School of Economics).

Marks, G. (1992) 'Structural Policy in the European Community', in A. Sbragia (ed.), *Euro-Politics: Institutions and Policymaking in the 'New' European Community* (Washington, DC: Brookings Institution), pp. 191–224.

Milward, A. S. (1984) *The Reconstruction of Western Europe, 1945–51* (London: Methuen).

Milward, A. S. (1992) *The European Rescue of the Nation-State* (London: Routledge).

Milward, A. S. and Sorensen, V. (1993) 'Interdependence or integration? A national choice' in A. S. Milward *et al. The Frontier of National Sovereignty: History and Theory, 1945–92* (London: Routledge), pp. 1–32.

Mitsos, A. (1993) 'Post-Maastricht process towards European Union and the economic and social cohesion of the Community', in P. Getimis and G. Kafkalas (eds), *Urban and Regional Development in the New Europe* (Athens: TOPOS), pp. 1–8.

Molle, W. (1990) *The Economics of European Integration* (Aldershot: Dartmouth).

Nanetti, R. Y. (1990) 'The Community Structural Funds and the Search for a European Regional Policy', paper presented at the Annual American Political Science Association Meeting, San Francisco, 30 August–2 September.

Nanetti, R. Y. (1992) *Coordination in Development Planning: An Evaluation of the Initial Implementation of the Community Support Framework*, (Brussels: Commission of the European Communities) October.

Nelson, R. R. (1991) 'Diffusion of development: post-World War II convergence among advanced industrial nations', *American Economic Review*, vol. 81, pp. 271–5.

Nevin, E. T. (1990) 'Regional Policy', in A. M. El-Agraa (ed.), *Economics of the European Community*, third edition (London: Philip Allan), pp. 325–46.

Papageorgiou, F. and S. Verney (1993) 'Regional Planning and the Integrated Mediterranean Programmes in Greece', in R. Leonardi (ed.), *The Regions and the European Community: The Response to the Single Market in the Underdeveloped Areas* (London: Frank Cass), pp. 139–61.

Pinder, D. (1983) *Regional Economic Development and Policy: Theory and Practice in the European Community* (London: George Allen & Unwin).

Plaskovitis, E. (1993) 'On-going evaluation of the Integrated Mediterranean Programmes: the Greek experience', in P. Getimis and G. Kafkalas (eds), *Urban and Regional Development in the New Europe* (Athens: TOPOS), pp. 67–76.

Quah, D. (1993) 'Galton's fallacy and tests of the convergence hypothesis', *The Scandinavian Journal of Economics*, vol. 95, no. 4 (December), pp. 427–443.

Ross, G., S. Hoffmann and S. Malzacher (1987) *The Mitterrand Experiment* (Oxford: Oxford University Press).

Shapiro, M. (1992) 'The European Court of Justice', in A. Sbragia, *Euro-Politics: Institutions and Policymaking in the 'New' European Community* (Washington, DC: Brookings Institution), pp. 123–56.

Smith, G. (1990) *The European Court of Justice: Judges or Policy Makers?* (London: Bruges Group).

Spinelli, A. (1965) *Rapporto sull'Europa* (Milan: Edizioni di Comunità).

Sutherland, P. D. (1986) 'Europe and the principle of convergence', *Regional Studies*, vol. 20, pp. 371–7.

Taylor, P. (1983) *The Limits of European Integration* (New York: Columbia University Press).

Tsoukalis, L. and R. Strauss (1985) 'Crisis and Adjustment in European Steel: Beyond Laisser-Faire', *Journal of Common Market Studies*, vol. 23, no. 3 (March), pp. 207–28.

Urwin, D. W. (1991) *The Community of Europe* (London: Longman).

Wessels, W. (1991) 'The EC Council: The Community's Decisionmaking Center', in R. O. Keohane and S. Hoffmann (eds), *The New European Community: Decisionmaking and Institutional Change* (Oxford: Westview Press), pp. 133–54.

2 Regional Disparities and Centre–Periphery Relations in the European Union

ECONOMIC DEVELOPMENT AND REGIONAL DISPARITIES

The literature on economic convergence and divergence has grown over the years. There is a significant debate not only on the direction of change but also on what causes change and how that change can be measured. In the past, the main factors explaining convergence or divergence have concentrated on physical factors such as infrastructure, financial capital and access to natural resources. In more recent times attention has begun to focus on the role of human capital (skills and entrepreneurial predispositions), institutional/political resources (formal constitutional structures of government) and social/cultural factors (associations, policy networks and views on social cooperation).[1] Theories concerning the institutionalisation of supranational decision making in Europe have also made explicit assumptions about the dynamic of economic growth and convergence and its link to the process of institution building in the EU.

In this chapter we will discuss the main economic and political-science theories that have been advanced to predict and explain the relationship between core and periphery within nation states and the EU, as well as positing the prospects of convergence of national and regional economies in an increasingly integrating European market. In the past, theories on convergence and divergence have been used to formulate hypotheses to analyse the economic and political prospects of peripheral states and regions in Europe. Recently though, these commonly accepted notions have been placed into question by empirical trends that have not conformed to the expectations or traditional notions concerning underdeveloped regions.

33

The economic theories that have searched for an explanation of the dynamic of regional growth (or the lack of it) and have been used as a basis for proposing regional policies can be divided into two basic categories. The first places emphasis on the process of convergence, or the move toward cohesion. Convergence is defined here as the end-product of socio-economic policies designed to reduce the socioeconomic disparities that exist among the regions and nations within Europe – that is, regional and national economies converge if the initially weaker economies benefit from appropriate economic policies designed to spur development, and if the economies of the peripheral states and regions grow at rates faster than those in the core areas. As a corollary, the prospect of convergence is enhanced if former core countries undergo economic decline as part of industrial restructuring or even deindustrialisation. In the debate on European Monetary Union the concept of convergence has been used to refer to the *increased similarity* in economic policies and, even more, to the *economic performance* of regional/national economies.[2]

Divergence, in contrast, is identified with the existence of increased disparities. Disparities increase as the logic of differentiated flows of factors of production serve to favour developed vis-à-vis underdeveloped regions or countries. The rich get richer and the poor get poorer. Divergence continues due to the fact that the regions and states undergoing decline are not endowed with the appropriate policies, conditions and performance levels necessary to reduce the gap and potential for growth that separates them from more developed areas.

Both sides of the debate have marshalled elaborate theoretical constructs in support of their points of view. But what is of concern here is which approach best describes the empirical reality of the pace and content of national and regional economic change during the past forty years, and how these levels of economic performance and outcomes are linked to European integration. Establishing the empirical record of disparities in Europe is crucial in testing the predictive capability of the two approaches and identifying the causal factors behind economic performance.

The basic question we are concerned with here is not the factors underlying change but rather whether economic integration at the European level helps or hinders the prospect of achieving a more cohesive EU. To answer this question, we need to understand the factors that fuel the course of economic development in Europe and how development has interacted with the pace and content of integration. Before beginning the analysis it will be worthwhile to have a brief look at some of the predictions made by both sides of the convergence/divergence debate.

CONVERGENCE THEORIES

A number of approaches have been advanced to explain the process of economic convergence in the context of developed nation-state systems. The four approaches discussed here are based on a mix of market, government and social factors that stimulate and maintain growth over time.

The first approach looks at the causes of growth and emphasises the role played in growth by industrialisation (Hoffmann, 1958; Bryce, 1960) and the creation of large industrial enterprises using economies of scale as their basic organising principle (Apter, 1987; Gupta, 1983).[3] According to this perspective, peripheral areas are underdeveloped because they lack the necessary industrial base that would allow them to compete with core areas (Hamilton, 1986). Thus an improvement in the comparative advantage of peripheral areas dominated by agriculture can be accomplished through replication of the industrialisation process.[4]

Prior to 1974 the industrialisation paradigm advocated in most developed economies focused on the adoption of economies of scale and Fordist production methods. National governments wanting to develop their economies pursued policies aimed at providing investment incentives, attracting capital from abroad and mobilising domestic capital for productive investments, raising the skill level of the workforce, protecting infant industries, creating a positive climate for entrepreneurship, and encouraging a sifting-out process among small and medium-sized enterprises in order to encourage the emergence of a dominate producer. Development in the other economic sectors (that is, agriculture and services) were considered useful, but in the final analysis development was based on the growth and evolution of traditional modes of industrialisation.

The success of the industrialisation process, it was argued, was based not on artisan shops or hand-crafted goods but on mass-produced goods able to compete on the world market because of their lower production costs.

More recent elaborations of this approach, such as that proposed by Grossman and Helpman (1991), have emphasised the role of integration in stimulating growth through a process of market scale whereby the removal of trade barriers allows peripheral economies to gain access to the large markets of core areas, eliminating redundancy (peripheral economies do not have to reinvent processes that have already been tested and applied elsewhere) and spurring the transfer of technology, thereby permitting peripheral regions to share immediately in innovations made elsewhere.

Other writers have, however, emphasised the difficulty of realising these objectives because of inherent rigidities in the free flow of factors of production. Vanhove and Klaassen (1980) place into question the mobility of labour, capital and prices, arguing instead that the economic reality in Europe reflects the inherent inflexibility of national wage bargaining and the production and distribution structures dominated by large national firms. These characteristics prevent firms from adequately adjusting their production and marketing strategies to take into account economic downturns, changes in demand, and increased competition from new producers and areas of production. Such built-in rigidities prevent the market from adequately compensating, in terms of wage and price levels, areas hit by recession.

Empirical evidence has shown that even if the job market and industrial production are contracting, the level of regional consumption remains the same. This is due to the compensatory role played by large welfare-state expenditure in the form of income-support programmes for the unemployed and their families. The end-result of the rigidities built into the market by governmental social policies is to decrease investment and increase regional disparities, unemployment and government deficits. Thus the 'invisible hand' of market economies, past levels of industrial production and the presence of a large working class are not guarantees that change will foster adaptation and growth. Instead the prospects for industrial restructuring are thwarted by governmental policies and the political expectations of citizens who have grown accustomed to high levels of consumption and governmental provision.

Since the early 1970s, with the two oil shocks and the restructuring of traditional industrial firms in Europe's older core areas, serious doubts have surfaced about whether industrialisation per se and industrialisation based on the Fordist model will really allow backward areas to catch up with the productivity and well-being of the developed parts of the EU. New industrialisation paradigms that focus on the role of small and medium-sized enterprises, high tech, and a mix between service and production firms have found support from policy makers and economists (Ross and Usher, 1986; Cross, 1981; Piore and Sabel, 1984; Garofoli, 1991). Even the role of agriculture as a stimulus to growth and other factors – such as social capital, the role of institutions and political arrangements – have been introduced to explain the 'residual' factors that have remained unaccounted for in the historical analysis of growth in industrialised societies.

The second major approach to spurring economic growth in Europe was the 'growth-pole' theory developed by Francois Perroux (1955).[5] The growth-pole theory accepted to a great extent the Fordist industrialisation paradigm, but in contrast with classical models of economic growth it introduced into the development equation a significant role for national economic planning and political decision making. Growth-pole policies set aside a central role for the public sector in attenuating the unbridled impact of market forces on underdeveloped areas. The ideas behind growth poles received their first extensive empirical implementation in Italy as an attempt to industrialise the south and Mezzogiorno (Carello, 1989; Saraceno, 1977). Growth-pole strategies have had a checkered career in both theory and practice in Italy and elsewhere. The Italian Mezzogiorno and other areas in the EU, such as Greece and Spain, have served as a vast European laboratory to test the validity of the growth-pole theory.

The theory basically states that growth can be planned and concentrated by geographic area into development poles, such as those that have been identified in urbanised, metropolitan areas (Pred, 1977). Underdevelopment, on the other hand, is usually manifested in rural areas where the level of urbanisation is low and there is a shortage of economic infrastructure, capital and skilled labour. Given the imbalance between urban and rural areas, growth-pole advocates suggest that governments must intervene to equalise the factors of production through direct action aimed at accelerating growth in less developed areas. Growth is therefore a byproduct of governmental policy rather than the unconscious consequence of private economic forces operating within the limits of market-driven calculations of costs and benefits .

In operationalising the growth-pole approach to development, government policies have concentrated on the creation of industries capable of mobilising labour from the surrounding community, raising the standard of living of the workforce, and generating incentives to stimulate local entrepreneurship in underdeveloped, non-urbanised areas. As a consequence of these actions, economies of scale and external economies can become manifest in the area around the growth pole, thereby stimulating both the development of spin-off enterprises engaged in subcontracting work for the growth pole industries and the formation of a more consumer-oriented thrust in complementary local industries.

The most extensive operationalisation of the growth-pole theory took place in southern Italy from 1950–93 through the activities of the Cassa per il Mezzogiorno and the Agency for the South. Roberto Camagni (1991) has argued that public intervention in the south was organised into three phases. The first, carried out in the 1950s, was the provision of basic infrastructure and overhead capital formation. The second and crucial stage (effected in the 1960s) was based on the intervention of publicly owned enterprises and attracting large branch plants of private corporations by providing generous financial incentives. The third, which ended in the 1970s, was organised around an attempt to create the conditions for a flowering of diffused forms of industrialisation based on small firms.[6]

In contrast with the growth-pole theory, the third approach to growth views the governments and public policy as hindrances to development. Government rules on investment, wages, working conditions, benefits, capital transfers and the nationality of investors can operate as significant inhibitors of development. Advocates of this approach (for example, Hirsch, 1976; Olson, 1982) emphasize the need to reintroduce market considerations into development policies and reduce state interference in economic activity. In countries with access to capital, technology and skilled labour – as is the case in Europe – and with the increasing need to compete at the world level against low-wage countries, growth is not based on significant governmental intervention in the creation of productive capacities or in industrialisation processes. Instead, governments need to concentrate on reducing structural impediments to economic growth, such as capital controls, regulations governing economic activity, labour laws, standardised wage scales, environmental standards ans so on. Government intervention in the economy and the necessity to adhere to regulations operate to throw economic development off-course and upset the natural equilibrium between economic factors.

This approach has gained great favour since the 1980s, and liberalisation has been reintroduced into EU welfare-state systems through the deregulation and privatisation policies pursued by governments of both conservative and progressive persuasion. Loukas Tsoukalis (1981) has argued that the growth of Spain, Portugal and Greece in the 1960s and 1970s was based on the reorientation of their markets toward greater interaction with the other countries of Western Europe through the elimination of autarkic economic policies. In a similar fashion, Krause (1968) and others have maintained that the growth of Europe in the postwar period was governed by the necessity of opening up national markets and internal economic and social activities to world trends and economic factors, leading to unparallelled growth and avoiding the economic disasters that afflicted Europe after the First World War, when national economic policies emphasised the protection of internal producers and markets from international competition.

The final theory of development has achieved prominence during the last decade and emphasises the role of endogenous, local factors in promoting growth. The endogenous theory of growth is to a certain extent a reaction to the Perrouxian growth-pole theory and other theories emphasising the role of state institutions and large capital-intensive concerns in determining development. Supporters of the endogenous-growth approach point to the important role of small firms and the interaction between grassroot groups in the social system and subnational political institutions in mobilising growth.

The point of departure of this school of development

theorists (Cappellin, 1993; Stoehr, 1990; Suarez-Villa, 1989; Wadley, 1986) is the same as the general critique of equilibrium theory: production factors are basically immobile. The basic components of development – physical infrastructure, labour, capital, technological inputs and so on – do not migrate from one area to another in response to anonymous market forces. Instead they tend to remain fixed in a particular location. Thus the challenge of governmental development policies is to create the conditions by which some of these factors are encouraged to migrate (that is, capital and technology) through appropriate incentive programmes. However the most important factor determining development is considered to be the ability of regions to promote the full employment of local resources and heighten the local prospects for innovation. Public policy designed to promote endogenous development needs to focus on lowering the barriers to firm creation and on helping existing firms to migrate into sectors of production where local areas have a comparative advantage. These objectives can be achieved through proactive research and development policies, up-to-date vocational education, increased producer services, aggressive foreign marketing strategies, public–private cooperation, and forward-looking territorial-development and environmental-protection strategies designed to increase the area's attractiveness to indigenous and external entrepreneurs (Garofoli, 1992).

Endogenous-growth theory differentiates itself from the previous three approaches by emphasising the role of subnational governments (that is, regional and local authorities) as active participants. The role of the region is to create an incentive structure and provide overall coordination of policies, while the role of local government is to build the social and physical infrastructure necessary for firms to maximise their external economies.

DIVERGENCE THEORIES

There are two basic groups of advocates of divergence theories. The first does not exclude the possibility of underdeveloped regions experiencing growth, but points to the difficulty of achieving this result. The second group has suffered a significant setback with the demise of the Soviet Union. In the past, Marxist theorists basically excluded the possibility of re-dressing regional differences as long as capitalism remained the dominant economic system.

The major argument used in the development of EC re-gional policy in the 1970s drew upon the theoretical work of Gunnar Myrdal. In 1957 Myrdal developed the cumulative causation theory, which is based on a criticism of the compara-tive advantage model in international trade (Myrdal, 1957; Holland, 1976; Vanhove and Klassen, 1980). Myrdal argues that market forces do not bring about an equal redistribution of production factors or incomes. The movement of capital, labour and services are the means through which developed regions are rewarded for their 'virtue' and less developed re-gions are robbed of their future potential for making progress. In other words, the success of the more developed regions is paid for by a reduction in the developmental potential of the less developed regions. As a consequence, a vicious cycle of underdevelopment is created that ripples through peripheral economies, producing a backwash effect that pushes capital, skilled labour, entrepreneurship, technology and so on toward core areas, reversing the impact of spread effects that encour-age production factors to move in the opposite direction – that is, from the developed core to the less developed periphery.

Myrdal also recognizes that economic growth in core areas has some positive effects for peripheral regions. These are labelled 'the spread effects of development'. The primary spread effects identified by Myrdal are less relevant in explain-ing development in Europe in the postwar period than might be the case for Third World countries. The initial spread ef-fect, emphasising the role of peripheral areas as exporters of raw materials and agricultural products to developed areas, has been counteracted since the early 1960s by (1) Europe's relatively low endowment of natural resources and the exist-ence of naturally endowed countries on its periphery (for example natural gas from the Maghreb and Russia, oil from the Middle East and wood and minerals from Africa) and (2) the impact of the Common Agricultural Policy. In fact, since the early 1970s underdeveloped areas such as southern Italy and Greece have become net importers of agricultural prod-ucts originating from core countries, rather than acting as the granaries, hot houses or fruit fields of Europe. The third spread effect mentioned by Myrdal – the spillover of technology into geographically contiguous areas – indeed manifested itself extensively in Italy, Spain and southern France as growth began to spread out from Europe's traditional core areas in the postwar period.

Myrdal's anticipated backwash effects from market integration have become the primary stimulators when formulating regional policies within nation states and at the European level. Governments have attempted to protect newborn industries from open-market competition and have encouraged local productive factors to remain in underdeveloped areas. Emphasis on the impact of backwash effects on the prospect of economic development have positively discouraged governments from considering economic integration as a solution to the problem of mobilising the potential of local growth. This has been based on three considerations.

First, the increased competition that is introduced by lowering tariff barriers (such as in a customs union) apply increased pressure on regionally depressed areas because these are the areas where firms with higher costs (due to the lack of economies of scale) are located. Once these higher-cost firms have to compete with lower-cost firms in more developed areas, they will be driven out of business and government will not be in a position to intervene due to restrictions on the use of government subsidies, monetary policies and manipulation of exchange rates.

Second, greater labour and capital mobility will push both to higher growth areas where returns are greater. Higher standard wages in an integrated market means increased wages in depressed areas, making it more difficult for the assembly of local factors to mount a response to the increased levels of competition.

Third, central areas have traditionally experienced greater growth and thus are in a better position to create external economies for even further growth. Thus they pull productive factors from underdeveloped areas by holding out the prospect of greater return and proximity to core markets.

According to the backwash logic developed by Myrdal, when underdeveloped countries or regions join an integrating market the main dynamic creates incentives for factors of production to move from peripheral to core areas.[7] Stephen Overturf has drawn out these implications by stating that European economic integration is simply not in the interest of Europe's peripheral economies:

> In any case, the concern is that with European integration the center will (and already has to some extent) become a Community-wide center leaving the existing periphery areas with the fate of even further decline. The new European center is seen to extend roughly along the Rhine and then across the Alps to include north-western Italy. If this were to occur to a large extent, it might leave entire countries in the 'periphery', a concept which, if accurate, might give pause to Spain, Portugal, and Greece, not to mention Britain and Ireland (Overturf, 1986, p. 126).

From this perspective, national and EU regional policies should have two fundamental goals: (1) efficiency – reducing the level of unemployment and the wasting of precious social capital due to fixed social costs (education and income-support policies) through the fostering of regional growth, and (2) fairness – redistributing the gains of national growth in a more equitable manner and avoiding potentially costly disruption of national unity.[8]

Radical and neo-Marxist theorists have adopted a similarly pessimistic view as that voiced by Myrdal on the chances of peripheral economies attaining the levels of development of core areas, but their critique of the prospects for development is system-oriented rather than based on an ability to balance backwash against spread effects in regional economies. For these theorists the entire system of disequilibrium, and therefore dependency, is based on a coercive relationship imposed over peripheral economies by the dominant core economic and military powers (André Frank, 1974). Through domination, the core countries and areas are able to extract and transfer to the benefit of capitalist development in the core the surplus value of production and extractive and agricultural activities in the periphery (Holland, 1976).

The 1974 Rosenthal Report looked at various explanations for economic underdevelopment, ranging from surplus extraction and polarisation, to unequal exchange and accumulation, to domination from abroad and disarticulation of internal economic systems, and concluded that development could not take place unless the costs were absorbed by the core of the world economic system through a system of economic and political cooperation (Lizano and Willmore, 1975). However, in the 1970s and early 1980s progress was not made toward greater political cooperation or economic development due to the attempt to emphasise the removal of political repression (in Chile, Argentina, Brazil, Uruguay and so on) over the needs of economic development and international economic co-operation. Such an approach cannot be readily applied in the EU, but it is often heard in some of the anti-integration rhetoric that emerges from the theme of internal colonialism, that is integration as a means of institutionalising the domination of the geographic core or of large-scale capital concerns versus more peripheral areas and smaller-scale enterprises (Holland, 1980, pp. 99–100).

Taken as a whole, the two approaches discussed above provide a series of hypotheses that can be tested in relation to the evolution of national economies around the world, as well as to the change in the economic levels of peripheral areas in more developed societies.[9] The rate of growth of underdeveloped countries vis-à-vis their more developed neighbours has not been sufficient to produce convergence on a global scale, but there have been significant exceptions to the rule, such as the Pacific Rim countries and southern China. The example of this group of countries raises the question of whether the poor economic performance of underdeveloped countries is due mainly to the economic forces discussed above or to non-economic factors such as corruption, administrative inefficiency or the lack of an adequate entrepreneurial culture. In fact the radical theorists point to political (military and political domination) rather than economic reasons when explaining the lack of growth.

THE ROLE OF PERIPHERAL STATES IN THE EUROPEAN UNION

The ratification of the Maastricht Treaty has brought to light a contradiction in the economics and political-science literature on peripheral states in Western Europe. Analyses of the political and economic structures of these states – Greece, Spain, Portugal, Ireland, and even Italy – have periodically emphasised the difficulty these countries have in inserting themselves into the centre of European economic development, participating fully and actively in EU policy making and influencing Europe's position on world issues. The conducting of European affairs continues to be seen as the preserve of northern countries – that is, those with the longest tradition of democratic institutions and strong economic structures – or rather by the 'big three': Germany, France and the UK.[10]

However, when we look at recent European events in greater detail these generalisations concerning southern and outer peripheral states cease to reflect empirical reality. For example, at the Edinburgh Summit Spain and the other peripheral states played a crucial part in reaching agreement on the Delors II budget package and in formulating a compromise solution to the Danish opt-out clauses on European citizenship and defence policies. The Maastricht ratification process demonstrated that it was exactly the more northern, core European countries that expressed the greatest reluctance (at both governmental and mass levels) to make the transition to full economic and political unity. In contrast, the peripheral and southern European states and publics continued to express widespread support for the European integration process.

As we have seen above with regard to the theories of economic divergence, a large part of the existing economics literature maintains that economic and political integration in the EU is not in the best interest of peripheral countries and regions. The dichotomy between centre and periphery on the one hand, and the gains and losses from integration on the other, is present in both economics and political-science literature on integration.

In the 1980s interest in the course of political and economic changes in southern European nation-states received a large boost due to the coming together of three independent phenomena: (1) the creation of democratic regimes throughout southern Europe (in the three years between 1974 and 1977 the authoritarian regimes in Portugal, Greece and Spain were replaced by parliamentary democracies); (2) the rise to power in the late 1970s and early 1980s of socialist governments throughout the south (from Portugal to Greece, and including

France and Italy); and (3) the performance of southern European economies, which began to outstrip the growth rates of northern European countries. As observed by Hudson and Lewis (1985, p. 35), during the 1960s and 1970s growth rates in southern Europe 'exceeded those in most major advanced capitalist nations, particularly in manufacturing, as Southern Europe assumed greater significance within the changing international division of labour'. In a similar manner, Allan Williams (1984, p. 1) posed the question of economic development in southern Europe in highly provocative terms:

> Before the 1950s it was appropriate to ask, 'why is southern Europe underdeveloped?'. But it has now been supplanted by the question, 'why has southern Europe developed so rapidly?'

The combination of economic growth and democratic development in southern European political systems and the added element of membership in the EU has placed into question the applicability of a number of theories derived from the traditional economic-development literature on the Third World, which emphasised concepts such as dependency and surplus extraction.[11] Today these theoretical approaches seem out of place, given the spectacular growth rates registered in Spain in the mid-1980s and Portugal at the end of the 1980s, and the support demonstrated by the general public for European integration.

The rate and pattern of economic growth in southern European countries in the 1980s makes it impossible to continue to attribute their growth to the equalisation of economic factors produced by the migration of labour and the return of remittances from abroad. Instead, large-scale labour migration has stopped and there has been significant capital investment. The products and services of these countries have established themselves in European-wide markets. In contrast with what we are seeing today in Eastern Europe, the transformation of southern Europe in the 1970s and 1980s provides an example of economic change keeping pace with political transformation in moving these societies forward toward a new economic and political equilibrium. In the case of southern Europe, this transition was facilitated and reinforced by the entry of Portugal, Spain and Greece into the EC.

The attempt to reconcile economic and political reality with theory has forced research on peripheral states to reconsider the theoretical assumptions and conclusions associated with explanations of economic and political performance. These reconsiderations now have to take into account a wider world economic context as well as new political and institutional structures influencing the behaviour of national governments, political parties and the public in EU countries.

CENTRE–PERIPHERY THEORIES IN POLITICAL SCIENCE AND ECONOMICS

One of the logical starting points in discussing the literature on centre–periphery relations on a European-wide basis is the work of Rokkan and Urwin (1982, 1983) and Tarrow (1977). The former combined a focus on the nation-state with an overall consideration of the changes taking place within and across Europe over the centuries, while the latter attempted to use the concept to analyse the relationship between centre and periphery in what at the time were highly centralised nation-states: France and Italy. In both studies the main objective was to formulate a formal model of territorial politics that could be used to analyse the evolving socioeconomic structure of physical space (that is, 'distance' between centre and periphery) in Europe and the political activity (government behaviour, political-party organisation and elite linkages with citizens) that followed from it.

The definitions of 'centre' and 'periphery' adopted by the authors highlight the problem endemic in territorial analyses of Europe: the two concepts are not defined in a manner that can be subjected to empirical testing. Rather they are expressed in terms of 'ideal types' that are already pregnant with the conclusions to be reached by the analysis. In the formulations of the concept by Rokkan and Urwin and Tarrow, the starting point is defining the centre and identifying a series of structural characteristics. In defining the centre, the following questions are asked. Where do the holders of key resources most frequently meet to negotiate and make decisions? Where do they convene for ceremonies that affirm the integral nature of the territory and the distinctive identity of its population? Where have they built the monuments that symbolise this identity (Rokkan and Urwin, 1983, p. 6; Tarrow, 1977, p. 18)? In answering these questions the authors point out that the location of major military–administrative, economic and cultural institutions (or the 'command centres') gives the first and most obvious clue to the identification of territorial centres. However their subsequent analysis of nation-state systems in Europe shows that there is significant variation among individual countries in the level of concentration of political, administrative, military, economic and cultural decision-making centres.

Rokkan and Urwin identify three types of territorial structure in describing the degree of concentration of key decision-making bodies. The first is called a *monocephalic* structure, in which there is a large concentration of command institutions in one small area. One finds in monocephalic centres a concentration of resource holders interacting over short distances, thereby permitting the national elites to share common facilities for communication, intermediation and influence.

The second type of territorial structure is marked by dispersion of the different types of arenas across a very wide geographical area. This type of system is called *polycephalic* and is characterised by 'a spatial segmentation of different types of resource-holders, and a chain of distinctive centres, each with its own profile of elite groups' (Rokkan and Urwin, 1983, p. 6).

The third variety of territorial structure is a mixed one in which the centre has more than one functional area in its territory, but it does not have a monopoly over all functions. Past state-building processes in these countries have not succeeded in removing all functions from the periphery and concentrating them into one geographic centre.[12]

Given that there are a variety of cores, it is also possible to identify a variety of peripheries. Rokkan and Urwin, in fact, point to the existence of two basic types of periphery: *interface* and *external*. The former describes peripheries located in central European areas that have the possibility of interacting with other peripheral territories, such as eastern Portugal/western Spain, Catalonia/Languedoc-Roussion and, on the other side of southern France, the Alpes-Cote d'Azur/Liguria region along the northern Mediterranean rim.[13] The term 'external periphery' is used to describe peripheral areas whose political borders are not shared because of their island, peninsular or external territorial status. This is the case with Ireland and regions on the periphery of mainland Greece, Italy and the UK as well as with the peripheral island territories of Portugal, Spain, Greece and France.

In both cases, external or interface regions find themselves at a disadvantage vis-à-vis the core. According to Tarrow (1977, pp. 15–38), the periphery is characterised by (1) physical distance from the centre; (2) an inferior allocation of economic, political and cultural resources; and (3) dependence on the centre for its livelihood and well-being. The circumstances of the periphery are in most cases not the result of random events but of a specific policy of subjugation on the part of the centre. The periphery is described by Rokkan and Urwin as territory penetrated, absorbed and dominated by the centre:

> It is often a conquered territory, as it were a kind of colony, administered by officials who are responsive less to the desires of the periphery than to instructions from a geographically remote centre. It will also tend to have a poorly developed economy, at the extreme either a subsistence economy standing outside the territorial network of economic exchanges and trade, or one that is dependent upon a single commodity that is sold in distant markets, and thus is more easily prey to frequent fluctuations in both demand and prices, over which the periphery itself will have little or no control. Finally, the periphery will also tend to have a marginal culture: without unified and distinctive institutions of its own, its culture will be fragmented and parochial (Rokkan and Urwin, 1983, p. 2).

In a similar manner, past treatments of the periphery go beyond a mere geographical definition of peripherality. As recognised by Tarrow, many of the commonly used definitions of the periphery propose an ideal type that may not be applicable everywhere and at different points in time. Peripherality as a structural characteristic of a particular area may exist in three distinctive domains: political, economic and cultural.[14] But whatever the domain, the essential feature is that the periphery depends upon one or more centres, which must be taken into account in any discussion of the periphery's situation, predicament and future.

In a similar fashion, Selwyn (1979) describes the economic characteristics of the periphery in the following way. The periphery is unable to exercise control over the use of its own resources; it lacks local innovation; it has weak internal linkages; it is dominated by information flows originating from the centre; and labour migrates from the periphery to the core. As the peripheral economy becomes absorbed into the national economy, its ability to resist structural dependency on the core is weakened until it eventually becomes dominated by the centre.

Concepts derived from core–periphery theories have been used not only to analyse the impact of market integration within nation-states, but also within the context of the EU. Seers (1979) asks 'what does a small, relatively unindustrialized country on the periphery gain from belonging to a system composed of technically advanced core countries?' The answer given is that, even if in the short run the periphery gains in terms of being able to raise its income levels through a strategy of labour migration and attracting outside capital, in the long run it subjugates itself to the economic, military and cultural hegemony of the core (Seers, 1979, p. xviii). During the 1980s the expectation of Seers and other writers on core–periphery economic relations was that membership in the EU would benefit capitalists and workers linked to multinational corporations operating within the peripheral countries, but the forced opening of peripheral markets would 'destroy many small businesses' and sectors (for example textiles and clothing) not prepared to face 'the full competitive power of the giant corporations of the core, despite the difference in wage levels' (ibid., p. 27).

These expectations of core–periphery analyses point to a set of economic conditions of cores and peripheries that can be (but seldom are) empirically tested on the basis of the historical record of European integration:

1. Have national growth rates suffered as national economies have first been opened to international trade and then incorporated into the EU?

2. Have small enterprises in the European periphery been destroyed by competition from large firms?
3. Has manufacturing in peripheral countries suffered from the opening and integration of national markets?
4. Has labour migration increased as economic integration has taken place?
5. Has the relationship between core and periphery within the EU and within nation-states deteriorated over time?

In a similar manner, we could analyse the political consequences of southern peripheral states' membership in a politically integrating community as predicted by extrapolations of centre–periphery theory in the political and administrative spheres:[15]

1. Have peripheral states become less important in the political decision-making process with regard to the allocation of resources in the EU?
2. Have they lost control over decisions affecting their economic conditions and socioeconomic well-being?
3. Have the southern European countries been relegated to increasingly subordinate political status in positions taken by the EU as a whole?
4. Have national publics in peripheral member states become less enthusiastic about European integration as they have experienced the impact of economic integration?

Rokkan and Urwin and other centre–periphery theorists do not attempt to answers these questions in relation to current developments in the EU nor in relation changing nation-state structures. The rise of regional movements and demands to decentralise the nation-state are attributed solely to the need of peripheries to mobilize against the centre in order to defend their residual rights, and not as a desire to fundamentally restructure the nation-state; nor are they necessarily seen as ethnic or linguistic mobilisation (Rokkan and Urwin, 1982; Urwin, 1985).

The authors admit that in the past the economic fortunes of nation-states and regions in Europe have changed on the basis of political/military events, the discovery of new trade routes and technological/economic change. Arrighi (1985) observes that during the last forty years the position of Europe's peripheral economies in the world economic system has undergone extensive change. Empirical evidence points to significant shifts in the position of countries such as Italy and Spain – which have moved, in Arrighi's terms, from semiperipheral to core status – and Portugal and Greece, which have been transformed from peripheral to semiperipheral countries (Arrighi, 1985).

Based on the analyses of Rokkan and Urwin (1983) and Arrighi (1985), it is possible to identify three major trends in the history of European development. Until the sixteenth century Europe was dominated by the east–west axis of economic and commercial activity founded on a string of important commercial centres along the Mediterranean coast. This axis gravitated northward with the rise of Islam in the eastern Mediterranean, the emergence of the nation-state system, the discovery of the New World and the opening of the Atlantic trade routes. The shifting of the east–west axis caused Mediterranean cities to lose their dominance over national capitals and trade centres in the north.

The second major trend in the subsequent centuries was the establishment of a north–south axis. This trend was greatly facilitated by the Reformation – when the links between state and religion were forged into a national identity – and was reinforced by the beginnings of the industrial revolution, which was grounded on coal as the primary energy source and iron ore as the necessary component in the manufacturing of capital goods. The industrial revolution and the introduction of railways as a major form of internal transport strengthened the position of the governmental, institutional core of the nation-state as the centralising structure to command national economic and political affairs and protect the political community from both internal and external enemies.

Centralisation hit its peak in the interwar period as part of the growing political/military tension among the European nation-states. As a result of domestic as well as international activities, the countries of the European periphery (Italy, Portugal, Spain and Greece) progressively cut themselves off from the rest of Europe and the world economy to pursue nationally inspired goals of political and economic autarky. In this phase of response to world economic conditions the state took precedence over market considerations, and greater provisions were made to protect national economic activity from the effects of international competition and penetration.

Trends toward autarky and centralisation in the European system were sharply reversed after the end of the Second World War, when countries were forced to open up their economies and political systems as part of the structural conditions imposed by the US for the reorganisation of political and economic life in Western Europe. Trade, monetary and security policies were allocated to international organisations such as GATT, IMF, OECD and NATO. Because of these changes the relationship between the European northern core and southern periphery began to shift.

In contrast with the interwar period, the role of the state in managing the economy has progressively declined since the Second World War. The state now supplements rather than substitutes for the market, and authoritarian rule has given way to democratic, parliamentary institutions and procedures throughout southern and eastern Europe.

The initial opening up of national economies to outside capital, labour migration and external trade had an impact on the structure of internal and external core–periphery relations. Data cited by Rokkan and Urwin and others (Cuadrado Roura and Suarez-Villa, 1992; Leonardi, 1993a) show that in the postwar period the differences between centre and periphery in nation-states started to decrease, and some of the largest decreases in socioeconomic differences between core and periphery took place in southern European countries (Williams, 1984; Arrighi, 1985).

Initial support for the conclusion that differences between core and periphery have been declining is provided by the study of ninety-seven regions, representing the six original EEC states, conducted by Biehl, Hussmann and Schnyder (1972). In looking at the change in 1960 vis-à-vis 1969 data on a measure of per capita gross internal product, they found that regional disparities had declined. The analysis also showed that the heart of the European economy had moved from the Rhur–Wallonie–Nord Pas de Calais triangle toward a nodal point located along the lower Rhine. From this core, in 1969 income gradients radiated out to the rest of the EC, though the predictive power of the gradient was disturbed by the existence of national capitals and major urban centres. A similar finding, covering the period 1950–70, is reported by Molle, van Holst and Smit (1980).

The above findings on the decrease in regional and national socioeconomic differences within the EC were never incorporated by Rokkan and Urwin into their theoretical formulations of centre–periphery relations. Nor was any attention paid to the impact of European integration on peripheral states or regions. They continued to see centre–periphery relations in nation-state terms as mostly a one-way street; the possibility that the periphery could gain as much or more from integration as the centre was never seriously contemplated.

Given its initial assumptions and methods of argumentation based on ideal types, the centre–periphery literature represents an approach that is significantly different from the one adopted by neofunctionalist integration theory. The latter stresses the fundamental role of economic growth in fuelling the process of institution building and changing existing political relations, thereby bringing about a transformation of the nation-state. Centre–periphery theories represent the equivalent in political-science literature of divergence theories in economics. Both theories draw the conclusion that economic and political integration has more negative than positive consequences for the periphery. However the empirical reality reported by longitudinal empirical studies have pointed in a different direction.

The move toward larger, integrated markets and institutional arrangements is seen by the peripheral countries/regions as offering more advantages than disadvantages (Leonardi, 1993b). Why then does survey research conducted in peripheral countries and regions report such a positive approach to European integration, while the dominant theories in the economics and political-science literature predict negative consequences arising from integration? In order to explain this we need to consider an alternative, convergence model of integration based on empirical rather than ideal definitions of centre and periphery and the processes by which they interact. Before we do that, we have to submit the existing economic theories to empirical verification in order to highlight the hypotheses that demonstrate the greatest predictive power, and begin to identify the factors that might account for the dynamic which we will discover.

NOTES

1. The author places himself in the latter category in emphasising the role of civic values and sense of community in the determination of institutional and economic performance. See Putnam, Leonardi and Nanetti, 1993, and Leonardi and Nanetti (eds), 1994.

2. Hodges (1981) uses convergence to refer to the adoption by member states of similar economic and monetary policies in addition to the more difficult goal of levels of economic performance.

3. Apter (1987, p. 105) has written that industrialisation is part of the modernisation process, but it is possible to modernise societies without much industry.

4. The logic of this position is, as expressed by Kindleberger (1965, p. 213), 'in order to increase efficiency on the farm one must start in the factory'.

5. For a discussion of Perroux and other traditional regional growth theories, see Holland, 1976.

6. There numerous works evaluating how well the growth-pole approach to regional development has stimulated regional development. For a recent treatment, see Millock and Olson, 1993. However it should be noted that in 1993 the Agency for the South – that is, the administrative instrument for the operationalisation of the approach – was abolished by the Amato government because of the lack of balance between the resources invested and the socioeconomic outcomes produced. The new policy links the allocation of further national regional development aid to the acceptance of the principles and programmes contained in the national and regional Community Support Frameworks. This move by the Italian government has for all practical purposes Europeanised Italy's regional development policies. For a discussion of regional development policies in the post-1993 period, see Camera dei Deputati (1994).

7. See the study by Krugman and Venables (1990) empirically testing this proposition.

8. It is argued below that current EU and regional-government development policies provide a third component, effectiveness (that is, more efficient and effective use of development resources), in the use of local, national and EU resources to achieve regional economic development. Derek Diamond and Nigel Spence (1983, p. 17) argue that regional policies have six empirical objectives: (1) to reduce unemployment in depressed areas; (2) to reduce congestion in developed areas; (3) to increase the rate of utilisation of national resources; (4) to reduce interregional differences and relieve inflationary pressures; (5) to preserve and strengthen regional cultures and identities; and (6) to achieve better balances between the population and the environment.

9. The work of Bairoch (1976) clearly demonstrates that between 1800 and 1975 the relative position of European national economies shifted considerably. Therefore the definition of core and peripheral areas in Europe is not static over time and space.

10.   The big states of the southern European periphery (Italy and Spain) are conspicuous by their absence.
11.   The manifestation of these two phenomena has not prevented students of southern Europe from applying dependency theories in an attempt to predict the development of Mediterranean countries. See Seers, Schaffer and Kiljunen, 1979.
12.   Based on the Rokkan and Urwin distinction, one could divide the countries into the following categories: (a) monocephalic countries – France, UK, Belgium, Austria, Denmark, Greece, Ireland, Portugal; (b) intermediate countries – Sweden, Norway, Finland; and (c) polycephalic countries – Germany, Italy, Netherlands, Switzerland and Spain. On the history of state-building in Europe, see Tilly, 1975.
13.   These are the classic border areas covered by Article 10 of the 1988 ERDF regulation trying to promote transborder cooperation discussed in Cappellin and Batey (1993).
14.   The treatment of peripherality as just an expression of ethno-linguistic mobilisation against the centre reflects only one part of the political aspects of periphery–centre relations. See Urwin, 1985.
15.   One of the basic weaknesses of centre–periphery theory in political science is that it has been used to explain past events rather than to predict and test present and future events. Given this orientation, the theory has never been subjected to systematic and careful verification on a longitudinal basis.

REFERENCES

André Frank, G. (1974) *Dependence and Underdevelopment: Latin America's Political Economy* (Garden City, NY: Doubleday).
Apter, D. (1987) *Rethinking Development* (London: Sage).
Arrighi, G. (ed.) (1985) *Semiperipheral Development: The Politics of Southern Europe in the Twentieth Century* (London: Sage).
Bairoch, P. (1976) 'Europe's Gross National Product: 1800–1975', *The Journal of European Economic History*, vol. 2 (Fall), pp. 273–340.
Biehl, D., O. Hussmann and S. Schnyder (1972) 'Zur Regionalen Einkommenverteilung in der Europaische Wirtschaftsgemeinschaft', *Die Weltwirtschaft*, pp. 64–8.
Bryce, M. (1960) *Industrial Developmnt: A Guide to Accelerating Economic Growth* (New York: McGraw-Hill).
Camagni, R. (1991) 'Regional deindustrialization and revitalization processes in Italy', in L. Rodwin and H. Sazanami (eds), *Industrial Change and Regional Economic Transformation: The Experience of Western Europe* (London: Harper Collins), pp. 137–67.
Camera dei Deputati, (1994) *Intervento nel Mezzogiorno e politiche regionali* (Rome: Camera dei Deputati).
Cappellin, R. (1993) 'Patterns and Policies of Economic Development and Cohesion Among the Regions of the European Community', in R. Leonardi, *The State of Economic and Social Cohesion in the Community Prior to*

the Creation of the Single Market: The View from the Bottom-Up, Part II (Brussels: Commission of the European Communities), pp. 1–64.

Cappellin, R. and P. W. Batey (eds) (1993) *Regional Networks, Border Regions and European Integration* (London: Pion Limited).

Carello, A. N. (1989) *The Northern Question: Italy's Participation in the European Economic Community and the Mezzogiorno's Underdevelopment* (Newark, NJ: University of Delaware Press).

Cross, M. (1981) *New Firm Formation and Regional Development* (Westmead: Gower).

Cuadrado Roura, J. and L. Suarez-Villa (1992) 'Regional Economic Integration and the Evolution of Disparities', Fourth World Congress of the Regional Science Association, Palma de Mallorca, 26–30 May.

Diamond, D. R. and N. A. Spence (1983) *Regional Policy Evaluation* (London: Gower).

Garofoli, G. (1991) 'The Italian Model of Spatial Development in the 1970s and 1980s', in G. Benko and M. Dunford (eds), *Industrial Change and Regional Development* (London: Belhaven Press), pp. 85–101.

Garofoli, G. (ed.), (1992) *Endogenous Development in Southern Europe* (Aldershot: Gower).

Grossman, G. M. and E. Helpman (1991) *Innovation and Growth in the Global Economy* (Cambridge, MA: MIT Press).

Gupta, L. C. (1983) *Growth Theory and Strategy: New Direction* (Delhi: Oxford University Press,).

Hamilton, I. (ed.) (1986) *Industrialization in Developing and Peripheral Regions* (London: Croom Helm).

Hirsch, F. (1976) *Social Limits to Growth* (Cambridge: Harvard University Press).

Hodges, M. (1981) 'Liberty, Equality, Divergency: The Legacy of the Treaty of Rome?', in M. Hodges and W. Wallace (eds), *Economic Divergence in the European Community* (London: Allen & Unwin), pp. 1–15.

Hoffmann, W. (1958) *The Growth of Industrial Economies* (Manchester: Manchester University Press).

Holland, S. (1976) *Capital Against Regions* (London: Macmillan).

Holland, S. (1980) *UnCommon Market: Capital, Class and Power in the European Community* (New York: St. Martin's Press).

Hudson, R. and J. Lewis (eds) (1985) *Uneven Development in Southern Europe: Studies of accumulation, class, migration and the state* (London: Methuen).

Kindleberger, C. (1965) *Economic Development* (New York: McGraw-Hill).

Krause, L. B. (1968) *European Economic Integration and the United States* (Washington, DC: The Brookings Institution).

Krugman, P. and A. Venables (1990) 'Integration and the competitiveness of peripheral industry', in C. Bliss and J. Braga de Machedo (eds), *Unity with Diversity in the European Economy: the Community's Southern Frontier* (Cambridge: Cambridge University Press), pp. 56–75.

Leonardi, R. (1993a) 'Cohesion in the European Community: Illusion or Reality?', *West European Politics* (October), pp. 492–517.

Leonardi, R. (ed.) (1993b) *The Regions and the European Community: The Impact of the Single Market on the Underdeveloped Areas* (London: Frank Cass).

Leonardi, R. and R. Y. Nanetti (eds) (1994) *Regional Development in a Modern European Economy: The Case of Tuscany* (London: Pinter).

Lizano, E. and L. N. Willmore (1975) 'Second Thoughts on Central America, The Rosenthal Report', *Journal of Common Market Studies*, vol. XIII, no. 3, pp. 280–307.

Millock, K. and S. Olson (1993) 'Why poor regions stay poor', *Journal of Regional Policy*, vol. 13 (January/March), pp. 51–72,

Molle, W., B. van Holst and H. Smit (1980) *Regional Disparity and Economic Development in the European Community* (Westmead: Saxon House).

Myrdal, G. (1957) *Economic Theory and the Underdeveloped Regions* (London: Duckworth).

Nanetti, R. Y. (1992) *Coordination in Development Planning: An Evaluation of the Initial Implementation of the Community Support Framework* (Brussels: Commission of the European Communities, October).

Olson, M. (1982) *The Rise and Decline of Nations: Economic Growth, Stagflation and Social Rigidities* (New Have, Conn.: Yale University Press).

Overturf, S. F. (1986) *The Economic Principles of European Integration* (New York: Praeger).

Perroux, F. (1955) 'Note sur la notion de pole de croissance', *Economie Appliquee*, no. 7.

Piore, M. and C. Sabel (1984) *The Second Industrial Divide* (New York: Free Press).

Pred, A. (1977) *City Systems in Advanced Economies* (London: Hutchinson).

Putnam, R. D., R. Leonardi and R. Y. Nanetti (1993) *Making Democracy Work: Civic Traditions in Modern Italy* (Princeton: Princeton University Press).

Rokkan, S. and D. W. Urwin (eds) (1982) *The Politics of Territorial Identity: Studies in European Regionalism* (London: Sage).

Rokkan, S. and D. W. Urwin (1983) *Economy, Territory, Identity: Politics of West European Peripheries* (London: Sage).

Ross, D. P. and P. J. Usher (1986) *From the Roots Up: Economic Development as if Community Mattered* (Croton-on-Hudson, NY: The Bootstrap Press).

Saraceno, P. (1977) *Risultati e nuovi obbiettivi dell'intervento straordinario* (Rome: SVIMEZ).

Sartori, G. (1976) *Parties and Party Systems: A Framework for Analysis* (New York: Cambridge Univesity Press).

Seers, D. (1979) 'Preface' in D. Seers, B. Schaffer and L. Kiljunen (eds) *Underdeveloped Europe: Studies in Core–Periphery Relations* (Hassocks: Harvest Press, pp. XIII–XXI.

Seers, D., B. Schaffer and L. Kiljunen (eds) (1979) *Underdeveloped Europe: Studies in Core–Periphery Relations* (Atlantic Highlands, NJ: Humanities Press).

Selwyn, P. (1979) 'Some Thoughts on Cores and Peripheries' in D. Seers, B. Schaffer and L. Kiljunen (eds) *Underdeveloped Europe: Studies in Core–Periphery Relations*, pp. 35–43.

Stoehr, W. (1990) *Global Challenge and Local Response* (London: Mansell).

Suarez-Villa, L. (1989) *The Evolution of Regional Economies* (New York: Praeger).

Tarrow, S. (1977) *Between Center and Periphery: Grassroots Politicians in Italy and France* (New Haven: Yale University Press).

Tilly, C. (ed.) (1975) *Formation of National States in Europe* (Princeton: Princeton University Press).

Tsoukalis, L. (1981) 'Economic Divergence and Enlargement' in M. Hodges and W. Wallace (eds), *Economic Divergence in the European Community* (London: Allen & Unwin), pp. 151–66.

Urwin, D. W. (1985) 'The Price of a Kingdom: Territory, Identity and the Centre–Periphery Dimension in Western Europe', in Y. Meny and V. Wright (eds) *Centre–Periphery Relations in Western Europe* (London: Allen & Unwin), pp. 151–70.

Vanhove, N. and L. H. Klaassen (1980) *Regional Policy A European Approach* (Montclair, NJ: Allenheld, Osmun & Co).

Wadley, D. (1986) *Restructuring the Regions* (Paris: OECD).

Williams, A. (ed.) (1984) *Southern Europe Transformed: Political and economic change in Greece, Italy, Portugal and Spain* (London: Harper & Row).

3 Methodology for the Study of Economic and Social Convergence

THE EMPIRICAL CRITERIA FOR EVALUATING CONVERGENCE

In making the transition between the predictions of economic and political theories and analysing what has been happening in regional economies in Europe, past research has not been sensitive to the need to test hypotheses in an empirical and dispassionate manner. In order to rectify this situation, the evaluation of convergence conducted in the next three chapters will be carried out by making a two-fold distinction. Chapters 3 and 4 will concentrate on defining and evaluating the *dependent* variable – that is, the variable or variables that provide evidence of a change (or no change) in the cohesion gap and the level of convergence – while in Chapter 5 attention will be paid to *independent* variables – that is, those variables that can explain or account for, on a statistical basis, the changes observed in the dependent variable.

Given the importance of knowing exactly what is happening to the dependent variable, much of this section will focus on developing an objective description of the level of regional social and economic development that meets the empirical criteria for measuring the state of convergence. In searching for the dependent variable, past studies and the Single European Act provide a clear guide. The goal of reducing regional economic and social disparities represents the starting point of the analysis.

In order to measure the concept of convergence, it is necessary to construct variables that contain data measuring the level of economic and social well-being on a longitudinal basis – that is, over different points in time. In selecting the dependent variables care must be taken to ensure the variables are *reliable* – that is, they have to be operationalised in the same

60

way over time – and *valid* – that is, they must tap the concept being analysed. To satisfy these criteria, the study identifies three factors that are made explicit and held constant in the collection and analysis of data.[1]

First, *the achievement of cohesion is conceived as a process that develops over time.* Cohesion is not a static state. It takes place (or does not take place) on a longitudinal basis as the convergence dynamic works itself through the economic system. Thus the dynamic of convergence has to be measured with time-series data. To evaluate whether convergence is taking place, it cannot be measured at only one point in time; nor can it realistically be measured over a relatively short period, for example over five to seven years. Given that economic cycles ripple through the various European national and regional economies at an uneven pace, national markets have been opened to international economic factors according to varying patterns, and countries have joined the EU at different points in time – maximising the accuracy of the measurement of trends requires a long-term series of data on national and regional economic conditions. The longer the period in which the variables are measured, the better the chance that the full course of an economic cycle and integration trends will be picked up as they work their way through the diverse national markets (Bayoumi and Eichengreen, 1991).

The Single European Act also posits economic and social cohesion as the result of a longitudinal process. The expectation expressed by the Single European Act is that, with the advancement of European integration, the creation of the Single Market and moves toward monetary union will enhance the chances of achieving socioeconomic cohesion. Simply stated: the gap between the EU's rich and poor areas will decrease, and it will decrease even faster as more economic resources are invested in peripheral countries and regions.

Though the expectations of the Single European Act and the Maastricht Treaty are projected toward the future, it is still possible to evaluate the prospect of achieving cohesion by assessing the success (or lack thereof) of the previous integration process in promoting a reduction in regional disparities or a convergence of socioeconomic conditions. Questions that arise in the light of past economic performance are:

1. If convergence was not promoted, even at a minimal level, within the European Common Market of six or nine member states, then what are the prospects that the union of twelve member states operating under the auspices of the Single Market and Monetary Union will achieve economic and social cohesion?
2. If progress was not made in reducing social and economic disparities under the European Common Market, the chances that the situation will change radically, even under conditions of full market integration, may be seriously questioned.
3. If convergence has not taken place in the past, the chance of achieving cohesion for the regions of Greece, Portugal and Spain is remote.

As a consequence achieving cohesion (or a significant amount of convergence), as expressed in the Rome Treaty, the Single European Act, the Maastricht Treaty and current EU policy pronouncements, constitutes only a theoretical prospect and not a concrete empirical expectation to be achieved during the next decade or two. Cohesion is, therefore, at best a ruse and at worst a cruel trick played on less developed economies to cajole them into providing their vital and scarce resources to feed the growth and expansion of the core economies.

The successful operationalisation of the first factor in evaluating the pace of convergence requires that the concept be measured over time using the same variable/s and the same cases.[2] If these basic principles of comparative research are not observed, then the components of the variable used to measure convergence over time undergo change. As a consequence the analysis measures different parts of the concept at different points in time. In a parallel fashion, if the definition of the *cases* or 'units of analysis' is changed over time, the analysis will measure cohesion for a differing mix of subjects rather than for the same ones over the time span considered.

Comparative analysis of cohesion that does not respect these simple principles – carrying out the analysis over an extended period of time and maintaining constant the definition of the variables and units of analysis – undermines the entire process of evaluation. The inevitable result of such changes is confusion as to what is taking place, what is being measured or how the results can be compared over time. The prospect of understanding the dynamic that is produced by market integration at the regional level is lost, and it becomes impossible to develop appropriate policy instruments for the EU's less favoured regions.

Second, *the appropriate level of analysis for the study of cohesion is the nation-state and the region.* While the determinants of growth continue to be the subject of continued debate, it is necessary to disentangle national from region-specific factors in the development process. As Paul Krugman (1991, p. 3) has argued, in trying empirically to measure and understand the differences in national growth rates and the impact of international specialisation on national and regional economies, the logical place to start is to look at what is happening at the subnational, regional level: 'The data will be better and pose fewer problems of compatibility, and the underlying economic forces will be less distorted by government policies'. To study economic changes that have taken place at the regional level vis-à-vis the national level we need a constant definition of the units of analysis over time. While the definition of the constituent nation-state has not changed within the EU during the last forty years, the same cannot be said for the regions.

As acknowledged by the EU in its definition of territorial levels through the distinction among NUTS I, II, and III, the term 'region' differs from one nation-state to another.[3] In some cases the region is a defined territorial space associated with a set of political and legal institutions with decision-making powers and policy-implementation roles, while in other cases it is only an arbitrary division of national territory into units used for the purpose of collecting and reporting statistical data. Nevertheless the importance of using a consistent definition of region is that it (1) allows the analysis to include the multidude of regions on which the EU has collected information, (2) permits evaluation of convergence trends beyond a limited number of cases and a short period of time, and (3) removes the restriction of basing the analysis on just a few regional case studies. Regional-level data provides the opportunity for an analysis of trends to move on to a more differentiated and detailed level of aggregation and focus on problem areas at the subnational level.

EUROSTAT and others have been collecting information at

the regional level for a number of years. The two data bases used in this study are (1) EUROSTAT's REGIO regional dataset, covering the period 1970 to 1988 and supplemented by EROSTAT 1989, 1990 and 1991 data, and (2) data published in Molle, van Holst and Smit (1980), covering the period between 1950 and 1970. These two sources provide an adequate data base to conduct a longitudinal analysis over a forty-year period. The two data sets will have to be analysed separately because of differing definitions of the dependent variable and slight variations in the units of analysis. However both data sets are very similar in structure, and taken together they can provide a clear indication of the course of regional and national disparities over the life of European imtegration.

In the analysis of the 1970–91 period a sub-sample of the 174 NUTS II statistical regions used by EUROSTAT was created and reworked, taking into account changes in the definition of NUTS II regions between 1970 and 1980. The sample covers eighty regions in the original nine member states over the period 1970–91. The regions of the other three member states (Greece, Portugal and Spain) can, with the present data, only be treated over a shorter, eleven-year period (1981–91). However, what is learned from the analysis of the nine member-state cases from 1950–91 can be easily applied when formulating predictions for the regions in the three new member states. In addition both sets of data (that is, for the nine member states and for the three southerm peripheral states) can be used to generate conclusions concerning the impact of economic convergence on less developed regional economies on the periphery of the EU. In many ways the past is still the best predictor of the future.

Third, *the rate of convergence can be measured in two basic ways*: it can be expressed in *absolute* terms, as measured by specific levels of productivity and consumption; or it can be expressed in *relative* terms through rank scores or the relative change in position on indexes vis-à-vis other regions.

In addition, absolute levels of development can be measured in comparative terms in two ways. The first is *externally* vis-à-vis other regions between a hypothetical Time 1 and Time 2 – that is, do a region's economic and social levels improve in comparison with those of neighbouring regions? The second is based on an *internal* comparison with the region's own development between Times 1 and 2 – that is, does the region in Time 2 enjoy a higher level of productivity and consumption than it did in Time 1? Thus from the beginning it is important to establish the point of reference (absolute versus relative comparison) and the frame of reference (internal or external comparison). Both sets of measures are important in analysing convergence because they measure various parts of the issue and can provide alternative scenarios for future policy intervention.

THE HYPOTHESES AND SCENARIOS FOR THE STUDY OF CONVERGENCE

In testing the hypothesis generated by the four sets of theoretical literature discussed above, it is necessary to make explicit reference to how change is expected to manifest itself in bringing about the results predicted by the hypotheses. For this purpose we have formulated three possible scenarios that could be followed in achieving convergence, plus one scenario for divergence and one for no change in the status quo. It is theoretically possible that, despite what is predicted by divergence and convergence theories, both sets of theories are wrong. Empirical analysis may show that there has simply been no change in disparities despite the massive resources invested in regional development. As a consequence we need to take into account the possibility of a third hypothesis that predicts no change over time.

Each hypothesis and its subset of scenarios will be discussed separately in terms of the starting point of the regions, the dynamic hypothetically characterising the most and least developed regions in the EU, and the increase or decrease of the 'cohesion gap' that is expected in projecting the results of the varying development trends. The three hypotheses will then be tested on the basis of empirical data presented in the following chapters.

The first hypothesis is the 'equivalent growth hypothesis' presented in Figure 3.1. In the figure both the most and the least developed regions experience growth, but that growth manifests itself at the same level in both sets of regions. Thus there is no net change in the cohesion gap that separates the

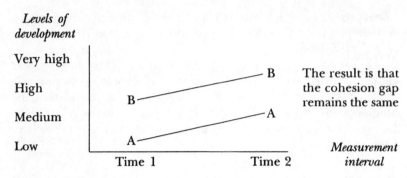

Figure 3.1   Equivalent growth hypothesis

regions at the two points in time when the measurement is made. In both cases the regions make absolute progress in their internal levels of, for example, productivity and well-being between Time 1 and Time 2. Despite making absolute and internal gains vis-à-vis where they were at Time 1, as measured by their position at Time 2, they do not make any progress with respect to each other because their relative positions remain the same, and as a consequence no progress is made in closing the cohesion gap between the regions at the top and those at the bottom of the ranking. Expressed in the criteria for analysing convergence over time, there is absolute change but no relative change, and internally there is change but externally there is no change.

The next hypothesis to be discussed is the one predicted by the economic convergence and neofunctionalist integration theories. In looking at the possible ways in which convergence can manifest itself, there are a number of alternative paths. The first scenario is the one that predicts convergence through a process of 'peripheral ascendancy'. Peripheral ascendancy predicts that the less developed regions will grow at an accelerated pace vis-à-vis the most developed regions, thereby reducing the gap between the two groups of regions as measurements are taken over time. There are two main ways in which the gap can be reduced. Figure 3.2 presents the first possibility: the closing of the cohesion gap through 'upward convergence'. The less developed regions experience accelerated rates of growth while the most developed regions undergo less spectacular growth. Figure 3.3, in turn, hypothesises a

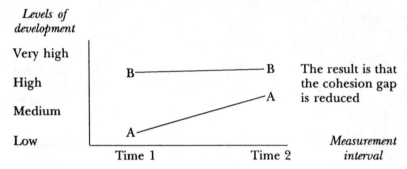

Figure 3.2   Convergence Hypothesis: Upward Convergence Scenario

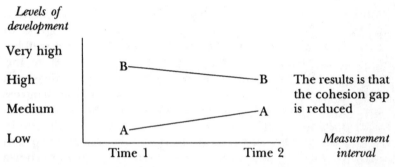

Figure 3.3   Convergence hypothesis: downward convergence scenario

similar end-result through 'downward convergence', with a decline in the strongest regions and modest growth by the less developed regions. The overall result of the dynamics illustrated by Scenarios 2 and 3 is the same, but the policy implications of the two hypotheses are radically different.

In Figure 3.2 reduction of the gap is posited on the basis of rapid growth on the part of the weakest regions: the rate of growth of the weakest between Time 1 and Time 2 outstrips the rate of development of the strongest regions, and the outcome is a reduction of the cohesion gap. According to this hypothesis, reduction is taking place in both internal and 'external' absolute terms. But there is still the theoretical possibility that it might not be taking place in relative terms: rank positions may remain unaltered in the process, while the gap between the regions is reduced. In statistical terms the

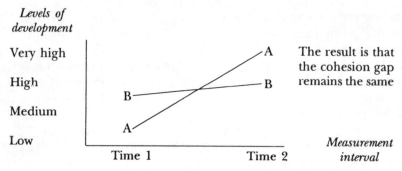

Figure 3.4   Convergence hypothesis: reversal of roles scenario

standard deviation, or the dispersion of the cases over the index, decreases.

In Figure 3.3 reduction of the cohesion gap is based more on the negative performance of the top regions than on any substantial increase in the weaker regions. In other words, convergence is due not to the sustained growth of the less developed regions but to the economic regression of the strongest regions toward the mean.

A convincing argument in support of Scenarios 2 and 3 was made by Jacques Delors in 1989, when he argued that the traditional factors (transport costs and economies of scale) fuelling the growth of the core versus the periphery have declined in importance in determining industrial-location decisions. Instead there has been growth in the importance of 'the deliberate strategies of the public authorities relating to market conditions and investments in human capital, R&D and economic infrastructure, and the reactions of mobile corporations to these strategies' (Delors, 1989, p. 83). A similar point is made by Tsoukalis (1991) in arguing that serious regional problems can be alleviated if EU policies aim at promoting both flexibility of product and factor markets and the effectiveness of EU and member-state regional policy instruments.

The last scenario to be discussed under convergence theory posits the existence of a combined upward and downward dynamic on the part of, respectively, the underdeveloped and developed regions. Scenario 3, which is presented in Figure 3.4, argues that the core runs into difficulty in maintaining its relative and even absolute standards of growth. In contrast, during the same period the periphery enjoys sustained growth to the point that the positions are reversed: the periphery become the core and the core declines into peripherality.[4] In such an eventuality the cohesion gap between rich and poor regions may remain the same, but the position of the regions changes radically. Thus the third scenario appropriately posits a reversal of roles.

The reversal-of-roles scenario represents the most extreme form of convergence or peripheral ascendancy. It asserts that a significant shift is occurring in the relative economic positions of the core and periphery.[5] This hypothesis may appear quite fanciful when we consider the current conditions of underdevelopment in Europe's peripheral regions, as described in the Periodic Reports (CEC, 1981, 1984, 1987, 1991a). However it may not be so fanciful when considering what is happening at other levels in the regional rankings – for example to regions at intermediate levels in the regional ranking. Here there may in fact be significant reversals of positions that represent an important component in the peripheral-ascendancy thesis. Rodwin (1991) has noted that the traditional dichotomy between core and periphery, or between northern and southern Europe, is no longer valid. The former industrial areas are now facing 'combined losses of job productivity and competitiveness' through declining investments, closure of plants, rising unemployment and emigration, declining revenues, and ageing and obsolete infrastructures. At the same time, formerly 'dependent', underdeveloped areas are turning out to be the most dynamic 'hot spots' of development. These regions, which often include 'sunbelt' areas, are relatively well endowed with infrastructure, climatically attractive and possess considerable amenities (Leonardi, 1994).

Figure 3.5 represents the more traditional hypothesis used in the discussion of regional disparities in the EU. This hypothesis stresses the increasing divergence between developed/centre/core regions and underdeveloped/peripheral regions. The 'core–periphery hypothesis' predicts a widening gap between rich and poor regions: the rich get richer and the poor get poorer in relative if not absolute terms. According to the hypothesis, the core/rich regions possess structural characteristics (economies of scale, skilled labour force, higher levels of technological development and so on) that continue to fuel

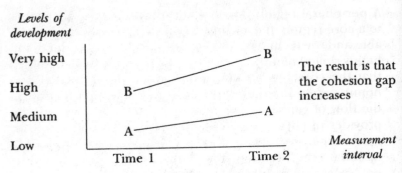

Figure 3.5 Divergence hypothesis: core–periphery scenario

their growth in a spiral of concentration and increased regional divergence at levels that cannot be achieved by poor regions because the latter are not blessed with the same advantages or external economies.

According to this hypothesis, even though the periphery may expand it cannot do so at the same level or pace as its rich neighbours. If poor regions grow in absolute terms and enjoy internal progress, this still does not compare with the expansion enjoyed by the rest of the EU. The position of the periphery is eroding in absolute terms: the gap between rich and poor regions increases over time. In this perspective, EU policies can help 'ease the pain' of the increasing gap through the use of transfer payments to improve living conditions, but they cannot change the basic logic or the dynamic of market factors. These transfer payments (development aid, training funds, infrastructure loans and so on) constitute the 'side payments' for the less developed countries so that they will not obstruct the integration of markets or protest over the loss of control of monetary (manipulation of exchange rates to make domestic products competitive on the world market) or fiscal policies (running budget deficits to sustain national investment and consumption levels) through integration.

The core–periphery concept has been used extensively to characterise situations where an unequal exchange occurs between regions. An example of the relationship between core and peripheral regions is provided by the work of Kielstra on Languedoc-Roussillon:

A peripheral region provides cheap products and/or labor to a core region in exchange for more expensive and profitable and/or technologically highly developed products and highly skilled and paid labor. Implicitly, it is usually assumed that the core region has a much more differentiated economic system than a peripheral region and that it controls the flow of capital in the economic system as a whole. As a provider of cheap products and/or labor and a market for more expensive products and labor, a 'periphery' fulfills essential economic functions for a 'center' though it does not receive a proportionate share in the social and economic benefits produced by the economic system as a whole (Kielstra, 1985, p. 246).[6]

In the past the EC has used the core-dominance hypothesis to argue for the need of additional funds to sustain its specific regional and more general Structural Fund policy (for example the Thomson Report in 1973). However some partial doubts on the viability of this explanation began to surface in a number of the studies spawned by the realisation of the Single Market (Padoa Schioppa *et al.*, 1987; Emerson, 1990).

In the formulations of the core–periphery thesis, the core of the EU is often viewed as centred on a triangular area along the Rhine, sometimes called the 'golden triangle', which is linked in economic and financial terms to a wider area stretching from the Ile de France to the Nordrhein-Westfalen Länder in Germany to the Saarland on the French–German border (CEC, 1991a, 1991b).[7] Despite some variations in the definitions used to delineate the core, there is agreement in defining the periphery as all or some parts of the EU's outer regions: Scotland, Ireland, Northern Ireland, Wales, the southern and western parts of France, Portugal, Spain, Italy (especially the Mezzogiorno) and Greece.[8] In other words, the greater part of the periphery is represented by Objective 1 areas.

More recent analyses (for example IFO, 1990; NIESR, 1991; Camagni, 1991) argue that core regions have consistently higher scores on population density, employment in industry, productivity and levels of well-being than their neighbours in the periphery, and the four Periodic Reports have contributed to the observation that over time the core continues to concentrate economic activity. It is held that once the industrial boom in the Western world slowed down in the wake of the 1974 and 1979 oil shocks, the main losers in the worldwide downturn continued to be the underdeveloped parts of the EC (Padoa Schioppa *et al.*, 1987). Thus the core-dominance hypothesis has practically achieved the status of a truism in analyses of the dynamic characterising the European regions.[9]

Apart from the Biehl, Hussman and Schnyder (1972) study cited in Chapter 2, the other main exception to the dominating divergence theories was the work of Molle, van Holst and Smit (1980), who argued that the gap between rich and poor regions – as well as the gap between rich and poor member states – has decreased. In summing up the results of their twenty-year survey of regional disparities in the initial nine member states, they unequivocally concluded that the core-dominance hypothesis is not at all supported by the data. They found that disparities decreased in a consistent manner at both national and regional levels:

> We have examined whether regions with similar growth rates also had other characteristics in common, such as their type of location with the EC. From the centre–periphery theory it might have been expected, for example, that integration would have the effect of making regions along the inner borders of the Community of the Six grow faster, and peripheral regions slower than average in the period 1960–70. The outcome of the analysis shows no such thing (Molle, van Holst, Smit, 1980, p. 161).

In subsequent writings Molle attributes the reduction of disparities to three factors: (1) the movement of capital – 'in all European countries manufacturing plants have moved from central to peripheral areas'; (2) the migration of workers – 'contrary to that of capital, labour movement was rather centripetal'; and (3) the creation of the welfare state – 'the provision of such welfare services as schools, hospitals, transfer payments, and social security systems has strengthened the economic base of the less affluent regions' (Molle, 1991, p. 422). Given the short treatment of the subject, Molle does not explain how the contradictory movements of capital and labour sort themselves out or how the creation of a welfare state increases economic productivity. In addition there is no discussion of other, more recent, peripheral 'pull' and core 'push' factors that might account for the reduction of disparities.

The insights generated by the Molle, van Holst and Smit study were not adequately developed in subsequent analyses by other students of regional disparities in the EU, nor by the Commission in preparing its Periodic Reports. Instead the bulk of the work on regional disparities drew the pessimistic conclusion that little could be done to increase the position of the peripheral regions in the system. Most of the literature continued to argue that the dynamic of market conditions favoured the core at the expense of the periphery. This argument was repeated in the Cecchini Report (1988) concerning economies of scale and the advantages of the Single Market.

The argument goes as follows: (1) if a larger market leads to better use of economies of scale, then the distribution of benefits from integration will be determined by the extent to which they are already exploited in the first place, and (2) countries that have not yet exhausted their use of economies of scale are likely to benefit the most. The core-dominance hypothesis predicts that the first option will be the dominant one in determining the distribution of economic benefits (Smith and Venables, 1988), while the peripheral-ascendancy thesis points to the latter option as the more important one in producing outcomes.[10]

Basically the centre–periphery theory, based on the traditional economies-of-scale argument, predicts that the gap between rich and poor can never be eliminated completely, or can only be eliminated with difficulty. In fact the hypothesis predicts that differences are most likely to expand over time.[11]

The problem with accepting the core-dominance hypothesis is, if the dynamic is at work in the EU, why isn't it also at work in a comparable, or even more integrated economy such as the US? The experience of the US manufacturing belt, as discussed in analyses of regional shifts in production, wages and migratory flows, suggests that – even where the market is a dominant factor in the location of economic activity – factor availability and changing production technology can be strong countervailing influences (Stough, 1993; Barro and Sala-i-Martin, 1991). If the analyses of European development trends are to be believed, there is a strong difference in the dynamics of the two markets. If this is the case, then analysis would have to show why the dynamic of economic integration in Europe is so diametrically opposite to that taking place in the US. Such an analysis suggests the existence of two different dynamics, logics and, conceivably, sets of rules for economic integration on the opposite sides of the Atlantic.[12]

Rather than embark on such a massive rethinking of economic theory, it is easier to test the convergence hypothesis that the dynamics of economic integration in the US and Europe are not different, but the same. All empirical work on the US has found that levels of social and economic well-being in the US have significantly converged during the last two decades (Barro and Sala-i-Martin, 1991; Stough, 1993). The testing of the convergence hypothesis thus emerges as the most logical starting point to explain the evolution of European regions under conditions of economic integration.[13]

Part of the answer to the apparent contradiction highlighted by the US vis-à-vis the European literature may be found in the fact that European analyses have had difficulty in considering the theoretical implications of convergence in the EU. Economists have discussed the theoretical possibility of European economic integration stimulating the economies of peripheral regions 'by enlarging the size of the market, facilitating the transfer of technology and eliminating redundancy in the development or imitation of ideas, products and organisational methods' (Abraham and Van Rompuy, 1991, p. 19), but this has not led to extensive empirical verifications of the eventuality in terms of the peripheral-pull and core-push factors.[14] Instead the emphasis has been on divergence to such an extent that empirical reality has been ignored.

In summary, the five scenarios presented above propose three different forms of change in the cohesion gap:

– Scenarios 2 and 3 predict a narrowing of the gap.
– Scenario 5 predicts an increase in the gap.
– Scenarios 1 and 4 hold out the prospect of no change in the gap (but for completely opposite reasons).

What differentiates Scenarios 1 and 4 is which regions find themselves at the bottom or at the top. According to Scenario 4, the gap remains the same but the regions that find themselves at the top and bottom of the ranking are quite different at the two different time points when the measurement is made. Scenarios 2 and 3 raise the possibility that the preconditions for a considerable narrowing of the gap are unfolding, and that the continuation of these trends will produce a significant shift in relations between the present alignment of core and peripheral regions. In addition, Scenario 4 poses an extreme form of peripheral ascendancy. Thus, out of the five scenarios, three (2, 3 and 4) predict a reduction in the gap between core and peripheral regions over time.

The scenarios that will be examined with particular interest here are the ones associated with the convergence hypothesis. If peripheral ascendancy is taking place in the EU, the periphery should demonstrate accelerated and sustained levels of growth, as measured by the dependent variable, and the changes in the variables should indicate a closing of the gap between rich and poor regions. This result is hypothesised to be the outcome of a number of factors that favour the growth of the peripheral regions vis-à-vis those located in the European core.

THE NEED TO REDEFINE CASES AND VARIABLES FOR THE ANALYSIS

The findings presented here are based on an analysis of raw data drawn for the 1950–70 period from Molle, van Holst and Smit (1980) and for the 1970–91 period from the REGIO dataset and other EUROSTAT-supplied data. Data from these sources have been used to calculate the dynamic of change over the forty-one-year period in which the member-states and regions of the EU were undergoing profound economic and social change. To carry out the analysis according to the criteria discussed above, a sample of EU regions was created in order to guarantee the use of the same variables and units of analysis over the same period of time.

Due to the changes in the composition of member states and difficulties in collecting data, reporting of the data in the Periodic Reports was not based on a constant definition of cases. During the time that elapsed between the preparation and publication of the First (CEC, 1981) and subsequent Periodic Reports (CEC, 1984, 1987, 1991a), the composition of the

EC changed. Greece joined in 1981, with Spain and Portugal following five years later. The need to include these three new members induced the Commission to redefine the units of analysis used in the study, and this was to have serious consequences for the understanding of the dynamic of regional change.

Economic growth at the regional level in Greece, Portugal and Spain was not evaluated and regions from these three new member states were not part of an integrated dataset until the Third Periodic Report (CEC, 1987). Thus the thirty-five new regions were not included in the analysis of regional disparities in the Second Periodic Report (CEC, 1984), and of course they were not part of the analysis contained in the First Report (CEC, 1981).

In addition the Second Periodic Report (CEC, 1984) made changes to the definition of 'historical' UK regions and to the collection of data for NUTS II regions in Belgium, Denmark and Germany. Thus without compensating for the greater level of detail introduced in the 1980s calculations of regional-level development and well-being – that is, maintaining constant the units of analysis for comparison with the previous analyses – it is not possible to compare the cohesion-gap data presented in the First Report with those in the Second, Third and Fourth Reports. The measurement of disparities between the least and most developed regions was carried out on the basis of different definitions of the units of analysis. In the period between the First and Third Periodic Reports the REGIO data set not only added new cases at the bottom of the index or rankings but also at the top.[15] As a consequence, changes in the number and definition of the cases falsified the measurement of the change in the gap between rich and poor regions and distorted the conclusions drawn by subsequent analyses. Attempts to measure the change in regional disparities over time (for example those carried out by Camagni, 1991; IFO, 1990; NIESER, 1991) are grounded on these shifting definitions of the units of analysis.[16]

The greater detail introduced in the analysis of the 1980s data vis-à-vis the units of analysis used to evaluate the 1970s data, *in and of itself* produced a widening gap between the most and least developed regions. The British regions were recategorised for the entire 1980s. The result was the move from eleven to thirty-four cases. In 1970 and 1977, using the older, larger classifications, there was only a single UK region above the European mean – the southeast. However in 1981, after the recategorisation had been carried out, there were two in the top twenty-five and eleven above the mean, a change not entirely attributable to the entry of Greece, Portugal and Spain. The number of German regions also increased from eleven to thirty-one, and the number of Belgian regions increased from three to ten due to a redefinition of what should be in the NUTS I and II categories. The thirty-four new regions slotting into the dataset at NUTS II with the accession of the three new peripheral states were more than counterbalanced (a two to one increase) by the addition of seventy-eight newly defined cases for the more developed member states. During the 1970s Germany, the UK and Belgium only accounted for twenty-five cases.

In order to be consistent in the definition of the cases to be analysed, the present analysis uses NUTS I level data for Belgium, the UK and Germany and NUTS II level data for France, Italy and the Netherlands.[17] The other three countries – Ireland, Luxembourg and Denmark – are treated at the NUTS I level.[18] In order to carry out the reorganisation of the data, the analysis was conducted on the basis of the raw data in the REGIO dataset and additional data was drawn from other EUROSTAT sources to extend the analysis to 1991.

Raw data from REGIO and EUROSTAT sources provided the basis for undertaking a full and systematic analysis over the twenty-one-year period required for comparative analysis. It was not possible to maintain over the same period the finer detail introduced in the 1980s REGIO dataset, which listed 174 possible cases at the NUTS II level. While the 1980s data could be reaggregated to the 1970 regional specifications – that is, reaggregating 1980s NUTS II level data back to NUTS I – it was not possible to disaggregate the 1970s NUTS I level data to the 1980s NUTS II level of differentiated cases. Thus the definition of cases used in this analysis allocates twenty to Italy, twenty-two to France, eleven to the UK, three to Belgium, eleven to Germany and ten to the Netherlands. Ireland, Luxembourg and Denmark are kept as one case each. In the latter instance, aggregating the regional data into one case is rendered necessary by the apparent lack of continuity between the definitions of the Danish regions between the 1970s and the 1980s.

The 1950–70 data analysis is based on the seventy-four cases used by Molle, van Holst and Smit (1980). Units of analysis are the same in the two time periods (1950–70 and 1970–9) for the UK, Germany, France, Italy, Belgium, Luxembourg and Ireland. Differences exist in the definition of cases for the Netherlands and Denmark. Molle *et al.* divide the Netherlands into four and Denmark into six regions. However, since the analysis of the two periods will not be presented in a 'continuous' manner – that is, values of index scores will not be directly compared over the two periods – what will be of concern here is a comparison between the relative rankings of the regions with respect to regional development and the trend over time – that is, whether differences in levels of development increase or decrease when comparing index scores at the beginning and end of the period under consideration.

The four Periodic Reports on the regions can serve as a starting point, but they cannot function as the sole data sources for the analysis. The stated purpose in undertaking the Periodic Reports was to assess the 'regions' capabilities to adapt their economies to changing circumstances and to develop their indigenous resources to the fullest extent possible' (CEC, 1981, p. 2). The addition of three member states led to a clear increase in disparities, given the increased number of regions and the addition of some of the poorest regions in Europe. Despite the possibility that many of the regions of the original nine member states might have improved their relative positions, this could never be evaluated due to the flood of new regions from an even more distant European periphery and to the redefinition of some of the original cases for the most developed countries.

As expected, the data analysed by the Periodic Reports showed that in the twelve member states the average level of regional income had declined. The ratio between the strongest and weakest regions had been inflated by the addition of a large number of sparsely populated mountainous zones, Mediterranean regions with weak agricultural structures, areas containing traditional industries that required restructuring and modernisation, and an appreciable increase in the number of regions coping with strong demographic pressures and high rates of unemployment and underemployment. In 1985 Spain, Greece and Portugal generated GDPs that were, respectively, 72 per cent, 57 per cent and 52 per cent of the EC average, in comparison with Italy's 103 per cent and Ireland's 65 per cent. The two latter countries had previously contained the weakest regions in the EC-9 (CEC, 1987, p. 9). The Third Periodic Report observed that by 1985 around one-fifth of the population were living in regions where income levels 'measured in terms of GDP per head of population trail behind the Community average by up to 60 per cent or more' (CEC, 1987, p. I).

Despite these changes, the Periodic Reports failed to evaluate how the regions had performed over the course of time.[19] In failing to carry out a longitudinal analysis, the Second, Third and Fourth Reports missed the opportunity to provide a measure of the impact that participation in the EC had had on regional economies in the less developed areas,[20] even though the Reports contained tantalising pieces of information that were in glaring contradiction to the official thesis of the Reports. For example, the Second Report made the observation, based on an analysis of changes in per capita GDP from 1970–83, that a group of fourteen regions located 'mostly in less densely populated and less urbanised or even more rural regions' on the extreme periphery of the EC 'performed best' (CEC, 1984, p. 67). However, given that such a finding contrasted with the expectation that the peripheral regions would be net losers rather than gainers from integration, this line of inquiry was never fully pursued, nor were these regions identified. In subsequent reports the emphasis was placed on the size of differences between core and peripheral regions and on a cross-sectional comparison of the gaps over time. The Periodic Reports did not track the same regions or a sample of regions over time to measure their performance vis-à-vis each other.

In retrospect it is possible to see that, if the gap was closing between the less developed regions of the original nine member states and their more prosperous neighbours, this might have provided an indicator of how participation in European integration improved the chances of economic development in underdeveloped areas, as foreseen by the original Common Market Treaty and reiterated in the Single European Act. It also could have provided an opportunity to evaluate whether the primary goal of EC regional policy ('to contribute to a higher degree of convergence between Member countries and to ensure a better balanced distribution of economic activities on the territory of the Community, through a reduction of regional disparities...', CEC, 1984, p. 4) was really being achieved. In the worst case, it would have supplied a measure of whether regional differences were in fact increasing due to the pull of market forces rather than to the mere addition of underdeveloped areas to the economic space.[21]

Despite its initial aims, the focus of each Periodic Report was much more on cross-sectional analysis than on a longitudinal evaluation of objective and consistent indicators of regional development. The mistakes made may also have been policy driven by the need to justify ERDF funding, based on the original arguments and motivations for the development of a regional policy contained in the 1973 Thomson Report. Whatever the reasons behind the mistakes made in the Periodic Reports, the Commission missed the opportunity to gain a clearer view of what was happening in the regions and what were the impacts of market integration on factor mobility in the European periphery.

NOTES

1.   These three factors are also important for the debate on the state of economic and social cohesion in the EU in fully operationalising the Single Market and moving toward economic and monetary union.
2.   This requirement might seem obvious to the reader, but it has not always been respected in analysis.
3.   See the discussion of the definition, level and size of regions presented in the Second Periodic Report (CEC, 1984, pp. 2–3).
4.   This is the scenario suggested by Rokkan and Urwin (1983) in explaining the consequences of the shift in development axis from an east–west to a north–south direction. See also Braudel, 1972.
5.   A realistic operationalisation of the hypothesis does not posit the full reversal of positions in the short run, nor the elimination of all of the characteristics of the two regional groupings, but it does introduce the prospect that over time there might be a dramatic change in positions in a manner similar to the one that has taken place in the US in the

rate of growth and investment in manufacturing in the 'frostbelt' versus the 'sunbelt' states.

6. Whether Kielstra would still characterise Languedoc-Rousillon as an exploited region in the 1990s is open to question, given the region's past economic performance.

7. The location of the Saarland as part of the 'golden triangle', with its 1970 per capita GDP ranking of 33rd out of 80 regions, serves to delineate statistically the triangle. Moving up through the ranking, the triangle would include Lombardia and Val d'Aosta in Italy. The line would then run up along both the French and German sides of the Rhine to Brussels, Luxembourg, a good part of Holland, and the southeast of the UK. Subsequent analysis will show that the territorial outlines of the golden triangle have tended to shift over time, and that recent data cast doubt on the existence of just one golden triangle in Europe. Indications are that the old single core has now broken down to form multiple cores – that is, there are a series of centres of development that are not necessarily territorially contiguous but do serve as the vital motors driving development and change in the EU (Abraham and Van Rompuy, 1991).

8. The five Länder of the eastern parts of Germany can now be added to the list of underdeveloped regions on the periphery of the EU.

9. This truism finds common expression in scholarly as well as the popular press. On 18 November 1991, in a *Financial Times* report entitled 'The likely costs of EMU for Europe's "periphery"', Edward Balls wrote that the peripheral countries – the UK and southern Europe – will pay a higher price for EMU than the core countries – Germany, France, Denmark and the Benelux – without discussing the off-setting benefits incurred by the periphery from EMU.

10. See Neven, 1990, who cancludes that the southern periphery will benefit the most, given its 'unexploited economies of scale'.

11. As suggested above, the hypothesis posits the allocation of regional development funds as a pay-off to keep the poorer countries happy, but in reality the funds do not eliminate the gap between rich from poor regions, nor do they represent the most efficient use of resources to spur economic development in the most dynamic regions of the EU. Thus, according to this logic, regional funds can only function in the short term to buy off the weaker countries and regions.

12. These observations give rise to consideration of three sets of hypotheses: (a) peripheral ascendancy is operating in both the US and Europe, (b) core dominance characterises both the US and Europe, or (c) peripheral ascendancy is operating in Europe while the US has witnessed peripheral ascendancy. Given the convincing nature of the US data, we believe that hypothesis (a) provides a better basis for understanding change in the EU, while a good part of the expectations underlying the Periodic Reports focused on hypothesis (b). An example is provided in the Third Periodic Report (CEC, 1987, p. 10) in the comparison made between the US and the EC: 'The much smaller disparities within the United States compared with the Community . . . suggest that the existence of a large and relatively uniform

market does not necessary [sic] lead in the long run to greater divergences. This does not exclude the possibility however, that on the
road to such a market some forces may also be released which may
lead to divergent developments'. Thus it seems that for a long time
the raison d'être of regional and overall Structural Fund aid to the
periphery of the EC was based on the expectation that differences
would inevitably increase rather than decrease over time as the result
of market integration.

13.   There is a growing body of literature in the US that explicitly takes the
US and European experience as the point of departure for comparative analysis. See the contributions by Bayoumi and Eichengreen (1991)
and Sala-i-Martin and Sachs (1991).

14.   Initial moves in this direction can be found in the work of Grossman
and Helpman (1990), but a lot more systematic work needs to be
done.

15.   The First Periodic Report also includes data on Greece with a differentiation of the country into nine regions (NUTS II). Subsequent
reports carried data on thirteen Greek regions (NUTS II). Thus the
only way to proceed with the Greek data is to reaggregate the nomoi
(NUTS III) into stable regional definitions before carrying out the
longitudinal analysis.

16.   Subsequent longitudinal analyses using REGIO data assumed that the
definition of the cases remained constant over time. However the use
of raw data for the three levels of data aggregation clearly shows that
the EUROSTAT definition of NUTS levels has not been constant over
time. There are significant gaps at different points in time in the
dataset. Unless analyses of the trend in regional disparities are based
on the raw data, the error in the assumption concerning the con-
stancy in the units of analysis remains undetected, thereby falsifying
the results of the analysis.

17.   In the First Periodic Report the eleven 'standard' UK regions were
described as NUTS II regions. See CEC, 1981, p. 5 and footnote 5.
However it is not important what number in the REGIO classification
scheme the regions are given (that is, NUTS I or II). What is important is that the boundaries of the physical territory from which data
are collected have not changed from one year to the next. Changes in
the boundaries of the regions constitutes a change in the units of
analysis, and such changes make it difficult to compare results over
time.

18.   For a description of the breakdown of NUTS I, II and III level data,
see CEC, 1991a, p. 84.

19.   In the Second Periodic Report the Forword, prepared by Antonio
Giolitti, states that 'Regional disparities in production levels [that is,
GDP per capita] did not diminish during the 1970s and are still very
marked' (CEC, 1984, p. iv).

20.   In this context it should be remembered that the original 1957 EEC
Treaty specified in the preamble that the creation of the Common
Market would lead to the alleviation of regional disparities. Interest-
ingly enough, though, this prediction was never tested by the EC at

the regional level. The Third Periodic Report concluded: 'As a result of the first oil shock and the major worldwide disequilibrium of the last fifteen years, the process of real convergence was interrupted and partly reversed' (CEC, 1987, p. 52), and it is repeated in the Fourth Periodic Report: 'During the 1980s, disparities in incomes per head in the Community increased slightly up to 1986 since when they have remained at around the same level' (CEC, 1991a, p. 1–1). The problem with these analyses is that they treat countries inside and outside the EC structure as equivalent in standing, while the 1957 Treaty and Single European Act specifically attributed to the integration process an accelerating force in the achievement of convergence.

21.   One of the other main weakness of the Periodic Reports is that, despite the fact that regional-level data are available, the analysis of trends in cohesion continues to be carried out at the national level. See the contradictory nature of the results reported in the Third Periodic Report (CEC, 1987, pp. 52–60).

REFERENCES

Abraham, F. and R. Van Rompuy (1991) 'Convergence-Divergence and the Implications for Community Structural Policies', Department of Economics, University of Leuven, Leuven, Belgium.

Bairoch, P. (1976) 'Europe's Gross National Product: 1800–1975', *The Journal of European Economic History*, vol. 2 (fall), pp. 273–340.

Barro, R. J. and X. Sala-i-Martin (1991) *Convergence Across States and Regions*, Brookings Papers on Economic Activity (Washington, DC: Brookings Institution).

Bayoumi, T. and B. Eichengreen (1991) 'Shocking Aspects of European Monetary Unification', University of California, Berkeley, Department of Economics. Paper for the Bank of England and International Monetary Fund.

Biehl, D., H. Hussmann and S. Schnyder (1972) 'Zur Regionalen Einkommenverteilung in der Europaische Wirtschaftsgemeinschaft', *Die Weltwirtschaft*, pp. 64–8.

Braudel, F. (1972) *The Mediterranean and the Mediterranean World in the Age of Philip II*, vols 1 and 2 (New York: Harper & Row).

Camagni, R. (1991) 'Interregional Disparities in the European Community: Structure and Performance of Objective One Regions in the 1980's', paper presented to the North American Regional Science Conference, New Orleans, 6–9 November.

CEC (1981) *Le Regioni d'Europa: Prima relazione periodic sulla situazione sociale ed economica nelle regioni della Comunita* (Luxembourg: Office of Official Publications of the European Communities).

CEC (1984) *The Regions of Europe: Second Periodic Report on the Social and Economic Situation of the Regions of the Community, Together with a Statement of the Regional Policy Committee* (Luxembourg: Office of Official Publications of the European Communities).

CEC (1987) *The Regions of the Enlarged Community: Third Periodic Report on the Social and Economic Situation and Development of the Regions of the Community* (Luxembourg: Office of Official Publications of the European Communities).

CEC (1991a) *The Regions in the 1990s: Fourth Periodic Report on the Social and Economic Situation and Development of the Regions of the Community* (Luxembourg: Office of Official Publications of the European Communities).

CEC (1991b) *The Regions in the 1990s* (Luxembourg: Office of Official Publications of the European Communities).

Cecchini, P. (1988) *The European Challenge: 1992* (Aldershot: Wildwood House).

Delors, J. (1989) 'Regional Implications of Economic and Monetary Integration', in CEC, *Report on Economic and Monetary Union in the European Community* (Luxembourg: Office of Official Publications of the European Communities), pp. 81–9.

Emerson, M. (1990) *The Economics of 1992* (Oxford: Oxford University Press).

Grossman, G. M. and E. Helpman (1990) 'Trade, Knowledge Spillovers and Growth', paper presented at the annual meeting of the European Economic Association, Lisbon, Portugal.

Hudson, R. and J. Lewis (eds) (1985) *Uneven Development in Southern Europe: Studies of accumulation, class, migration and the state* (London: Methuen).

IFO (1990) *An Empirical Assessment of Factors Shaping Regional Competitiveness in Problem Regions*, volumes I–V (Munich: IFO).

Kielstra, N. (1985) 'The Rural Languedoc: Periphery to "Relictual" Space', in R. Hudson and J. Lewis (eds), *Uneven Development in Southern Europe: Studies of accumulation, class, migration and the state* (London: Methuen), pp. 246–62.

Krugman, P. (1991) *Geography and Trade* (Cambridge, MA: MIT Press, 1911).

Leonardi, R. (1994) 'Networking and the European Single Market: Tuscany as the vanguard Mediterranean region' in R. Leonardi and R. Y. Nanetti (eds) *Regional Development in a Modern European Economy: The Case of Tuscany* (London: Pinter), pp. 238–55.

Molle, W. T. M. (1991) *The Economics of Economic Integration: Theory, Practice, Policy* (Aldershot: Dartmouth).

Molle, W. T. M., B. van Holst and H. Smit (1980) *Regional Disparity and Economic Development in the European Community* (Farnborough: Saxon House, Teakfield).

Neven, D. J. (1990) 'EEC Integration Towards 1992: Some Distributional Aspects', *Economic Policy* (April), pp. 13–46.

NIESR (1991) 'A New Strategy for Social and Economic Cohesion after 1992', Final Report for the European Parliament, National Institute of Economic and Social Research, London.

Padoa Schioppa, T. with M. Emerson *et al.* (1987) *Efficiency, Stability, Equity* (Oxford: Oxford University Press).

Richardson, H. W. (1969) *Elements of Regional Economics* (London: Penguin).

Rivera-Batiz, L. A. and P. M. Romer (1990) 'Economic Integration and Endogenous Growth', NBER Working Paper No. 3528.

Rodwin, L. (1991) 'European industrial change and regional economic transformation: an overview of recent experience', in L. Rodwin and H. Sazanami (eds), *Industrial Change and Regional Economic Transformation: The Experience of Western Europe* (London: Harper Collins), pp. 3–36.

Rokkan, S. and D. W. Urwin (1983) *Economy, Territory, Identity: Politics of West European Peripheries* (London: Sage).

Sala-i-Martin, X. and J. Sachs (1991) 'Fiscal Federalism and Optimum Currency Areas: Evidence for Europe from the U.S.', National Bureau of Economic Research, Working Paper No. 3855.

Smith, A. and A. J. Venables (1988) 'Completing the Internal Market in the EC, Some Industry Simulations', *European Economic Review*, vol. 32, pp. 1501–25.

Stough, R. (1993) 'Rise of the Southern Periphery in the United States: Understanding the Frostbelt-Sunbelt Shifts', in R. Leonardi, *The State of Economic and Social Cohesion in the Community Prior to the Creation of the Single Market: The View from the Bottom-Up* (Brussels: Commission of the European Communities), Chapter 2.

Tsoukalis, L. (1991) *The New European Community: The Politics and Economics of Integration* (Oxford: Oxford University Press).

4 The Findings: Dependent Variables

DEFINING THE DEPENDENT VARIABLES

The aim of the this chapter is to undertake a systematic analysis of the dynamic of convergence at the regional level by looking in greater detail at the actual empirical changes that have taken place over time. Defining the dependent variables was handicapped by a lack of adequate data over an extended period of time. As a consequence only two indicators could be used: per capita GDP at market prices and exchange rates was tracked from 1970 to 1991; and data on per capita purchasing-power standards (PPS) was analysed over an equivalent twenty-one year period. Most of the longitudinal empirical studies conducted on core–periphery relations in Europe have used the same dependent variables, while Molle, van Holst and Smit (1980), Biehl, Hussmann and Schnyder (1971) and Bairoch (1976) built their dependant variable on per capita GDP expressed in US dollars.[1]

Regional disparities during the 1950–70 period are analysed on the basis of one dependant variable (per capita GDP in US dollars), while for the period 1970–91 two dependant variables are used: per capita GDP and per capita PPS. Apart from the fact that other alternatives in selecting data for longitudinal analysis were not available, these two measures were adopted for two reasons. First, per capita GDP is the only measure that has been used consistently by other authors (CEC, 1981–91a; NIESR, 1991; Tsoukalis, 1991; Molle, 1991) to track regional disparities over time.[2] Second, the arguments presented for the use of GDP and PPS in the Periodic Reports were persuasive.

The First Periodic Report chose per capita GDP as a means of assessing the regions' potential to adapt to changes in the international economy and develop indigenous resources to the highest possible degree. This measure, the First Periodic Report argued, demonstrated the income-generating capacity of an economic unit in the international arena. The assumption that underpinned its adoption was that integration was

86

succeeding if all firms took the levels and changes of international prices as a reference point. This was particularly relevant because the EC faced increasing challenges from the international economy, and even if an area was not directly involved in international markets international prices affected regional producers through interregional linkages.

The Fourth Report, on the other hand, applied per capita PPS as its key indicator for income disparities. PPS compares prices for the same basket of goods and services in the different member states and therefore takes into account the impact of internal inflation and external depreciation of national currencies on the calculation on national income measures. Income is expressed in terms of its ability to purchase that basket. PPS then, is an indicator of the standard of living because it examines the internal purchasing power of a region's residents. The First Report argued that purchasing power is not an adequate indicator for comparing economic performance and potential. However it is a good indicator of social development, especially if the objective of regional and social policies is to promote convergence of living standards, income and productivity.[3] The analysis employed here will use both measures in order to draw a more complete picture of what happened to the cohesion gap at the EC regional level between 1970 and 1991.

The issue of concern is whether the analysis of the empirical data shows a decrease or an increase in cohesion over time. To meet the criteria for systematic comparative analysis outlined above, both core and periphery are given precise names and positions on indexes and rankings that are then evaluated over time for their persistence or change. Comparisons of the regions' index scores for GDP and PPS, plus their ranking on these scores, will provide an unambiguous basis for drawing conclusions on whether the cohesion gap is widening or narrowing in the EU.

FOUR DECADES OF CONVERGENCE

Analysis of eighty cases over the twenty-one year period 1970–91 using the variables per capita GDP in ECU and per capita PPS, plus seventy-four cases over the 1950–70 period, shows that there was a significant *reduction* of the cohesion gap between core and peripheral regions in the EU. All three peripheral-ascendancy scenarios presented in Chapter 3 describe some aspect of what happened at the regional level in the EC between 1970 and 1991. Scenario 2, positing the prospect of an upward convergence, describes the comparative, absolute growth rates of the less favoured regions. Scenario 3, arguing downward convergence, is supported by a comparison of the relative position of regions on the per capita GDP and per capita PPS indexes over time. The regions in the upper parts of the index fall – that is, their values on the index fall – while the regions at the bottom experience an upward movement in their index scores. Scenario 4 – reversal of roles – is supported when the absolute and relative positions of the regions in the middle and upper parts of the rankings are analysed. Regions that in 1950 and 1970 were in the middle or lower part of the rankings, by 1991 had been elevated to positions above the mean, and regions that had enjoyed relatively high positions in the early 1950s and 1970s had fallen toward the middle or lower part of the rankings. Verification of all three scenarios of the convergence hypothesis strongly suggests that convergence is not only a hypothesis that is supported by longitudinal data on US manufacturing and income levels; it can also be used to describe the changes that have taken place in EC over the past forty-one years.

Table 4.1 presents the per capita GDP figures (in US dollars) for the seventy-four regions analysed to measure the dynamic of regional disparities in the 1950–70 period covered by the Molle, van Holst and Smit study. In 1950 the centre of development was located on either side of the English Channel, around the capital cities and their hinterlands: Region Parisienne (Paris), Brabant (Brussels), Southeast (London) and Luxembourg. The other top regions were those containing traditional industrial concentrations, such as heavy industrial and mining activities: Wallonie, Nord, West Midlands and Yorkshire-Humberside. In these regions industrial employment accounted for over half of those employed. Only one German Land (Hamburg) was among the top regions, while a number of others were below the average for member states.

The bottom of the index scores was composed of all of Italy's southern regions. At the absolute bottom were the three

Table 4.1   Changes in per capita GDP in European regions, 1950–1970 ($US, EU = 100)

	1950	1960	1970	Change in index scores 1950–70
Schleswig-Holstein	59	90	99	+40
Hamburg	144	174	182	+38
Niedersachsen	66	94	105	+39
Bremen	119	148	144	+25
Nordrhein-Westfalen	95	120	129	+34
Hessen	79	113	136	+57
Rheinland-Pfalz	66	84	114	+48
Baden-Wurtemberg	82	114	129	+47
Bayern	70	96	119	+49
Sued	75	104	123	+48
Saarland	100	104	103	+3
W. Berlin	83	111	128	+45
Region Parisienne	194	169	169	−25
Nord	137	122	112	−25
Champagne	111	105	114	+3
Picardie	111	101	104	−7
Haute Normandie	120	127	131	+11
Centre	88	95	103	+15
Basse Normandie	92	85	90	−2
Bourgogne	95	89	99	+4
Lorraine	134	113	108	−26
Alsace	128	106	112	−16
Franche-Comte	110	100	102	−8
Pays de la Loire	94	90	97	+3
Bretagne	86	77	81	−5
Poitou-Charentes	82	81	89	+7
Acquitaine	91	99	100	+9
Midi-Pyrennes	80	79	82	+2
Limousin	100	83	86	−14
Rhone-Alpes	119	109	118	−1
Auvergne	99	88	87	−12
Languedoc-Roussillon	88	86	83	−5
Provence-Alpes C. D'Azur	115	111	106	−9
Corse	97	87	81	−16
Piemonte	90	85	91	+1
Valle d'Aosta	96	90	92	−4
Liguria	104	89	94	−10
Lombardia	95	91	96	+1

Table 4.1   (Cont.)

	1950	1960	1970	Change in index scores 1950–70
Trentino-Alto Adige	68	59	73	+5
Veneto	56	58	70	+14
Friuli-Venezia Giulia	63	62	77	+14
Emilia-Romagna	67	70	83	+16
Toscana	66	61	74	+8
Umbria	54	46	63	+9
Marche	53	45	61	+8
Lazio	69	71	75	+6
Campania	42	42	48	+6
Abruzzo	41	41	54	+13
Molise	34	35	44	+10
Puglia	40	39	50	+10
Basilicata	35	29	46	+11
Calabria	34	30	41	+7
Sicilia	41	37	52	+11
Sardegna	46	43	55	+9
Nord	74	76	92	+18
Oost	72	77	91	+19
West	97	94	112	+15
Zuid	84	81	93	+9
Vlaandern	131	98	107	−24
Wallonie	149	102	97	−52
Brabant	175	137	127	−48
Luxembourg (GD)	177	144	129	−48
North of England	109	106	71	−38
York and Humberside	131	121	78	−53
East Midlands	115	118	81	−34
East Anglia	112	101	79	−33
Southeast England	158	131	98	−60
Southwest England	94	104	78	−16
West Midlands	134	127	88	−46
Northwest England	127	116	80	−47
Wales	92	103	72	−20
Scotland	114	101	77	−37
Northern Ireland	80	74	61	−19
Ireland	71	62	60	−11
Sjaell	158	135	143	−15
Fyn	144	117	125	−19
Jylland	137	111	123	−14

Table 4.1   (Cont.)

Summary of changes in index scores

	1950	1970
Top/bottom 1	5.7/1	4.4/1
Top/bottom 5	4.7/1	3.4/1
Top/bottom 10	3.7/1	2.8/1

predominantly mountainous regions of Italy: Calabria, Molise and Basilicata. Not far from the southern regions in index score were those in the central part of the country, such as Marche, Umbria and Veneto. Emilia-Romagna and Toscana began the 1950s with, respectively, 67 per cent and 66 per cent of the EC mean on the GDP index. The low scores for these and other low-scoring regions were due to the preponderance of agriculture vis-à-vis industrial and service activities. Agriculture employed 52 per cent of the workforce in Emilia-Romagna, 62 per cent in the Marche and 54 per cent in Umbria.

During the following ten years there was a slight shift in the concentration of the strongest regions toward the southern side of the English Channel. In 1960 Hamburg was joined by Bremen, while the other German Länder improved their index scores throughout the ranking. The weaker regions in Italy, on the other hand, showed absolute gains in per capita GDP, but these increases did not offset the gains enjoyed in the other regions. The list and ranking of the southern Italian regions remained constant and their relative scores decreased, rapid industrial growth still being restricted to the northern triangle (Lombardia, Piemonte and Liguria). All that was left to the south was an improving infrastructure base grafted on to poor and undermechanised agriculture. Industry was just beginning to make its presence felt in the south, but vast numbers of southern workers migrated to the north to find jobs and opportunities. As a result, emigration and transfer payments from relatives who had already emigrated to other parts of Italy and Europe were the main sources of, respectively, hope and income, but these were not sufficient to maintain the south's position relative to other regions in Europe.

By 1970, though, there was a significant improvement in the position of the less developed regions. Average index scores went up considerably, and the gap between the top and bottom ten regions, which stood at 3.7/1 in 1950 was reduced to 2.8/1 in 1970. For the top and bottom five regions the change was from 4.7/1 in 1950 to 3.4/1 twenty years later. Molle, Van Holst and Smit (1980, p. 80) conclude that 'the disparity between the countries of the European Community decreased markedly in the period under study . . . , and so did the disparity between the regions of each of the four large countries'. The causes of this change during the 1950–70 period are identified as largely due 'to a shift in the distribution of people and employment from regions with low to regions with high GDP per head, and only for a small part to GDP redistribution, while on the national level the decrease in disparity between the EC member countries is entirely due to the "redistribution" of GDP among these countries' (ibid., p. 85). Regions where growth was greatest are located in Germany, while the traditional manufacturing areas along the English Channel continued to grow, but at lower levels. During the second decade the southern Italian regions witnessed a significant improvement, which allowed them to overcome the decline they had experienced during the 1950s because of emigration and the transfer of financial resources to the north. Conditions also began to improve significantly in the central part of the country.

Turning to the second group of data, which covers eighty regions between 1970 and 1991, we find in Table 4.2 a parallel form of convergence taking place. The index scores were calculated for eight different points in time, and the presence of a number of data points allows us to trace in some detail the variations in relative development levels. The EC average was calculated on the basis of raw data for the eighty cases, and each region's index score was calculated vis-à-vis the EC average. By calculating the gap separating the different groups of developed and underdeveloped regions – that is, the single, the top five, and the top ten most developed regions in comparison with their equivalent number among the less developed – and comparing the ratios over the twenty-one year period, the results show, once again, a clear *reduction* of the gap between developed and underdeveloped regions. This

Table 4.2 Regional index scores on GDP per inhabitant in ECU, 1970–1991 (EU = 100)

Region	1970	1977	1981	1984	1986	1988	1990	1991	Diff. 91-70
Schleswig-Holstein	108	118	101	103	104	104	102	103	–5
Hamburg	211	207	188	200	201	202	191	211	0
Niedersachsen	111	114	103	105	108	108	105	108	–3
Bremen	174	169	151	155	161	162	154	160	–14
Nordrhein-Westf.	130	132	117	118	120	120	116	116	–14
Hessen	126	144	130	137	141	142	141	150	+24
Rheinland-Pfalz	109	118	107	109	111	112	118	105	–4
Baden-Wurtemberg	137	140	125	127	132	132	129	131	–6
Bavaria	114	125	115	121	125	125	125	128	+14
Saarland	106	115	110	112	115	116	113	113	+7
W. Berlin	147	146	130	137	138	138	120	96	–51*
Ile de France	179	165	167	163	172	165	164	159	–20
Champagne-Arden.	122	117	113	103	105	102	109	106	–16
Picardie	109	109	106	96	99	95	94	91	–18
Haute Normandie	137	130	125	111	120	116	104	103	–34
Centre	107	107	105	102	105	102	110	98	–9
Basse Normandie	95	98	95	97	90	87	95	91	–4
Bourgogne	103	102	102	95	99	96	98	94	–9
Nord-Pas-de-Calais	110	99	99	90	91	88	89	86	–24
Lorraine	114	108	105	95	95	92	95	89	–25
Alsace	121	115	119	112	117	113	113	108	–13
Franche-Comte	105	111	106	98	98	95	101	99	–6
Pays de la Loire	99	99	102	95	98	94	95	93	–3

Table 4.2 (Cont.)

Region	1970	1977	1981	1984	1986	1988	1990	1991	Diff. 91-70
Bretagne	82	91	94	89	92	89	91	87	+5
Poitou-Charentes	90	93	92	89	91	88	88	86	-4
Acquitaine	102	106	108	107	104	100	99	99	-3
Midi-Pyrennes	85	88	94	93	91	88	89	91	+6
Limousin	85	86	88	86	88	85	85	83	-2
Rhone-Alpes	123	114	116	109	114	109	108	105	-18
Auvergne	92	93	92	90	91	88	89	87	-5
Languedoc-Rous.	85	89	89	88	89	85	86	81	-4
Provence-Alpes C.	107	108	110	103	104	100	100	97	-10
Corse	-	-	84	75	80	77	77	76	-
Piemonte	105	88	95	100	104	106	115	116	+11
Valle d'Aosta	110	108	115	111	116	120	121	125	+15
Liguria	115	84	97	103	104	106	112	113	-2
Lombardia	110	92	101	113	120	123	131	131	+21
Trentino-Alto A.	79	74	86	104	103	105	113	119	+40
Veneto	81	73	81	97	101	104	111	114	+33
Friuli-Venezia G.	89	75	89	97	101	104	113	118	+29
Emilia-Romagna	92	86	98	110	111	114	123	124	+32
Toscana	87	76	86	97	101	104	108	106	+19
Umbria	70	67	79	87	88	88	93	96	+16
Marche	72	68	78	88	92	95	98	102	+30
Lazio	87	71	80	97	101	105	111	115	+28
Campania	55	48	55	61	59	60	63	69	+14

Abruzzo	56	56	65	77	78	79	84	88	+32
Molise	46	46	58	67	69	70	75	77	+31
Puglia	55	49	56	62	63	65	69	72	+17
Basilicata	46	48	56	61	56	57	59	63	+17
Calabria	42	43	49	50	51	52	54	55	+13
Sicilia	54	46	54	61	61	63	65	66	+12
Sardegna	54	53	56	67	67	67	71	72	+18
Groningen	121	251	240	231	181	174	129	130	+9
Friesland	80	105	84	80	84	80	78	80	0
Drenthe	82	117	110	101	100	96	84	84	+2
East Netherlands	91	111	89	85	86	82	82	85	-6
Utrecht	96	124	104	101	101	97	92	102	+6
North Holland	115	138	118	122	119	114	113	108	-7
South Holland	119	134	110	108	108	104	105	101	-18
Zeeland	108	125	104	104	102	98	105	102	-6
North Brabant (NL)	100	113	92	92	96	92	91	95	-5
Limburg (NL)	87	105	88	87	90	87	90	90	+3
Flanders	106	124	104	95	98	98	101	100	-6
Wallonia	97	104	88	78	80	81	81	80	-17
Brussels	133	188	164	143	149	149	157	156	+23
Luxembourg (GD)	135	125	112	111	114	113	119	121	-14
North of England	78	66	89	82	72	80	76	77	-1
York and Humbers.	87	67	88	83	77	83	80	79	-8
East Midlands	94	68	92	88	79	86	85	85	-9
East Anglia	85	69	93	93	83	90	90	89	+4
Southeast England	106	82	116	110	100	112	106	105	-1
Southwest England	85	65	91	88	79	88	84	85	0

Table 4.2 Regional index scores on GDP per inhabitant in ECU, 1970–1991 (EU = 100)

Region	1970	1977	1981	1984	1986	1988	1990	1991	Diff. 91–70
West Midlands	95	68	87	83	75	83	81	80	−15
Northwest England	95	68	91	86	78	85	79	81	−14
Wales	85	60	80	77	69	76	73	74	−9
Scotland	90	69	94	88	79	86	81	84	−6
Northern Ireland	75	55	74	71	64	69	65	67	−8
Ireland	57	48	57	61	61	59	63	62	+5
Denmark	137	143	120	129	138	134	132	127	−10

Summary of changes in index scores:

	1970	1991
Top/bottom 1	5.0/1	3.8/1
Top/bottom 5	3.5/1	2.3/1
Top/bottom 10	2.7/1	1.9/1

* The 1991 calculation for West Berlin also includes East Berlin. Thus, in the calculations of changes in index scores the last value used for West Berlin is the 1990 score, which did not contain data from East Berlin. Otherwise the comparison over time would have been falsified by the entry of the eastern part of Berlin rather than by a systemic convergence dynamic.

is true for both dependent variables: per capita GDP and PPS.

According to the per capita GDP variable the gap between the single most developed and the single least developed region fell from the 1970 level of 5.0/1 to 3.8/1 in 1991; for the five most developed and five least developed regions the drop went from 3.5/1 to 2.3/1. The differences between the top and bottom five regions in the intervening years are characterised by the following trend: 1977, 4.2/1; 1981, 3.4/1; 1984, 3.0/1; 1986, 3.0/1; 1990, 2.6/1; and 1991, 2.3/1. In 1977 the gap grew, due in part to the ripple effect of the 1974 energy crisis caused by the quadrupling of oil prices. These effects are reflected clearly in the sharp increase experienced by Groningen (production of natural gas), which moved from a 1970 index score of 121 to 251. In 1990 Groningen fell back to 129 down on the per capita GDP index scores as gas prices stabilised. As expected, the trend is in the same direction if one compares larger groups of regions. For example, the gap between the average of the top ten most developed and bottom ten least developed regions decreased from 2.8/1 in 1970 to 1.9/1 in 1991.[4]

Figure 4.1 presents the change in the distribution of regional inequalities by comparing the 1991 with the 1970 per capita GDP data on the basis of a Lorenz curve.[5] Figure 4.1 shows that the changes in GDP were most pronounced in the middle range of regions, but that there was a consistent reduction of differences throughout the curve.

What happened to change the structure of peripheral regional economies so dramatically? The basic response is that there was a profound transformation of the structure of the three economic sectors and of the balance between the northern and southern part of Europe. If we take the two extreme cases in 1950 of industrial development (UK) and agricultural underdevelopment (Italy) and compare them with the situation in 1990, we see in Table 4.3 that an extraordinary change took place. On the one hand the UK regions deindustrialised, and on the other the Italian regions were no longer dominated by agricultural production when employing the workforce. During the last forty years Italy has become more industrialised. In both cases, though, the regions saw enormous growth in the service sector. The North, York and Humberside, and

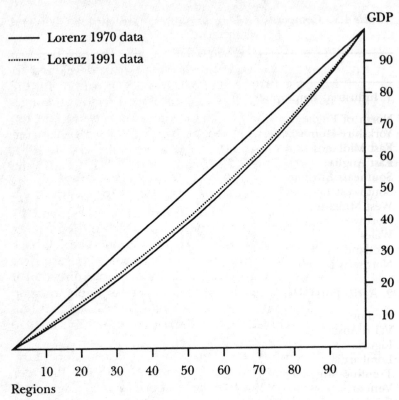

Figure 4.1   Lorenz curve for GDP per capita data, 1970–1991

the West Midlands had similar levels of service employment to Lombardy, Emilia-Romagna and Tuscany. However, what the data do not tell us is what activities comprised the service sector in that period. Was service-sector employment taking place in research activities and services for industry or did it represent lower value added employment that was not directly fed into industry? The answers to these questions are important if we are to evaluate the ability of regions to continue to meet the needs for growth and development, but they can only be provided by a careful, comparative analysis of service sectors in each region.

In other core countries the trend over time was similar to that registered by the UK. The data presented in Table 4.2

Table 4.3   Comparison of UK industrial and Italian agricultural employment, 1950–90

	1950	1960	1970	1981	1990
1. Industrial Employment in the UK Regions:					
North of England	55	55	50	40	37
Yorkshire-Humberside	59	57	53	40	36
East Midlands	60	59	57	44	38
East Anglia	37	38	43	32	30
Southeast England	44	44	40	29	27
Southwest England	41	41	42	30	29
West Midlands	63	63	59	44	39
Northwest England	57	55	51	38	34
Wales	51	51	48	35	33
Scotland	50	50	49	34	32
Northern Ireland	50	48	46	29	29
2. Agricultural Employment in Italy:					
Piemonte	33	25	12	10	7
Val d'Aosta	38	23	14	13	8
Liguria	18	14	8	7	6
Lombardia	20	11	5	4	3
Trentino-Alto Adige	42	35	17	15	11
Veneto	47	30	16	12	7
Friuli-Venezia Giulia	33	23	12	9	5
Emilia-Romagna	52	35	21	13	10
Marche	62	53	30	16	10
Toscana	42	28	13	11	6
Umbria	58	48	24	15	8
Lazio	34	22	11	9	6
Campania	48	36	26	20	11
Abruzzo	64	51	32	20	11
Molise	79	71	46	32	21
Puglia	60	47	35	22	17
Basilicata	72	59	40	32	21
Calabria	64	48	34	28	23
Sicilia	51	38	27	19	15
Sardegna	53	40	26	16	15

show that between 1970 and 1991 the index scores for core regions generally fell. Germany maintained five of its Länder in the top ten of the index, but the majority of the German Länder (eight out of eleven) experienced a decrease in their index scores. A similar phenomenon characterised the French regions: of the twenty-one regions for which data are available, sixteen saw their index scores drop.[6] In Belgium, the index scores of Flanders and Wallonia fell, as did those of Luxembourg and Denmark, while Brussels' score rose. The British and Dutch regions were almost evenly split between those regions that fell and those that rose on the index.

The main benefactor of the change in index scores was the EC-9 periphery. Ireland and seventeen of the twenty Italian regions witnessed significant increases in their index scores. Even the southern Italian regions – long relegated to the bottom of the rankings of nine or even twelve member states – made strong gains, especially those positioned along the Appennine mountain range. During the twenty-one year period, Abruzzo went from 56 per cent to 88 per cent on the index, Molise from 46 per cent to 77 per cent and Basilicata from 46 per cent to 63 per cent. Given that in 1970 all five of the weakest regions were located in the Italian Mezzogiorno, the fact that their index scores increased while those of the strongest regions fell during the last two decades, helps once again to explain the reduction of the cohesion gap as predicted by the peripheral ascendancy thesis and convergence theories. In addition, it should be remembered that in 1970 two central Italian regions (Umbria and Marche) were respectively ranked ninth and tenth among the bottom one-eighth of the least developed European regions. In 1991 their GDP scores were at the European mean.[7]

The reduced gap between strong and weak regions can also be seen in the relative ranking of the regions on the per capita GDP index. Table 4.4 provides a detailed breakdown of the regions' relative ranking over the twenty-one years and shows the significant drop in ranking (defined here as a drop of over ten positions in the ranking) registered by regions that in the 1970s occupied the middle or upper parts of the rankings, such as Champagne-Ardennes, Nord Pas-de-Calais, Lorraine, Picardie, Flanders, Wallonia, East Netherlands, West Midlands, Basse Normandie and Sardegna. Using the same measure, there

Table 4.4 Regional ranking on GDP per inhabitant indexes, 1970–1991

Region	1970	1977	1981	1984	1986	1988	1990	1991	Diff. 91-70
Schleswig-Holstein	27	20	37	28	28	29	34	31	−4
Hamburg	1	2	2	2	1	1	1	1	0
Niedersachsen	21	26	33	25	23	23	31	22	−1
Bremen	3	4	5	4	4	4	4	2	+1
Nordrhein-Westfalen	10	12	13	12	11	12	16	17	−17
Hessen	11	7	7	7	6	6	5	5	+6
Rheinland-Pfalz	26	19	25	22	21	21	15	27	−1
Baden-Wurtemberg	6	9	9	9	9	9	8	7	−1
Bavaria	19	15	16	11	10	10	10	9	+10
Saarland	33	24	20	15	17	14	22	21	+12
W. Berlin	4	6	6	6	7	7	13	42	−38
Ile de France	2	5	3	3	3	3	2	3	−1
Champagne-Ardennes	13	22	18	29	25	33	26	26	−13
Picardie	25	30	26	41	41	42	45	48	−23
Haute Normandie	7	13	8	16	12	15	33	30	−23
Centre	30	33	28	31	24	34	37	39	−9
Basse Normandie	44	41	41	40	54	56	44	47	−3
Bourgogne	36	38	34	42	40	40	41	44	−8
Nord-Pas-de-Calais	23	39	38	49	52	55	52	56	−33
Lorraine	20	31	29	43	46	46	42	50	−30
Alsace	15	23	11	14	15	19	19	23	−8

Table 4.4 (Cont.)

Region	1970	1977	1981	1984	1986	1988	1990	1991	Diff. 91–70
Franche-Comte	34	23	27	35	42	43	36	37	−3
Pays de la Loire	39	40	35	45	43	45	43	45	−6
Bretagne	62	45	43	51	48	49	49	54	+8
Poitou-Charentes	50	42	48	52	50	53	55	55	−5
Acquitaine	37	34	24	24	29	35	39	38	−1
Midi-Pyrennes	59	47	44	46	49	52	53	46	+13
Limousin	56	49	59	61	56	61	57	62	−6
Rhone-Alpes	12	25	14	21	19	22	28	28	−16
Auvergne	46	43	49	50	51	51	54	53	−7
Languedoc-Rous.	57	46	55	56	55	60	56	63	−6
Provence-Alpes C.	29	31	22	30	30	36	38	40	−11
Corse	–	–	64	70	62	69	69	71	
Piemonte	35	48	42	34	27	25	17	16	+19
Valle d'Aosta	24	32	17	18	16	13	12	11	+13
Liguria	18	51	40	30	26	24	23	20	−2
Lombardia	22	44	36	13	13	11	7	6	+16
Trentino-Alto Adige	66	55	63	27	31	27	21	14	+52
Veneto	64	56	66	38	37	28	24	19	+45
Friuli-Venezia G.	51	54	56	39	34	31	20	15	+36
Emilia-Romagna	47	50	39	19	20	17	11	12	+35
Toscana	54	53	62	36	33	32	27	25	+29

Umbria	70	64	69	59	57	50	46	41	+29
Marche	69	62	70	53	47	44	40	33	+26
Lazio	52	57	67	37	35	26	25	18	+34
Campania	73	75	78	78	78	76	78	75	-2
Abruzzo	72	69	72	68	66	68	60	52	+20
Molise	77	76	73	73	71	71	71	70	+7
Puglia	74	72	77	74	75	74	74	74	0
Basilicata	76	73	76	75	79	78	79	78	-2
Calabria	78	78	80	79	80	79	80	80	-2
Sicilia	75	77	79	76	76	75	76	77	-2
Sardegna	61	71	75	72	73	73	73	73	-12
Groningen	14	1	1	1	2	2	9	8	-6
Friesland	65	36	65	66	59	66	68	67	-2
Drenthe	63	21	21	32	39	41	61	60	+3
East Netherlands	48	29	53	62	58	64	62	57	-9
Utrecht	41	18	30	33	36	39	47	32	+9
North Holland	17	10	12	10	14	16	18	24	-7
South Holland	16	11	23	23	22	30	32	35	-19
Zeeland	28	14	31	26	32	37	30	34	-6
North Brabant (NL)	38	27	47	48	45	47	48	43	-5
Limburg (NL)	55	35	60	58	53	57	51	49	+6
Flanders	31	17	32	44	44	38	35	36	-5
Wallonia	40	37	58	67	61	65	64	66	-26
Brussels	9	3	4	5	5	5	3	4	+5

104

Table 4.4 (Cont.)

Region	1970	1977	1981	1984	1986	1988	1990	1991	Diff. 91–70
Luxembourg (GD)	8	16	19	17	18	18	14	13	–5
North of England	67	66	54	65	70	67	70	69	–2
York and Humber.	53	65	57	64	68	62	66	68	–15
East Midlands	45	63	50	57	65	58	58	58	–13
East Anglia	56	59	46	47	60	48	50	51	+5
Southeast England	32	52	15	20	38	20	29	29	+3
Southwest England	58	67	52	55	63	54	59	59	–1
West Midlands	42	60	61	63	69	63	65	65	–23
Northwest England	43	61	51	60	66	60	67	64	–21
Wales	60	68	68	69	72	70	72	72	–12
Scotland	49	58	45	54	64	59	63	61	–12
Northern Ireland	68	70	71	71	74	72	75	76	–8
Ireland	71	74	74	77	77	77	77	79	–8
Denmark	5	8	10	8	8	8	6	10	–5

was an equally significant movement upward in the ranking by Groningen, Lombardia, Southeast England, Saarland, Trentino-Alto Adige, Emilia-Romagna, Veneto, Friuli-Venezia Giulia, Lazio, Toscana, East Anglia, Southwest England, Bretagne and Marche. The most spectacular gains were experienced by regions in the middle or lower end of the scale, thus providing a confirmation of the applicability of Scenario 4, or role reversal, in explaining the changes taking place in the intermediate parts of the rankings.

Parallel conclusions can be drawn from the analysis of PPS data (see Table 4.5). Comparisons using the PPS variable were conducted over a similar period. In comparing 1970 index scores with those in 1991, the gap between the most and least well-off region declined from 4.2/1 to 3.6/1. Among the top and bottom five regions, the ratio fell from 3.1/1 in 1970 to 2.3/1 in 1991, and for the ten most and ten least developed regions the ratio went from 2.5/1 to 1.7/1.[8] The regions that qualified for the top ten rankings remained fairly stable. Six of the top ten in 1970 were still part of the group in 1991. The four new members were one German Land (Hessen) and three Italian regions (Lombardia, Valle d'Aosta and Emilia-Romagna). The general rise of northern and central Italian regions in relation to the overall EC mean is evident throughout the ranking. The Italian 'high flyers' on the PPS index were once again regions in northeastern and central parts of the country, where industrialisation focused on various light industries situated in industrial districts that had sprung up in the 1970s and 1980s. The southern regions also increased their overall scores. Two notable cases in the Mezzogiorno were the increases enjoyed by Abruzzo (+31 PPS points) and Molise (+30 PPS points) during the twenty-one year interval between the first and last calculation of PPS scores. In addition to the continued upward thrust of the Ile de France area, important progress was made by the regions in the French periphery, but a reduction was registered for regions in the northeastern part of the country. The PPS high flyers in France were Midi-Pyrennes (+19), Bretagne (+17) and Acquitaine (+11).

A comparison of the summary scores presented at the bottom of Tables 4.2 and 4.5 shows that, in general, the gap in per capita GDP tends to be larger than that in per capita PPS in all of the comparisons. This is due to the fact that the

Table 4.5 Regional index score on PPS per inhabitant, 1970–90

Region	1970	1977	1981	1984	1986	1988	1990	1991	Diff. 91–70
Schleswig-Holstein	95	96	92	92	91	93	95	96	+1
Hamburg	185	168	171	179	176	170	178	197	+12
Niedersachsen	97	93	93	94	94	95	98	101	+4
Bremen	152	138	138	138	141	139	144	149	−3
Nordrhein-Westf.	113	107	107	106	105	105	108	108	−5
Hessen	110	117	118	122	124	126	132	140	+30
Rheinland-Pfalz	95	96	97	97	98	97	110	98	+3
Baden-Wurtemberg	120	114	113	114	116	116	120	122	+2
Bavaria	100	101	105	108	110	111	116	119	+19
Saarland	93	93	100	100	101	99	105	105	+12
W. Berlin	128	119	118	122	121	110	112	90	−38
Ile de France	158	153	154	158	161	158	162	162	+4
Champagne-Arden.	107	108	104	100	99	101	108	108	+1
Picardie	96	101	98	93	93	93	93	92	−4
Haute Normandie	121	120	115	108	113	107	103	105	−16
Centre	94	99	97	98	99	98	100	100	+6
Basse Normandie	84	91	88	93	85	91	94	92	+8
Bourgogne	91	94	94	92	93	95	97	96	+5
Nord-Pas-de-C.	97	92	92	87	85	85	88	87	−10
Lorraine	100	100	97	92	89	89	94	91	−9
Alsace	106	108	110	108	110	110	112	110	+4

Franche-Comte	92	103	98	94	92	97	100	101	+9
Pays de la Loire	87	91	94	92	92	90	94	95	+8
Bretagne	72	85	87	86	86	88	90	89	-17
Poitou-Charentes	79	87	85	86	86	87	87	87	+8
Acquitaine	90	98	100	103	97	98	98	101	+11
Midi-Pyrennes	74	82	87	90	86	89	88	93	+19
Limousin	75	80	81	84	82	82	84	84	+9
Rhone-Alpes	108	106	107	106	107	101	107	107	-1
Auvergne	81	86	85	87	85	87	88	89	+8
Languedoc-Rous.	75	83	82	85	84	84	85	83	+8
Provence-Alpes-C	94	100	101	99	97	96	99	99	+5
Corse	–	–	78	73	75	77	77	78	–
Piemonte	106	118	119	111	115	118	117	116	+10
Valle d'Aosta	112	145	144	124	127	125	123	125	+13
Liguria	117	113	122	115	115	115	114	113	-4
Lombardia	112	124	127	126	132	136	133	131	+19
Trentino-Alto A.	80	100	108	116	114	116	114	119	+39
Veneto	82	97	101	108	111	115	113	113	+31
Friuli-Venezia G.	90	101	112	108	111	116	114	118	+28
Emilia-Romagna	92	116	123	123	122	127	125	124	+32
Toscana	88	102	109	109	112	111	110	106	+28
Umbria	71	89	99	97	96	96	95	96	+25
Marche	73	92	98	99	101	101	100	102	+29
Lazio	89	96	101	109	111	114	112	114	+25
Campania	56	64	69	68	64	65	64	68	+12

Table 4.5 (Cont.)

Region	1970	1977	1981	1984	1986	1988	1990	1991	Diff. 91–70
Abruzzo	57	75	81	86	86	87	85	88	+31
Molise	46	62	73	74	76	77	76	76	+30
Puglia	56	66	70	69	69	72	70	72	+16
Basilicata	47	65	70	68	62	61	60	63	+16
Calabria	43	58	62	56	56	56	55	55	+12
Sicilia	55	61	68	68	67	67	66	66	+11
Sardegna	63	71	71	75	73	73	72	72	+9
Groningen	123	216	234	226	179	131	131	131	+8
Friesland	82	90	82	78	83	80	79	80	–8
Drenthe	83	101	107	99	99	86	85	85	+2
East Netherlands	92	95	87	83	85	85	83	86	–6
Utrecht	98	107	102	98	100	98	93	103	+5
North Holland	117	119	116	119	118	116	115	108	–9
South Holland	121	116	107	106	107	107	106	102	–19
Zeeland	109	107	102	102	101	107	106	103	–6
North Brabant (NL)	101	97	90	90	95	94	93	95	–6
Limburg (NL)	88	90	86	85	89	92	91	91	+3
Flanders	95	98	97	99	98	100	103	103	+8
Wallonia	86	82	82	81	80	80	82	82	–4
Brussels	120	148	153	149	149	153	160	161	+41
Luxembourg (GD)	126	110	111	115	119	122	120	123	–3

		1991							
North of England	80	93	87	87	86	90	84	93	+13
York and Humberside	89	93	86	88	93	94	89	83	−6
East Midlands	96	95	90	93	95	98	94	89	−7
East Anglia	87	96	90	98	100	102	100	93	+6
Southeast England	109	114	112	116	121	128	118	110	+1
Southwest England	87	91	88	93	96	100	93	89	+2
West Midlands	97	96	85	88	91	96	89	84	−13
Northwest England	97	95	89	92	94	97	88	85	−12
Wales	86	85	77	81	83	87	81	78	−8
Scotland	92	96	91	94	95	99	90	88	−4
Northern Ireland	76	78	72	75	77	78	72	70	−6
Ireland	60	60	62	62	61	63	66	68	+8
Denmark	118	107	102	108	112	107	104	104	−14

Summary of changes in PPS scores:

	1970	1991
Top/bottom 1	4.2/1	3.6/1
Top/bottom 5	3.1/1	2.3/1
Top/bottom 10	2.5/1	1.7/1

existence of wide gaps in standards of living among citizens living within the same political space can be 'politically hazardous'. Politicians are well aware of the need to improve living standards in order to improve their prospects of reelection. Also, during the last two decades national governments have made a significant effort to build up welfare states and engage in substantial transfers of wealth in order to diminish disparities within national boundaries. This effort has also been underwritten by the EU in its attempt to increase the development potential of lagging regions.

What is interesting to note here in relation to the change in per capita PPS and GDP scores is that in both cases the trend over the two-decade period was toward a reduction of the gap between regions at the top and bottom of the scale. The shift in positions was less marked using the PPS indicator because of a lower initial differentiation between the top and bottom of the scale and a greater tendency toward stability on the PPS measure among the regions at the top of the index. The two index scores had a very high correlation and the relative rankings of the regions on the two dependent variables were very similar.

Table 4.6 helps to summarise the dynamic of the forty-one years covered here. The composition of the top ten regions in both data sets shows how the epicentre of European economic strength gradually moved from either side of the English Channel to more southerly locations along the Rhine, and more recently even leapfrogging the Alps into northern Italy. With the exception of the natural-gas producing region of Groningen, the list of regions appearing in the 1991 top-ten list looks surprisingly like the north/south line of city–state/regional conglomeration that dominated economic activity and trade in Europe during the Renaissance period – that is, prior to the consolidation of the nation-state system. This is evident when we look at the following group of top regions, (that is, those ranked from 11th to 20th) in which we find the rest of north-central Italy and the remaining German Länder.

In a parallel fashion, Table 4.7 shows that as development has migrated south, relative underdevelopment has migrated north. In 1950 and 1960 the lowest levels of growth were concentrated in the Italian Mezzogiorno. In the 1970s the island of Ireland appeared on the list due to the slower than average

Table 4.6 Europe's most developed regions, 1950–91

Top ten	1950	1950 top ten in 1960	1950 top ten in 1970
1950: The Channel industrialised zone			
Region Parisienne	194	169	169
Luxemburg	177	144	129
Brabant	175	137	127
Southeast England	158	131	98
Sjaell	158	135	143
Wallonie	149	102	97
Hamburg	144	174	182
Fyn	144	117	125
Jylland	137	111	123
Nord	137	122	112
Mean score	157	134	119

	1960
1960: The Channel–Rhine axis	
Hamburg	174
Region Parisienne	169
Bremen	148
Luxembourg	144
Brabant	137
Sjaell	135
Southeast England	131
Haute Normandie	127
West Midlands	127
Nord	122
Mean score	141

	1970 Molle Index	*1970* Leonardi Index
1970: Rhine development zone*		
Hamburg	182	211
Region Parisienne	169	179
Bremen	144	174
Sjaell	143	137
Hessen	136	126
Haute Normandie	131	137
Luxembourg	129	135

Table 4.6   (cont.)

Top ten	1950	1950 top ten in 1960	1950 top ten in 1970
Nordrhein-Westf.		129	130
Baden Wuerttemberg		129	137
West Berlin		128	147
Mean score		142	151

1981: North-Rhine axis

	1981
Groningen	240
Hamburg	188
Ile de France	167
Brussels	164
Bremen	151
W. Berlin	130
Hessen	130
Haute Normandie	125
Baden Wurtemberg	125
Denmark	120
Mean score	154

1991: Rhine/Po River core

	1991
Hamburg	211
Bremen	160
Ile de France	159
Brussels	156
Hessen	150
Lombardia	131
Baden-Wurtemberg	131
Groningen	130
Bavaria	128
Denmark	127
Mean score	148

* The list of most developed regions includes eleven that are identical on both index score calculations.

Table 4.7   Europe's least developed regions, 1950–91

Bottom 10	1950	1950 bottom ten in 1960	1950 bottom ten in 1970
1950: South-Central Italy			
Calabria	34	30	41
Molise	34	35	44
Basilicata	35	30	41
Puglia	40	39	50
Abruzzo	41	41	54
Sicilia	41	37	52
Campania	42	42	48
Sardegna	48	43	55
Marche	53	45	61
Umbria	54	46	63
Mean score	42	39	51

1960: South-Central Italy (no change from 1950)

1970: The Catholic Periphery

	1970 Molle Index	1970 Leonardi Index
Calabria	41	42
Basilicata	41	46
Molise	44	46
Campania	48	55
Puglia	50	55
Sicilia	52	54
Abruzzo	54	56
Sardegna	55	54
Ireland	60	57
Northern Ireland	61	70 (Umbria)
Mean score	51	53

1981: The North/South Catholic Periphery

	1981
Calabria	49
Sicilia	54
Campania	55
Basilicata	56

Table 4.7   (cont.)

Bottom 10	1950	1950 bottom ten in 1960	1950 bottom ten in 1970
Puglia		56	
Sardegna		56	
Ireland		57	
Molise		58	
Abruzzo		65	
N. Ireland		74	
Mean score		58	

1990: North/South Periphery

	1991
Calabria	55
Ireland	62
Basilicata	63
Sicilia	66
N. Ireland	67
Campania	69
Puglia	72
Sardegna	72
Wales	72
Molise	77
(North England)	77
Mean score (10)	68

Change in index scores between the 10 most and 10 least developed regions on the Molle and Leonardi indexes[1]

	Molle Index			Leonardi Index		
	1950	1960	1970	1970	1981	1991
Most developed	142	140	140	152	154	148
Least developed	42	39	51	53	58	68
Differences in points on index scores	100	101	89	99	96	80

Table 4.7   (Cont.)

Change in index scores between the 10 most and 10 least developed
regions in 1950 on the Molle and Leonardi indexes[2]

	Molle Index			Leonardi Index		
	1950	1960	1970	1970	1981	1991
Most developed	142	130	119	152	140	140
Least developed	42	39	51	53	58	75
Differences in points on index scores	100	91	68	99	82	65

Notes

1. The regions included in the calculation of the index scores vary over the years, as indicated by the list of regions presented in the previous tables.
2. The regions included in the calculation of the index scores remain constant over the time covered by the two indexes.

growth of its productive apparatus. By 1991 low levels of growth were being recorded across the Irish Sea in Wales and the north of England, and in areas that forty-one years previously had been above the European mean in development and economic well-being. In the second group of ten regions with the lowest per capita GDP there are a series of regions located in the old coalmining and industrial areas of the UK, Belgium and Holland. These findings confirm the need for the EU to be increasingly sensitive to the problems of industrial restructuring, and to develop alternative economic activities in areas suffering from industrial decline and reconversion.

In comparing the evolution of developed and underdeveloped regions over the forty-one years, it is necessary to analyse the index scores and rankings of the regions on both sets of indexes. The 1950–70 and 1970–91 lists show that, though index scores may have varied, the listing or ranking of regions did not. Apart from the problems caused by a different breakdown of the regions in Denmark and the Netherlands, the lists are very similar. This result provides an indication that the phenomenon of growth and regional transformation in both studies has been captured in an adequate and parallel manner.

Apart from a weakening of the position of the less developed regions in 1960 and a strengthening of the most developed regions in 1981, the trend demonstrated by the two indexes is clear – over time cohesion has increased and regional economies are slowly converging, as predicted by the convergence hypothesis. Over the forty-one years covered by the regional analysis, significant shifts took place in large areas of the EC. The industrial model based on mass production and regimented workers gave way to one emphasising flexibility and smaller-scale production. The flexible-specialisation model was adopted in areas that were previously characterised by agricultural production or a mixed economy (Becattini, 1994; Amin, 1994). As argued by David Jones, economic growth is not merely a product of quantitative increases in production. Rather, it is the outcome of a transformation of economic structures in which new products and production methods are evolved on the basis of a creative interaction between social, institutional, and economic forces:

> Transformation involves the introduction of new products and new production methods utilising different input combinations and human skills, a redistribution of resources from one industry to another and the adaptation to changing trade patters. Social and institutional factors play a key role in this transformation process (Jones, 1981: 41).

From the 1970s the position of top and bottom regions in our nine-nation data set remained fairly stable. The decrease in the gap between developed and underdeveloped regions can be explained by the significant upward movement of the bottom regions, as described by the upward-convergence model discussed in Chapter 3.

THE TREND IN INTRA- AND INTERSTATE DISPARITIES

Before turning to an analysis of what has happened to economic disparities at the national level, it is worthwhile considering the observation made by Rokkan and Urwin (1982) that, as the periphery is absorbed by the centre, disparities are likely to grow within a nation-state. Even if disparities are decreasing within the EU, is there a similar parallel pattern within the nation-state?

To provide an answer to this, a calculation of the trend of dispersion around the mean is applied to the analysis of intranational differences. The data show that during the 1970–91 period, as had been the case between 1950 and 1970, divergences also decreased within the larger nation-states. There was, however, one exception to this rule – in 1970 the UK recorded the lowest dispersion rate around the mean of any of the large EC countries. Its standard deviation score was 9.97, in contrast with 24.56 for Germany, 20.53 for France and 30.18 for Italy. During the twenty-year period, as the standard deviation scores for the other member states decreased the score for the UK increased, though at the end of the 1980s the UK still had lower standard deviation scores in relation to those recorded by equivalent-sized EC countries.

The present data base can also help us to answer the question of whether cohesion was also being achieved at the nation-state level. Parallel to the conclusions drawn by Hallett (1981) in analyzing national economic performance data up to the end of the 1970s, our analysis shows that there was a comparable reduction in the cohesion gap at the national level, that is, there was as much convergence at the national as there was at the regional level. Given the wider initial gap between top and bottom regions on the index scores, the rate of convergence at the regional level kept pace with the reduction of differences at the national level. National-level data show that between 1970 and 1991 the gap between the most (Luxembourg) and the least (Ireland) developed countries went from 2.4/1 to 1.8/1. Thus the gap that in 1991 separated the top countries from the bottom ones was equivalent to the gap that separated the top ten from the bottom ten regions.

Using dispersion around the mean, or standard deviation, to measure the convergence of nation-states within the EC over a longer forty-two year period, we find a similar phenomenon. The data in Table 4.8 have been used to plot the trend in the level of dispersion of nation-states around the EC mean, and it shows that dispersion declined up to 1974, the year of the oil shock. During 1974 the level of dispersion rose in a manner very similar to the one reported by Padoa Schioppa

Table 4.8   Evolution of the development gap among EC member
states based on per capita GDP, 1950–92[1]

Year	Standard deviation	Min.	Max.	Spread min/max
1950[2]		28	160	132
1960	37.661	39	158	119
1961	35.357	39	150	111
1962	33.610	40	141	101
1963	32.033	41	138	97
1964	32.865	41	141	100
1965	31.627	43	136	93
1966	30.597	44	133	89
1967	29.715	46	132	86
1968	28.944	48	132	84
1969	29.561	47	140	93
1970	29.041	49	141	92
1971	27.158	51	131	80
1972	26.840	53	134	81
1973	27.120	56	142	86
1974	29.226	54	153	99
1975	24.916	52	127	75
1976	25.195	52	126	74
1977	24.168	53	119	66
1978	23.574	53	119	66
1979	23.921	54	119	67
1980	23.570	55	118	63
1981	23.215	56	117	61
1982	23.431	56	119	63
1983	23.842	55	118	63
1984	24.711	52	121	69
1985	24.886	52	122	70
1986	25.608	52	126	74
1987	24.584	54	123	69
1988	24.333	54	124	70
1989	24.478	54	130	76
1990	23.572	53	125	72
1991	24.102	52	128	75
1992[3]	24.332	52	130	77

Notes
1. The 1960–92 figures are calculated from data presented in CEC,
   1992, and the 1950–70 figures are from Molle, Holst and Smit,
   1980.
2. The 1950 figure is based on per capita GDP expressed in US
   dollars. (Molle, Holst and Smit, 1980, p. 322).
3. From 1960–92 the standard deviation changed from 37.661 to
   24.332; minimum GDP/capita changed from 39 to 52 and the
   maximum changed from 158 to 130.

et al. (1986). But our data show that *after* 1974 the downward trend continued unabated until 1981, the year in which there was a decline in the rate of development of the four (and in most cases, future) peripheral EC states: Greece, Portugal, Spain and Ireland. However the table also shows that seven years later (possibly as a result of membership and participation in the doubling of the Structural Funds) the performance of three of the four countries began to improve once again at rates above the EC mean. In contrast, the position of Greece continued to deteriorate. The next section will attempt to find explanations for the divergent performances of the three peripheral member states in the mid-1980s and the continued decline of Greece.

THE DEPENDENT VARIABLES: THE GREEK, SPANISH, AND PORTUGUESE REGIONS, 1981–91

In the past, much of the public support in countries such as Greece, Spain and Portugal for entry into the EC was based on the expectation that accession would provide a positive stimulus to the growth of national and regional economies by providing larger markets for domestically produced goods and attracting outside investment into the local manufacturing and service sectors. If we look at Table 4.9, we find that the growth rates reported in the 34 regions added by the last two accessions (1981 and 1986) compared quite favourably with those of other regions in the EC. The Greek growth rates between 1975 and 1985 are of note, and do not paint the 'gloom and doom' picture favoured in descriptions of the Greek case.

The one major exception to this generalisation was the Attiki (Athens) area, which represents over half of the Greek population and the bulk of Greek production. Attiki experienced very low and even negative growth over the period concerned, and its lack of performance may have been due to an over-saturation of economic activity combined with urbanisation and political control in the area around the national capital. Greece is a highly monocephalic country, and Athens is in many ways an example of a national core area that has used development funds in an increasingly unproductive manner – expansion in Athens has led to diminishing returns. This should

Table 4.9   Change in per capita GDP (ECU, 1985 prices)
(per cent per annum)

Region	1975–85	1985–89
Schleswig-Holstein	1.6	3.5
Hamburg	2.8	2.5
Niedersachsen	2.4	3.2
Bremen	2.5	3.6
Nordrhein-Westfalen	1.8	2.8
Hessen	2.3	3.2
Rheinland-Pfalz	2.1	3.0
Baden-Wurtemberg	2.3	3.1
Bavaria	3.1	3.4
Saarland	3.0	2.3
W. Berlin	2.7	0.6
Ile de France	2.2	3.1
Champagne-Ardenne	1.0	2.2
Picardie	1.1	2.7
Haute-Normandie	1.8	1.8
Centre	2.3	2.4
Basse-Normandie	2.3	0.7
Borgogne	2.0	2.8
Nord Pas de Calais	1.0	2.2
Lorraine	0.7	2.7
Alsace	1.9	3.2
France-Comte	1.1	2.1
Pays de la Loire	1.9	2.7
Bretagne	1.9	3.2
Poitou-Carentes	1.7	2.9
Aquitaine	2.5	1.4
Midi-Pyrennes	2.6	2.0
Limousin	2.2	3.8
Rhone-Alpes	1.7	3.0
Auvergne	1.8	3.6
Languedoc-Roussillon	1.9	2.9
Provence-Alpes-Cote d'Azur	1.3	1.6
Corse		2.4
Piemonte	2.7	2.9
Val d'Aosta	5.5	2.9
Liguria	7.5	3.5
Lombardia	2.8	3.1
Trentino-Alto Adige	3.0	4.2
Veneto	4.8	4.3

Table 4.9 (cont.)

Region	1975–85	1985–89
Friuli-Venezia Giulia	5.8	5.1
Emilia-Romagna	0.3	3.8
Toscana	2.9	2.4
Umbria	−0.5	2.0
Lazio	4.7	4.9
Campania	3.0	1.2
Abruzzo	6.3	3.2
Molise	9.4	3.9
Puglia	3.9	4.1
Basilicata	4.1	5.8
Calabria	1.2	−1.4
Sicilia	0.5	4.7
Sardegna	3.1	4.0
Groningen	2.8	−6.3
Friesland	0.8	4.6
Drenthe	3.1	0.7
East Netherlands	0.8	2.9
Utrecht	0.7	2.1
North Holland	2.1	2.0
South Holland	0.5	3.5
Zeeland	−0.1	4.1
North Brabant	0.9	3.7
Limburg	1.2	3.7
Flanders	2.1	3.0
Brussels	1.7	3.4
Wallonie	1.7	3.9
Luxembourg	2.2	3.3
North of England	1.8	3.0
York and Humberside	1.8	2.6
East Midlands	1.6	2.4
East Anglia	2.3	3.0
Southeast England	2.2	4.1
Southwest England	2.3	3.5
West Midlands	1.5	3.2
Northwest England	1.6	3.1
Wales	1.5	3.4
Scotland	1.8	2.8
Northern Ireland	1.5	2.7

Table 4.9   (Cont.)

Region	1975–85	1985–89
Ireland	1.0	2.6
Denmark	2.4	0.8
Anat. Mak. Thraki	5.2	2.6
Kentriki Maked.	2.1	2.6
Kytiki Makedonia	1.1	2.6
Thessalia	3.1	2.6
Ipeiros	3.0	2.6
Ionia Nisia	3.6	2.6
Dytiki Ellada	2.6	2.5
Sterea Ellada	2.4	2.6
Peloponnisos	3.1	2.6
Attiki	0.4	−0.1
Voreio Aigaio	3.1	2.5
Notio Aigaio	3.4	2.5
Kriti	3.1	2.7
Galicia	2.1	4.2
Asturias	3.0	2.9
Cantabria	1.8	0.9
Pais Vasco	0.5	3.9
Navarra	−0.1	4.1
Rioja	3.6	1.7
Aragon	1.5	4.2
Madrid	0.6	4.1
Castilla-Leon	2.0	3.3
Castilla-La Mancha	−0.9	5.9
Extremadura	7.4	2.3
Cataluna	−0.6	4.6
Comunidad Valenciana	−0.1	5.3
Baleares	6.1	5.1
Andalucia	0.5	4.1
Murcia	−2.3	5.8
Norte	1.6	3.9
Centro	4.5	5.4
Lisboa e Val do Tejo	2.2	3.9
Alentejo	0.2	5.3
Algarve	0.1	4.5

Source: PA Cambridge Economic Consultants (1989).

suggest that it would be wise for the Greek government and the EU to locate new industries in, and even transfer older industries to, other areas of the country. Also, the weight of Attiki in the calculation of national GDP is of great importance and might be a dominant factor in the overall negative figures that have been reported for Greece. The relatively poor performance of Athens weighs heavily on the overall national index score. Data on GDP per capita in the thirteen Greek regions between 1970 and 1991 show that a significant amount of convergence has taken place within Greece during the past twenty-two years (Konsolas, 1993 and Konsolas, Papadaskalopoulos and Rondos, 1994).

Another explanation for the poor performance of the Greek economy in relation to the other new member states is the relatively low amount of foreign investment in Greece. For foreign firms to invest in Greece, it is not only important that investments be profitable but that firms be certain that the local economy and public sector are capable of guaranteeing a series of factors necessary for successful operation:

– structural economic factors, such as adequate infrastructure, skilled labour, acceptable labour costs, access to markets, investment grants and subsidised loans, favourable taxing provisions and so on;
– amenities for managers and technicians, that is, cultural and sports facilities, quality residential areas and schools, life-style considerations;
– quality administrative and political processes guaranteeing transparency in governmental procedures.

It could be argued that Greece does not lack the structural economic factors and social amenities needed to attract capital and industry. The reluctance of foreign investors to enter Greece and the low level of domestic investment may have more to do with doubts about the transparency of political and administrative processes than with the profitability of Greek investments.

The data presented in Table 4.10, which compares direct foreign investment with Structural Funds payments and fixed domestic capital formation, show that foreign investment in Greece lags far behind that in the other peripheral states: the rate of investment in Greece is less than half that in the other member states. In a similar vein, when comparing the amount of Structural Funds (EC funds made available through the Regional, Social and Agricultural-Guidance Funds) payments versus the rate of foreign direct investment we find, once again, that the mix of foreign investments and Structural Funds payments are substantially different in Greece than they are in the other three peripheral member states. Structural Funds payments far outweigh foreign direct investment in Greece, while in the other countries foreign investment has on average outstripped EC payments. In Spain, foreign direct investment was already seven times higher than EC contributions during the first year of membership in 1986, and it has maintained a strong position ever since. Portugal and Ireland, in turn, have experienced a greater balance between the two types of investment, but as Table 4.10 shows the beginning of the substantial investment programmes put into place by the 1989 Community Support Frameworks produced a dramatic upswing in private foreign investment in the two countries.

Returning to Table 4.9, the data there confirm that the Spanish regions went through a difficult period in the late 1970s and the first part of the 1980s, but that there was a significant improvement in growth in the post-1985 period. However even in the period 1975–85 a few Spanish regions (Extramadura and the Baleares Islands) performed outstandingly on the per capita GDP indexes. From 1985–9 the outstanding performers were the regional economies of Murcia, Comunidad Valencia and Castilla-La Mancha, which registered average growth rates of above 5 per cent.

Portugal also showed significant growth rates for a good part of the same period. The Lisboa e Val do Tejo, Norte and Centro regions recorded consistently good performances. Starting in 1985, they were joined by the other two regions – Alentejo and Algarve – in registering above-average EC growth rates. Subsequent data on the growth of per capita GDP from 1986–90 show that Portugal's growth rate rose at a rate of 1.5 per cent above the EC average, bringing the country's index score from 52.0 per cent of the EC average in 1985 to 56.3 per cent in 1991 (Madureira-Pires, 1992, p. 6).[9]

The problem with using the annual percentage increase in per capita GDP as an adequate measure of economic growth across regions is that it provides information on internal

Table 4.10 Foreign direct investment, EC Structural Funds payments and gross domestic fixed capital formation in peripheral countries, 1985–90 (in milliards of ECU at current prices and exchange rates)

Year	Foreign direct investment	Structural funds payments	Gross fixed capital formation
Spain:			
1985	2.50	–	41.87
1986	3.39	0.49	45.81
1987	3.77	0.68	52.87
1988	5.69	1.04	66.11
1989	7.21	1.62	83.41
1990	NA	2.32	95.42
Portugal:			
1985	0.34	–	5.90
1986	0.23	0.30	6.64
1987	0.37	0.44	7.69
1988	0.70	0.63	9.48
1989	1.42	0.78	10.87
1990	NA	1.06	12.39
Ireland:			
1985	0.54	0.36	4.74
1986	0.09	0.35	4.63
1987	0.52	0.47	4.31
1988	0.49	0.40	4.69
1989	1.45	0.48	5.69
1990	NA	0.59	6.38
Greece:			
1985	0.21	0.47	8.33
1986	0.34	0.50	7.41
1987	0.19	0.52	6.88
1988	0.15	0.59	7.87
1989	0.34	0.55	9.45
1990	NA	1.06	10.23

changes but does not tell us very much about external changes or how regions compare with each other. The lack of comparable regional-level data for the 1970s in the case of Greece, Spain and Portugal restricts longitudinal analysis of economic performance to the shorter 1981–91 period. Data in Tables 4.11 and 4.13 suggest that substantial change also took place in the three new member states between 1981 and 1991.

The data in Table 4.11 cannot be added to the data for the nine EC member states analysed in the previous sections because in order to incorporate Greece, Portugal and Spain a new index score had to be calculated for the EC-12 countries. In adding the thirty-four new regions to the calculations the EC average is lowered, and therefore so are the index scores for all the other regions. For example, in the previous EC-9 analysis the index score for Hamburg was 188 in 1981 and 195 in 1989, but when the new regions are included the index scores for Hamburg jump to 228 in 1981 and 238 in 1989. In this case the absolute GDP values for Hamburg have not changed. What has changed is its relative index score vis-à-vis the EC mean and vis-à-vis the newcomers that have been introduced into the calculation.[10]

The comparison between the regional per capita GDP index scores shows that, even with the addition of the thirty-four regions of the three new members, the ratios between the top and bottom five regions dropped from a level of 6.7/1 in 1981 to 5.1/1 in 1991 due to the upward push of the Portuguese regions.

Table 4.11 shows that during the 1980s the regions of Portugal and Spain witnessed a substantial improvement in their per capita GDP index scores, with most of the improvement taking place during the last two years. The only exception to this rule was Alentejo, which slid down two points on the index. Increases in Spain were nationwide and substantial in nature, affecting both Objective 1 and non-Objective 1 areas. Apart from the island regions of the Canarias and Baleares, substantial rises were registered by the interior and Mediterranean regions of Navarra, Aragon, Madrid, Cataluna, Murcia and Valencia. The regions with single-digit increases were those in the north and northwest of the country – Galicia, Asturias, Cantabria and Rioja.

The pace and depth of change in Spain has led some

Table 4.11 Index scores for GDP/inhabitant in ECU for regions in Greece, Spain and Portugal, 1981–91 (EC = 100)

Region	1981	1984	1986	1987	1988	1989	1991	Diff. 1991–81
Anat. Mak. Thraki	44	52	42	41	42	44	37	−7
Kentriki Maked.	48	49	40	38	39	41	39	−9
Dytiki Makedonia	46	43	35	34	35	37	40	−6
Thessalia	48	48	39	37	38	41	38	−10
Ipeiros	39	39	32	30	31	33	31	−8
Ionia Nisia	44	46	38	36	37	40	37	−7
Dytiki Ellada	45	46	38	36	37	39	36	−9
Sterea Ellada	65	62	51	49	50	53	50	−15
Peloponnisos	54	52	43	41	42	45	41	−13
Attiki	52	54	44	42	44	45	46	−6
Voreio Aigaio	35	37	30	29	30	32	30	−5
Notio Aigaio	47	51	42	40	41	44	41	−6
Kriti	43	45	37	35	36	38	37	−6
Galicia	55	52	54	55	59	56	61	+6
Asturias	70	64	66	68	72	68	75	+5
Cantabria	71	65	61	63	67	62	77	+6
Pais Vasco	82	73	75	77	82	78	92	+10
Navarra	81	73	74	76	81	78	101	+20
Rioja	81	77	76	78	83	78	88	+7
Aragon	67	67	68	70	74	72	90	+23
Madrid	74	69	72	73	78	74	100	+26

Table 4.11   (cont.)

Region	1981	1984	1986	1987	1988	1989	1991	*Diff. 1991–81*
Castilla-Leon	60	60	60	61	65	62	70	+10
Castilla-La Mancha	52	47	51	53	56	55	67	+15
Extremadura	40	41	41	42	45	42	52	+12
Cataluna	73	69	71	73	77	75	98	+25
Comunidad Valenciana	64	60	63	65	69	67	81	+17
Baleares	81	87	92	95	101	95	106	+25
Andalucia	49	46	49	50	53	51	62	+13
Murcia	56	53	56	57	61	59	76	+20
Ceuta y Melilla	43						66	+23
Canarias	54						80	+26
Norte	28	25	25	25	26	25	39	+11
Centro	27	24	30	30	31	32	30	+3
Lisboa e Val do Tejo	44	38	42	42	43	41	59	+15
Alentejo	28	25	27	28	28	29	26	−2
Algarve	31	24	27	28	28	28	37	+6

observers to predict that during the 1990s Spain will be transformed into one of Europe's most important economic entities. Luis Suarez-Villa and Juan Cuadrado Roura have observed that the transformation of Spain's economic and political status in the EU will have significant implications for the conceptualisation and operationalisation of growth strategies in the future:

> Spain has experienced deep economic, political, and social transformation in the postwar era. One of Europe's poorest and most agrarian economies barely three decades ago, it has become an important advanced nation and a model of rapid political and economic change (Suarez-Villa and Cuadrado Roura, 1993, p. 121).

In contrast with Ireland, Portugal and Spain – its partners in the European periphery – the relative performance of the Greek national and regional economies was negative across the board. The regions registering double-digit contraction were Thessalia, Sterea Ellada and the Peloponnisos, while the remainder were in single-digit but significant decline.

The overall decline of the Greek scores suggest the presence of a strong 'national' factor. One of the most obvious places to look for the source of this national factor was the declining value of the Drachma vis-à-vis the ECU over the entire twenty-one year period. The Spanish pesata increased in value against the ECU from 1987–91, as did the Portuguese escudo and the Irish punt from 1990 (see Table 4.12).

Despite the fact that per capita GDP scores decreased for the Greek regions over time, the PPS scores reported a mixed response. Some regions (for example Anatolia Makedonia Thraki, Ionia Nisia, Voreio Aigaio and Kriti) increased their scores while others continued to decline over the same period (Sterea Ellada, Thessalia, Dytiki Ellada, Peloponnisos and Attiki) (see Table 4.13). This suggests that the decline in exchange rates had a negative impact on the GDP scores of Greece, while the level of well-being, as measured by PPS, did not decline in a consistent and substantial manner. Convergence was still taking place in the 1980s, though, in the countries participating in ERM, while convergence was less evident in Greece, which had not yet joined. Thus one conclusion suggested by the analysis is that exchange-rate stability is necessary

Table 4.12   ECU GDP exchange rates for member states

Year	BFr	DKr	DM	DR	PtA	FFr	IR£	ItL	LFr	HFl	Esc	UK£
1970	51.1	7.67	3.74	31	71	5.68	0.43	639	51.1	3.70	29	0.43
1977	40.9	6.86	2.65	42	87	5.61	0.65	1007	40.9	2.80	44	0.65
1881	41.3	7.92	2.51	62	102	6.04	0.69	1263	41.3	2.77	68	0.55
1984	45.4	8.14	2.23	88	127	6.87	0.73	1381	45.4	2.50	115	0.59
1986	43.8	7.94	2.12	137	137	6.80	0.73	1461	43.8	2.40	147	0.67
1988	43.4	7.95	2.07	168	138	7.04	0.77	1537	43.4	2.33	170	0.66
1990	42.4	7.86	2.05	201	129	6.91	0.77	1521	42.4	2.31	181	0.71
1991	42.2	7.90	2.05	225	128	6.97	0.77	1533	42.2	2.31	178	0.70

in order to measure effectively the extent of convergence of regional economies; otherwise the growth of these economies as expressed in GDP per capita in ECUs is masked by changes in the value of the national currency.

As the above analysis has established, the most developed regions experienced a reduction in their index scores in terms of individual as well as groupings of top regions. The drop in the index scores of the top regions serves to validate part of the 'downward-convergence' scenarios discussed above. But in analysing the index scores of the former bottom regions of the EC-9, an 'upward-convergence' trend can be seen in the index scores of the previously less developed regions. A similar trend is illustrated by the data on the three southern peripheral states.

It is worth noting from the data presented in Tables 4.11 and 4.12, that among the outstanding performers on the two indicators were the vacation 'capitals' of Spain – the Baleares and Canarias islands – as well as the metropolitan areas of Madrid and Catalonia, the Spanish territory Ceuta y Melilla and the peripheral region Murcia.[11] All these regions have a strong tourism factor in their regional economies.

Tourism seems to have become increasingly important in spurring the development of formerly underdeveloped regional economies in Spain. It may also have served to compensate the country for the downturn in industrial production and expansion of unemployment during the mid-1980s.[12] The Spanish case suggests that Greece should develop its tourist industry as a primary pump-priming strategy to spur the economic development of peripheral areas (CEC, 1993).

A second consideration to be taken into account when comparing the performance of the Portuguese and Greek regions with their Spanish counterparts is that the Spanish regions have at their disposal a series of potential levers for development that are not available in Greece and Portugal. Regions in Spain have institutional infrastructure that permits them to undertake their own 'self-help' projects or to experiment in alternative forms of economic development. Administrative and political autonomy gives the regions the power to experiment with policies rather than having to wait for the national government to come up with appropriate solutions. Greek and Portuguese regions do not have access to these alternative instruments and might, therefore, have to rely on

Table 4.13   Index scores for PPS/inhabitant for regions in
Greece, Spain and Portugal, 1980–91 (EC = 100)

Region	1980	1991	Diff. 1991–80
Anat. Mak. Thraki	41	45	+4
Kentriki Maked.	52	47	−5
Dytiki Makedonia	48	48	0
Thessalia	48	45	−3
Ipeiros	38	38	0
Ionia Nisia	41	44	+3
Dytiki Ellada	45	43	−2
Sterea Ellada	72	60	−12
Peloponnisos	52	49	−3
Attiki	59	55	−4
Voreio Aigaio	42	44	+2
Notio Aigaio	36	36	0
Kriti	45	49	+4
Galicia	61	61	0
Asturias	77	75	−2
Cantabria	78	77	−1
Pais Vasco	89	92	+3
Navarra	90	100	+10
Rioja	88	87	−1
Aragon	76	89	+13
Madrid	81	100	+19
Castilla-Leon	70	70	0
Castilla-La Mancha	61	66	+5
Extremadura	45	52	+7
Cataluna	83	98	+15
Comunidad Valenciana	71	80	+9
Baleares	86	106	+20
Andalucia	56	62	+6
Murcia	65	76	+11
Ceuta y Melilla	50	66	+16
Canarias	59	79	+20
Norte	44	54	+10
Centro	42	42	0
Lisboa e Val do Tejo	69	82	+13
Alentejo	49	36	−13
Algarve	48	52	+4

state-generated development schemes. These usually take longer to have an impact at the regional level and cannot be customised to the exigencies of regional economies and society.[13]

Thirdly, it must be remembered that even though the development of these regions was monitored over an eleven-year period, the nation-states were not members of the EC during the same period. Portugal and Spain only joined in 1986, and one of our working hypotheses is that integration in and of itself serves as a positive stimulus to peripheral regional economies and accounts for a significant part of convergence.[14]

For Spain and Portugal, index scores on the whole deteriorated up to 1986, but started to move upward when the two countries became full members of the EC. One could also argue that the scores began to firm up when Spain and Portugal joined the ERM, so ensuring exchange-rate stability. Therefore, in these two cases most of the data in the tables refers to regional economic levels prior to membership in the EC, prior to participation in any specifically oriented EC programme, and prior to membersship of the ERM.

Subsequent EC allocations in the form of Structural Fund aid made a substantial contribution to economic investment and overall GDP in the three nations, accounting in 1993 for 3.7 per cent (Portugal), 0.8 per cent (Spain) and 2.9 per cent (Greece) of GDP.[15] This, in combination with national contributions (+3.1 per cent in Portugal, +0.8 per cent in Spain and +2.2 per cent in Greece) and the amounts already allocated by the EC, acted as a significant stimulus to the national economies, explaining in part the surge of these countries toward convergence.

Despite the positive economic effects of CSFs and other EC funding programmes, GDP scores in Greece improved neither nationally nor regionally. According to official figures, Greece's high moment of convergence vis-à-vis other national economies occurred in 1978, while it was negotiating its entry into the EC. During that year its per capita GDP index hit 58.6, but since then it has been in decline.

Given that Greece has been a member of the EC since 1981 and has been the recipient of major funding programmes, the question remains, why hasn't its economy responded to the flow of EC investment funds and why is it the only country that has consistently performed in contradiction to convergence theories? To begin with, Greece joined at the start of a general European-wide recession. Thus the weaker Greek economy was not able to take advantage of the expanding European market and the greater availability of resources (Gorman and Kiljunen, 1983; Seers and Vaitos, 1982; Tsoukalis, 1979).[16]

Secondly, Greece's ability to make full use of EC grants to spur development has always been less than adequate. When the Integrated Mediterranean Programmes were introduced (3.3 billion ECU were allocated to Greece over a seven-year period), the country had the lowest level of overall implementation of the IMP measures when compared with France and Italy (Bianchi, 1993). Once again, Greece's inadequate institutional infrastructure at the subnational level served to retard growth and slow implementation of EC programmes, when what was needed was a quick turnover of programmes in order to establish a momentum for development (Papageorgiou and Verney, 1993).

Thirdly, the entrepreneurial base in Greece is not adequately organised to operate as an effective instrument to link individual entrepreneurs, associations and sectoral groups to European-level programmes aimed at spurring investment. This is made abundantly clear by Greece's relative lack of success in gaining access to European Investment Bank (EIB) loans. The amount received by Greece is much lower than that allocated to other underdeveloped countries, such as Portugal and Spain, and the types of project financed by the EIB are infrastructure oriented rather than designed to stimulate business or, in the Bank's own words, spur 'industrial competitiveness and European integration'.[17] Special attention should therefore be focused on organizing and networking Greek entrepreneurs and business interests into the emerging EU framework and encouraging the integration of Greek economic concerns into the opportunity structures offered by the Single Market.

Fourthly, as discussed above, the expenditures associated with the Community Support Framework have not resulted in increased foreign investment – that is, EU and national investments have not been translated in Greece into knock-on effects spurring private investment from abroad. Foreign capital has remained aloof from Greece. Some of the blame for this may be attributed to the lack of administrative transparency and the exclusion of the Greek currency from the ERM, but the rest could be attributed to the lack of forward-looking investment programs in the periphery.

The fluctuating performance of the European peripheral countries and the original nine member states suggests that, when comparing the rate and intensity of convergence, account must be taken of the time needed for positive economic stimuli and negative economic shocks to work their way through national economies. Until full transition is made to EMU, regional economies in Europe still have to operate within national contexts and are therefore heavily influenced by national exchange-rate fluctuations and national-level difficulties in implementing adequate monetary and fiscal policies.

The data presented in this chapter suggest that recession and growth cycles tend to ripple through the peripheral economies with some delay vis-à-vis the core countries. The Fourth Periodic Report (CEC, 1991) claims that from 1986–7 the growth rate of the top twenty-five regions was close to that of the weaker twenty five: the difference was only 0.2 per cent, and the weaker twenty-five's growth rate from 1986–7 was higher than the European average. In contrast our data for 1985–9, show that the growth rate of the regions at the bottom of the ranking was significantly higher than for those at the top, and that this positive trend continued into the 1991–2 period for Portugal and Ireland. The discrepancy between the data presented in the Fourth Periodic Report and ours demonstrates the importance of constantly monitoring economic trends in order to capture the impact of the delayed ripple effects running through the various European economies. Taking into account the lag inherent in ripple effects, it is clear that regional economies in the EU periphery have substantially changed their development prospects. Regions in Spain and Portugal are developing rapidly, and by the end of the second phase of the Community Support Frameworks in 1999 they will be much closer to the European mean than was the case when they joined the European integration process.

The performance of Greece does not fit the convergence model, but this may be due more to national-level administrative and political difficulties and a weakening drachma than to the performance of individual entrepreneurs and local economies. The unstable political situation in the Balkans might continue to discourage foreign investment. Developments in former Yugoslavia, the closure of the overland routes linking Greece with the rest of the EU, political tension over Macedonia and increased military expenditure in response to increased conflicts with Turkey do not bode well for the ability of Greece to concentrate on strengthening its economy within the European framework in the short to medium term.

NOTES

1. Molle, van Holst and Smit (1980, pp. 14–15) write that their GDP figures are 'all defined according to the 1958 System of National Accounts (SNA) published by the OECD. They represent the gross value added at factor cost produced in the area under consideration. National GDP figures have been made internally comparable by counting them all in US$ with the help of official exchange rates (fortunately very stable in the period of the study). Regional GDP figures have been established by applying to these national figures the percentage shares that each region had in that year in the national GDP. In order to calculate real growth, all growth rates at current price GDP figures have been corrected for the general Western European inflation rate'.

2. The Periodic Reports spawned a whole series of studies based on secondary analysis of regional trends in the EC. These accepted uncritically the conclusion that regional disparities were on the increase in the EC.

3. The Second and Third Periodic Reports ranked the regions according to a synthetic index of the intensity of regional problems. The index was comprised of several variables including GDP and employment rates. Why it was not repeated in the Fourth Report is not known. Molle, Van Holst and Smit (1980, p. 165) expressed the view that Purchasing Power Parities (PPP) would have provided a better basis for measuring regional disparities than GDP, but at the time of writing they were not available for the nine member-states.

4. In 1970 West Berlin was ranked fourth out of the eighty regions. Given that the 1991 GDP figure for Berlin combines what was formerly East and West Berlin, the 1990 figure for West Berlin was used in the calculation. Through the incorporation of East Berlin, the ranking of (West) Berlin went from thirteenth to forty-second in per capita GDP. The same adjustment was made when calculating PPS scores over time.

5. The Lorenz curve was developed in 1905 to measure disparity in income distribution. The closer the line to the diagonal, the greater the *equality* in distribution; and the more the line curves, the greater the

inequality. The advantage of the Lorenz curve is that it permits a comparison of unequal distributions across cases or across time.

6. Corse was dropped from the calculation due to the lack of 1970s data.

7. These figures on GDP per capita scores differ radically from those reported by Carello (1989: 169) in relation to the Italian regions for the period 1971–81. Why Italy as a whole and the southern regions, in particular, register decreases in their GDP scores in Carello's calculations is unclear.

8. The change in the country scores between 1970 and 1991 shows that the ratio went from 2.1/1 to 1.8/1. The lowest country on the PPS index was, once again, Ireland while the highest index score went to Luxembourg.

9. In 1960 Portugal had an index score of 38.7; in 1970 it was 48.9 (CEC, 1992, Appendix, p. 1).

10. The addition and subtraction of cases in and by itself tends to change rank scores. Thus extreme care must be used when making comparisons over time when the number and composition of the units are not kept constant. The problem was heightened in 1991 with the addition of the five East German Länder, which in absolute terms have the lowest GDP scores in the EC. Just through their addition, the impact on regions in the three southern European peripheral states has been to raise their relative index scores. The calculations used for 1991 exclude the GDP scores for the five East German Länder in order to provide an homogeneous and consistent comparison over time.

11. The data on the Spanish regions suggest a strong movement toward *internal cohesion* within Spain as a result of the process of integrating Spain into the EC.

12. A survey (EUI, 1992) conducted by the author on tourism flows and receipts in the Mediterranean shows that while the total number of tourists decreased slightly from 1989 to 1990, gross receipts from tourism increased by 25 per cent.

13. For an in-depth discussion of the relationship between economic growth and regional institutions, see Leonardi and Garmise, 1993; Cuchillo, 1993; Keating, 1993.

14. On this point, see Yannopoulos, 1989.

15. The 1993 figure for Ireland was 2.7 per cent of GDP. Prior to the initiation of the Community Support frameworks the four peripheral countries received in 1986 EC Structural Funds contributions amounting to 2.1 per cent in Portugal, 0.5 per cent in Spain, 1.7 per cent in Ireland and 1.5 per cent in Greece (Pimpāo, 1994).

16. In fact some observers predicted that integration into an already integrated market would have serious negative impacts on weaker economies such as Greece: 'The plan for Western European integration, which is geared to industrialised countries and was established at a time of extensive economic growth, does not include the instruments required to protect a Community of countries at different levels of development against serious backwash effects or even a tendency towards disintegration at a time of relative stagnation. It is becoming more and more evident that existing and growing imbalances resulting

from the dynamic impact of regional concentration and the structural economic disparities imply permanent structural crisis. These prejudice the development opportunities of the acceding countries and impede the coordination of national economic and monetary policies' Musto (1982, p. 68).

17. See 'Annual Report, 1990', European Investment Bank, 1991, pp. 80–101.

REFERENCES

Amin, A. (1994) 'Santa Croce in context or how industrial districts respond to the restructuring of world markets', in R. Leonardi and R. Y. Nanetti (eds) *Regional Development in a Modern European Economy: The Case of Tuscany* (London: Pinter, 1994), pp. 170–80.

Bairoch, P. (1976) 'Europe's Gross National Product: 1800–1975', *The Journal of European Economic History*, vol. 2 (fall), pp. 273–340.

Batley, R. and G. Stoker (eds) (1991) *Local Government in Europe: Trends and Developments* (London: Macmillan).

Becattini, G. (1994) 'The development of light industry in Tuscany: an interpretation', in R. Leonardi and R. Y. Nanetti (eds) *Regional Development in a Modern European Economy: The Case of Tuscany* (London: Pinter), pp. 69–85.

Bianchi, G. (1993) 'The IMPs: A Missed Opportunity? An Appraisal of the Design and Implementation of the Integrated Mediterranean Programmes', in R. Leonardi (ed.), *The Regions and the European Community: The Regional Response to the Single Market in the Underdeveloped Areas* (London: Frank Cass), pp. 47–70.

Biehl, D., D. Hussmann and S. Schnyder (1972) 'Zur Regionalen Einkommenverteilung in der Europaische Wirtschaftsgemeinschaft', *Die Welwirtschaft*, pp. 64–8.

Carello, A. N. *The Northen Question: Italy's Participation in the European Economic Community and the Mezzogiorno's Underdevelopment* (Newark, N.J.: University of Deleware Press, 1989).

CEC (1981) *Le Regioni d'Europa: Prima relazione periodic sulla situazione sociale ed economica nelle regioni della Comunitàe*, (Luxembourg: Office of Official Publications of the European Communities).

CEC (1984) *The Regions of Europe: Second Periodic Report on the Social and Economic Situation of the Regions of the Community, Together with a Statement of the Regional Policy Committee* (Luxembourg: Office of Official Publications of the European Communities).

CEC, (1987) *The Regions of the Enlarged Community: Third Periodic Report on the Social and Economic Situation and Development of the Regions of the Community* (Luxembourg: Office of Official Publications of the European Communities).

CEC (1991) *The Regions in the 1990s: Fourth Periodic Report on the Social and Economic Situation and Development of the Regions of the Community* (Luxembourg: Office of Official Publications of the European Communities).

CEC (1992) 'Community Structural Policies: Assessment and Outlook', Brussels, 18 March, COM(1992) 84 final.

CEC (1993) 'The Evolution of Holiday Travel Facilities and in the Flow of Tourism Inside and Outside of the European Community' (Brussels: DG XXIII).

Cuchillo, M. (1993) 'The Autonomous Communities as the Spanish Meso', in L. J. Sharpe (ed.), *The Rise of Meso Government in Europe* (London: Sage), pp. 210–46.

EUI (1992) 'Tourism in the Mediterranean: Past Trends and Future Opportunities', mimeo, (Florence: European University Institute, February).

Gorman, L. and M. Kiljunen (eds) *The Enlargement of the European Community: Case-Studies of Greece, Portugal and Spain* (London: Macmillan, 1983).

Hallett, E. C. 'Economic Convergence and Divergence in the European Community: A Survey of the Evidence' in M. Hodges and W. Wallace (eds) *Economic Divergence in the European Community* (London: Allen & Unwin, 1981), pp. 16–31.

Jones, D. T. 'Industrial Development and Economic Divergence' in M. Hodges and W. Wallace (eds) *Economic Divergence in the European Community* (London: Allen & Unwin, 1981), pp. 32–57.

Keating, M. (1993) 'The Continental Meso: Regions in the European Community' in L. J. Sharpe (ed.), *The Rise of Meso Government in Europe* (London: Sage), pp. 296–312.

Konsolas, N. (1993) *Regional Development Policies in Greece* (Athens: Regional Studies Institute).

Konsolas, N., A. Papadaskalopoulos and K. Rondos (1994) 'Greek Regional Development: Strategies and Policies in the European Context', paper delivered at the Second Meeting of the Network on Economic and Social Cohesion, Florence, Italy, 3–4 June.

Leonardi, R. and S. O. Garmise (1993) 'Conclusions: Subnational Elites and the European Community' in R. Leonardi (ed.), *The Regions and the European Community: The Regional Response to 1992 in the Underdeveloped Areas* (London: Frank Cass), pp. 247–274.

Madureira-Pires, L. (1992) 'European Community Development Policies: The Case of Portugal', Paper presented at the European Research Seminar, London School of Economics, Department of Government, February 28.

Molle W. (1990) *The Economics of European Integration* (Aldershot: Dartmouth).

Molle, W., B. van Holst and H. Smit (1980) *Regional Disparity and Economic Development in the European Community* (Westmead: Saxon House).

Musto, S. (1982) 'Structural Implications' in D. Seers and C. Vaitos (eds) *The Second Enlargement of the EEC* (New York: St. Martin's Press), pp. 67–91.

NIESR (1991) 'A New Strategy for Social and Economic Cohesion after 1992', Final Report for the European Parliament, National Institute of Economic and Social Research, London.

PA Cambridge Economic Consultants (1989) 'The Efficiency of Regional Policy in Member Countries of the European Community', mimeo, Cambridge.

Padoa Schioppa, T. with M. Emerson *et al.* (1987) *Efficiency, Stability, Equity* (Oxford: Oxford University Press).

Papageorgiou, F. and S. Verney (1993) 'Regional Planning and the Integrated Mediterranean Programmes in Greece', in R. Leonardi (ed.), *The*

Regions and the European Community: The Regional Response to the Single Market in the Underdeveloped Areas (London: Frank Cass), pp. 139–61.

Pimpão, A. (1994) 'Analysis of Regional Convergence in Portugal', paper delivered at the Second Meeting of the Network on Economic and Social Cohesion, Florence, Italy, 3–4 June.

Rokkan, S. and D. W. Urwin (1982) *The Politics of Territorial Identity: Studies in European Regionalism* (London: Sage).

Seers, D. and C. Vaitos (eds) (1982) *The Second Enlargement of the EEC* (New York: St. Martin's Press).

Suarez-Villa, L. and J. Cuadrado Roura (1993) 'Thirty Years of Spanish Regional Change: Interregional Dynamics and Sectoral Transformation', *International Regional Science Review*, vol. 15, no. 2, pp. 121–56.

Tsoukalis, L. (ed.) (1979) *Greece and the European Community* (Farnborough: Saxon House).

Tsoukalis, L. (1991) *The New European Community: The Politics and Economics of Integration* (Oxford: Oxford University Press).

Yannopoulos, G. (ed.) (1989) *European Integration and the Iberian Economies* (New York: St. Martin's Press).

5 The Italian Mezzogiorno: Does it Fit the Convergence Model?

SOUTHERN ITALY IN COMPARATIVE PERSPECTIVE

The Italian Mezzogiorno has a number of characteristics similar to those manifested by the other regions located in Objective 1 areas along the southern periphery of the EU. Until the accession of Greece, Portugal and Spain, Italy's southern regions had the lowest levels of development, the highest levels of unemployment and among the lowest supply of economic and social infrastructure in all of the EC. In 1950 the level of development of southern Italy was approximately one third of the average for the first nine member states. Its main resource, labour, was freely exported to the northern regions of Italy (especially the industrial triangle formed by the regions of Lombardy, Piedmont and Liguria) and industrialised EC countries (Romero, 1993). In other European countries Italians flocked to fill jobs in coalmining (Belgium and France), manufacturing (Germany), construction (Switzerland) and services (UK).

Since 1950 the bottom rankings in European regional development have been occupied almost exclusively by Italian regions. The situation changed in 1970 when the two central regions of Umbria and Marche went from the bottom toward the middle of the GDP and PPS rankings. On this occasion the eight regions of the Mezzogiorno were joined by Northern Ireland and the Republic of Ireland to form the ten lowest-ranked regions. In 1991 Abruzzo left the bottom ten and was replaced by Wales, and Molise was on the point of exiting, to be replaced by the north of England.

The experience of Italy's southern regions represents a paradox in the evolution of Europe's regions. On the one hand they are emblematic of the change that has taken place in the overall European rankings. The cases of Abruzzo and Molise demonstrate that peripheral ascendancy has been operating since the early 1970s in at least some of the Italian south, as had earlier been the case with regions in the centre and north of the country. On the other hand the bulk of the southern regions still maintain their relative position at the bottom of the rankings. This suggests that the alternative hypothesis, that underdevelopment is a permanent state of the European periphery, could be supported by the case of the Italian south.

Has the convergence dynamic bypassed the Mezzogiorno? Why has the south remained so underdeveloped vis-à-vis the north, despite the extensive emigration of workers from the south to the north, the massive transfer of wealth to the south through income maintenance and pension schemes, and the substantial investments made in the south by the Italian state since the 1950s? The position of the south has improved in relation to where it was in 1950 and 1960, but the change has not been sufficient to remove it from the bottom of the European rankings. With the extension of the EC in the 1980s to include the other three southern-European states, the Mezzogiorno now faces the prospect of being overtaken by the other Objective 1 regions. This chapter will look at these issues by analysing the comparative performance of the southern regions vis-à-vis their northern neighbours and discuss the reasons advanced to explain the poor performance of the southern regional economies.

The economies of the south have converged toward the European mean, but they have done so more through government provision than through significant economic growth. In 1950 the Italian south was characterised by the lowest levels of industrialisation, the highest dependence on agriculture and the highest birth rates in the six states that shortly thereafter were to form the European Coal and Steel Community. Ten years later the relative position of the south as a whole worsened as emigration and capital flight bled the area of its vital human and capital resources (Conti, 1979). Only Molise, Abruzzo and Campania were able to maintain their position while the other regions underwent a decline.

The performance of the Italian Mezzogiorno during the 1950s offers a pertinent illustration of how labour migration and remittances from abroad *per se* do not operate as substitutes for infrastructure development and capital investments in helping regions to grow and converge towards the more developed parts of Europe (Barucci, 1978; Saville, 1967). The land-reform programme initiated in the 1950s served to alleviate pressure from subsistence farmers who wanted to own their own land, but it did not resolve the economic problems of providing a base for a rationalisation of the sector and spurring growth in other activities. To a great extent the land-reform scheme served to resolve the south's social and political problems (Amato *et al.*, 1979; King, 1973; Tarrow, 1967), but it failed to resolve the traditional problems of agriculture being tied to small landholdings, the lack of agricultural research to improve existing products and develop new plant varieties, poor commercialisation of agricultural products through government monopolies (*federconsorzi*) and an inadequate infrastructure network in transporting goods to other markets in Italy and Europe. The competitive weakness of Italy's agricultural sector was compounded in the 1960s through the adoption of the CAP, which encouraged farmers to produce for short-term gain through the price-support mechanism rather than to conquer new markets in Italy and Europe.

In terms of per capita GDP, the 1960s represented an inversion of the economic and social conditions affecting the south. The infrastructure gap was slowly closed through the actions of the Fund for the South and the overall national investment programme. Investment in the growth poles, concentrating on large industrial plants, began in earnest and seemed to be about to transform the economic face and destiny of the area (D'Antonio, 1991; Podbielski, 1974). By 1970 the South was enjoying levels of income that were close to one half of the EC average.

During the decades 1970–91 the regions in the Mezzogiorno continued to improve their absolute and relative levels of prosperity, to the point that in 1991 a majority had passed the threshold of 75 per cent of the EC average in levels of development.[1] This was the case for Abruzzo (95 per cent), Molise (82 per cent), Sardegna (78 per cent) and Puglia (77 per cent). The remaining three – Basilicata, Sicily and Calabria – had lower scores but were well within reach of the 75 per cent mark. In the second round of Community Support Frameworks (1994–99), Abruzzo was designated an Objective 1 region for only three more years, rather than the six years allocated to the other regions receiving Structural Fund aid. The restriction of the second CSF to three years was intended to permit Abruzzo to make a controlled transition from Objective 1 to non-Objective 1 status – that is, to a fully competitive position in the market (CEC, 1993). Though above the 75 per cent threshold in 1992, Molise and Sardegna have not been excluded from the second phase of the CSFs because the eligibility criterion (that is, per capita GDP) used in 1991 to rank the regions was raised on a de facto basis from 75 per cent to 80 per cent of the EC average.[2]

Despite these increases, there are other aspects of the economic structure of the Mezzogiorno that do not bode well for the future. In comparing the eight southern regions with their counterpart in Greece, Spain and Portugal on the combined 1991 GDP index scores, we can see from Table 5.1 that the south is losing its advantage over the Spanish regions. The GDP and PPS scores for the bulk of Italy's southern regions remained static over the five years prior to 1991, while those of the Spanish regions grew substantially. Internal cohesion has made significant progress in Spain. In 1991 the only regions in Spain that remained behind the lowest Italian region, Calabria, on the GDP index were Extremadura, Galicia and Andalucia.

The situation is even more serious when we take into consideration the data in Table 5.2, which show that the socioeconomic situation in southern Italy is deteriorating vis-à-vis that of its southern peripheral counterpart. The Mezzogiorno has a lower level of employment in industry, a lower percentage of the population active in the economy and a substantial proportion of its workforce in agriculture. In addition, from 1985–91 unemployment in the other Objective 1 areas decreased, but in southern Italy it increased. The prospects for the future are therefore not encouraging, despite the fact that the south is adjacent to one of Europe's most dynamic productive regions.

ITALY'S DUAL ECONOMY

What are the causes of the south's low socioeconomic performance? The answer to this question must be sought in the duality of Italy's economy and in the characteristics of the

Table 5.1   Per capita GDP for peripheral regions in the
European Union, 1991

	GDP index score	GDP ranking
Italian Mezzogiorno		
Abruzzi	107	53
Molise	93	75
Campania	83	82
Puglia	87	81
Basilicata	76	90
Calabria	67	95
Sicilia	80	86
Sardegna	88	80
Spain		
Galicia	63	97
Asturias	77	89
Cantabria	79	87
Pais Vasco	95	73
Navarra	103	59
Rioja	90	79
Aragon	92	77
Madrid	103	60
Castilla-Leon	72	92
Castilla-La Mancha	69	93
Extremadura	54	99
Cataluna	101	65
Comunidad Valenciana	83	83
Baleares	109	50
Andalucia	64	96
Murcia	78	88
Ceuta y Melilla	68	94
Canarias	82	84
Portugal		
Norte	40	110
Centro	31	119
Lisboa e Val do Tejo	61	98
Alentejo	26	121
Algarve	38	114
Greece		
Anatolia Makedonia Thraki	38	112
Kentriki Makedonia	40	107
Dytiki Makedonia	41	106
Thessalia	39	111

Table 5.1   (Cont.)

	GDP index score	GDP ranking
Ipeiros	32	118
Ionia Nisia	37	115
Dytiki Ellada	37	117
Sterea Ellada	51	100
Peloponnisos	42	104
Attiki	47	101
Voreio Aigaio	31	120
Notio Aigaio	42	105
Kriti	38	113
Germany		
Brandenberg	44	102
Mecklenburg-Vorpommern	40	108
Sachsen	40	109
Sachsen-Anhalt	42	103
Thuringen	37	116
Ireland	75	91
N. Ireland	81	85
Corsica	93	76

socio-political structure that dominates the south. To a great extent the south contains within itself all of the contradictions of uneven growth of a country that has undergone two significant industrial transformations. The first was the period of industrialisation during the 1950s, which was dominated by large enterprises taking advantage of the economies of scale to be found in the northern industrial triangle. The second was in the 1970s when large industries in the north were decentralised and industrial districts populated by small and medium-sized enterprises began to appear in substantial numbers in the northeast and centre of the country. These two industrial 'miracles' helped to propel Italy into the forefront of European business and manufacturing, and it opened up a period of unparalleled prosperity. By the 1980s industrialisation seemed to be on the verge of spilling over into the Mezzogiorno to open the way to a third economic miracle.

The reason why that miracle failed to materialise can be detected in the data presented in Table 5.3. It shows that the

	Ireland	Spain	Portg.	Greece	Italy South	EU 12
Level of activity						
1991	51.9	47.2	59.5	47.4	47.8	55.1
1985	(52.0)	(47.2)	(58.8)	(50.6)	(38.7)	(53.6)
Unemployment						
1993	18.8	17.8	4.5	7.7	16.3	9.4
1986	(18.7)	(21.5)	(8.7)	(7.5)	(14.9)	(10.0)
Youth						
1992	26.2	32.3	9.9	24.6	42.9	18.1
1990	(23.8)	(38.7)	(11.9)	(25.9)	(54.2)	(16.1)
Female						
1992	18.8	25.5	6.1	12.9	30.0	11.5
1986	(20.2)	(25.3)	(11.2)	(11.3)	(26.1)	(13.2)
Employment sector						
Agriculture						
1991	13.8	10.7	17.5	21.6	15.3	6.4
1986	(16.0)	(23.9)	(21.5)	(28.5)	(17.8)	(8.1)
Industry						
1991	28.9	33.1	33.7	28.6	23.3	33.3
1986	(29.6)	(27.5)	(33.9)	(26.2)	(24.2)	(33.7)
Services						
1991	57.1	56.3	48.7	49.8	61.4	60.3
1986	(53.9)	(48.6)	(44.5)	(45.3)	(58.0)	(57.7)

Sources: Data on unemployment, April 1992 figures from EUROSTAT, *Basic Statistics of the European Community*, 30th edition (Luxembourg: Office of Official Publications of the European Communities, 1993); all other data from EUROSTAT, *Regions Statistical Yearbook, 1993* (Luxembourg: Office of Official Publications of the European Communities, 1993).

Table 5.3 Socioeconomic indicators comparing the Italian south with the national average

(a) Distribution of national GDP (1985 prices)

	1982	1983	1984	1985	1986	1987	1988	1989	1990	1991	1992
South	24.5	25.2	25.5	25.2	25.1	25.2	25.1	25.0	24.9	25.2	24.9
North	75.5	74.8	74.5	74.8	74.9	74.8	74.9	75.0	75.1	74.8	75.1

(b) Characteristics of the Italian Mezzogiorno:

	1980	1991	1992
Percentage of national total			
Population	35.4	36.7	36.7
Students	39.9	43.9	–
Percentage of national workforce in			
Agriculture	49.4	49.2	50.3
Industry	21.5	22.2	22.4
Services	29.5	30.8	30.8

Percentage of unemployed			
Of total	48.6	40.2	59.2
Youth	49.4	61.9	60.8
Percentage of national value added in			
Agriculture	42.5	45.0	41.2
Industry	17.6	18.3	18.2
Services	26.8	27.7	27.5
Percentage of national:			
Family consumption	28.2	28.9	28.6
Investments	27.8	27.3	26.9
Percentage of national trade			
Exports	10.4	8.9	8.7
Imports	17.2	12.4	12.2
Percentage of national tourism			
All tourists	18.2	18.4	18.8
Foreign tourists	14.4	13.8	13.6
Percentage of national infant mortality	54.2	54.1	51.6
Percentage of telephones	25.0	29.5	29.6

Source: Author's calculations using data in SVIMEZ (1993)

eight southern regions have been consistent underperformers when compared with northern and central Italian regions in terms of the structure of economic production, investment and exports. With 36.2 per cent of the Italian population, the south only contributes 25 per cent of national GDP, 8.7 per cent of exports, 13.6 per cent of foreign tourism, and 22.4 per cent of value added in industry. However, at the same time it represents 41.2 per cent of value added in agriculture, 59.2 per cent of unemployment, 60.8 per cent of youth unemployment and 51.6 per cent of infant mortality. The south also accounts for the bulk of the country's homicides (72 per cent) and armed robberies (63 per cent). In 1992, murders committed by criminal organisations in three southern regions (Sicily, Calabria and Campania) outnumbered those in the whole of the centre and north of the country. The south is at the national average when it comes to levels of consumption, telephone and car ownership, and savings. Thus the south is modern and comparable to the centre–north when it comes to the personal consumption and accumulation side of the ledger.

The reason behind the contradiction between patterns of consumption and production in the south is, of course, the breadth and depth of state intervention. The state has intervened in the Italian south to sustain consumption levels through an extensive series of social and economic policies that range from industrial aid to generous 'disability' pensions. Critics of the Italian government's intervention in the south have argued that a good part of the southern economy 'lies outside of the market' (Wolleb and Wolleb, 1990, p. 31) as a direct result of central-government planning and control, government grants to business, public subsidisation of manufacturing, absorption of successive cohorts of the unemployed into the bureaucracy, and public enterprises that show constant deficits. In the south socio-political considerations tied to the national political and administrative decision-making structures have been effectively substituted for entrepreneurship as a means of accessing resources and raising personal wealth. Thus if southerners are at a disadvantage vis-à-vis their compatriots to the north in terms of economic performance, they have found alternative ladders of socioeconomic mobility through the political system, state apparatuses (that is, public administration, the courts, the police and the armed forces)[3] and the intellectual community.

The social well-being enjoyed by the south during the last decade has significantly changed its traditional characteristics: emigration has stopped and birth rates have declined. In the 1960s the population numbers were held steady – large out-flows of workers were compensated for by higher than average birth rates. The 1970s saw the rate of emigration fall, but the population did not increase as there was a parallel decline in the birth rate. Throughout the 1980s and early 1990s there was a small yearly increase in the south of approximately 1.5 per cent, while the population in the north remained unchanged or even declined.

The increased homogeneity between north and south in social patterns was not accompanied by a parallel move in the economy. During the 1980s the Italian economy experienced an upturn in production and investment in a fashion similar to that which took place in the other major industrialised countries of Europe. By the end of the decade France, the UK and Italy had started to slow down. The one exception was Germany, which continued to expand until the end of 1991. Germany's continued growth was influenced by the economic impetus provided by the monetary and economic reunification of the two parts of Germany. Once the flush of reunification was over, Germany's growth rates fell toward the European mean.

Growth continued above the EU mean in the early 1990s in the small peripheral economies of Ireland, Portugal and Greece, but Spain's growth rate slowed significantly in 1991, and in 1993 the country's economic base actually contracted.

In Italy the slowdown of the late 1980s was marked by a lack of synchronisation between regional-level economies, and especially between north and south. It took the south much longer to emerge from the 1981–3 recession, and when its economy did rebound growth was short-lived. The economic performance of the south paralleled, to a certain extent, the Spanish example in registering a substantial increase in GDP in 1991: +2.6 per cent compared with 0.8 per cent in the centre–north of the country. However in 1992 the south underwent a contraction in GDP while the centre–north returned to a positive 1.3 per cent level of expansion. The impact of these changes are evident from Table 5.4, which illustrates the growing gap between the levels of the individual southern regions and the overall scores for the Mezzogiorno vis-à-vis the North.

The south's delay in registering the impact of the European-wide recession as well as the resilience of its productive capacity is in large part due to the restricted 'openness' – that is, the impact of imports and exports in relation to regional GDP – of its economy. As illustrated in Figure 5.1, many southern Italian regions are significantly below the national average in the openness of their markets. As a result they are less sensitive to international economic shocks caused by a downturn in production and levels of consumption in other countries.

The impact of the international economic shock was finally relayed to the south in 1992–3 through a significant decline in production levels in agriculture, industry and construction. These declines were further exacerbated by the cutback in transfer payments and public investments upon the termination of Italy's forty-two-year history of national attempts to spur economic development through the Fund for the South (1950–80) and the Agency for the Development of the South (1986–92). Levels of economic well-being in the south are much more dependent upon institutionalised transfer payments from the Italian government than is the case in other parts of the country. In 1989 the south received 36.0 per cent of state transfers while contributing only 19.9 per cent of revenue. Thus the need to reduce overall government spending and the accumulated deficit in preparation for EMU has hit hardest in the south, where government spending on services, pensions, unemployment compensation and public-sector employees represents a higher proportion of regional GDP.

Taking into account differentials in the rates of population increase, development in the south has not decreased the gap between northern and southern Italy in terms of per capita income and levels of productivity. Between 1980 and 1992 per capita income in the south fell approximately two and a half points in relation to that of the centre–north, and increases in the levels of productivity in the south have not kept pace with those in the north. The negative impact of the gap is being further exacerbated by the higher levels of unemployment that continue to be registered in the south.

The unemployment levels recorded in the south are of

Table 5.4 Comparison of Italian economic indicators, 1980–92

	South			Centre–north			Italy		
	1980	1991	1992	1980	1991	1992	1980	1991	1992
Level of activity	35.7	38.6	38.7	41.8	44.7	44.6	39.7	42.5	42.4
Percentage of value added									
Agriculture	9.1	12.0	10.7	3.9	3.4	3.6	5.2	4.5	4.5
Industry	26.7	24.8	24.4	38.7	37.3	36.6	35.8	34.2	33.6
Services	64.2	63.2	64.9	57.4	59.3	59.8	59.0	61.3	61.9
Level of unemployment									
Total	11.1	19.9	20.4	5.4	6.5	7.1	7.2	10.9	11.5
Youth 14–29	27.2	42.0	42.9	13.6	14.3	15.5	18.1	24.1	25.3
Females	53.9	53.0	52.1	63.1	63.0	62.1	57.9	57.0	56.2
GDP per capita	70.5	68.7	67.9	116.2	118.1	118.6	100.0	100.0	100.0

Source: Author's calculations using data in SVIMEZ (1993)

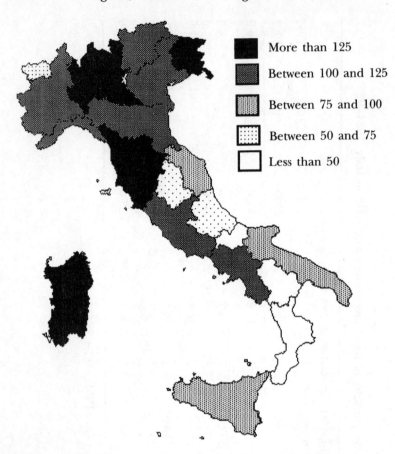

Figure 5.1   Import–export index in Italy's regions, 1987 (imports + exports/regional GDP. Italy = 100)

particular concern when compared with the trend in other underdeveloped parts of the EU. As we saw above, southern Italian unemployment appears to present a 'special case' in Europe. While in the mid- to late 1980s unemployment was decreasing in the rest of Europe, it was increasing in the Italian south, reaching 20 per cent by 1989.

The same pattern was registered for capital investment. As is illustrated in Table 5.5 while the centre–north underwent a

Table 5.5 North–south comparisons of fixed investments and GDP in Italy, 1984–92

(a) Levels of fixed investments (1980 prices, % increases)

	1986	1987	1988	1989	1990	1991	1992
Italy	+2.2	+5.0	+6.9	+4.6	+3.0	+0.6	-1.4
South	+0.8	+4.3	+3.3	-0.2	+2.4	-0.8	-3.1
Centre–north	+2.8	+5.3	+8.5	+6.4	+3.2	+1.2	-0.8

(b) GDP per capita for the southern Italian regions, 1984–92 (Italy = 100)

	1984	1986	1991	1992
Abruzzo	79.1	83.8	86.9	86.6
Sardegna	75.3	73.7	73.8	74.7
Molise	71.8	71.0	70.3	70.6
Puglia	69.7	70.5	72.2	71.4
Sicilia	69.4	66.5	67.5	66.4
Campania	68.3	65.6	66.8	65.4
Basilicata	68.6	56.2	59.0	60.6
Calabria	57.9	55.2	57.8	56.6

Sources: Author's calculations using data in SVIMEZ (1993), EUROSTAT (1994), ISTAT (1992, 1986).

phase of intense renovation with an acceleration of investment during the 1987–8 period, the south lagged behind by about two years. As a consequence the southern Italian economy became even more vulnerable and weak. Taking into account value-added in industrial production, productivity has consistently been approximately 25 per cent lower in the south than in the centre–north, and this gap continued to widen in the 1980s.

As was discussed in the previous chapter, the situation in the Mezzogiorno is not homogeneous. There are regions (for example Abruzzo and Molise) that have experienced considerable growth since the early 1970s, and there are areas, such as the Adriatic coast, that have seen the diffusion of small and medium size firms (King, 1987). Small and medium-sized enterprises have begun to make their appearance in the south, though not at the level enjoyed in the north (King, 1985). Modern agricultural methods and products have been introduced in dynamic agricultural areas in the south, such as those found in Metaponto in Basilicata, the province of Foggia in Puglia and the Vittoria-Comiso area in Sicily.

The example of Abruzzo, the northernmost southern Italian region, is emblematic of the prospects for growth in the Mezzogiorno. In Abruzzo the average rate of industrial productivity and growth have been higher than those registered by other southern regions.[4] The structure of the economy in Abruzzo does not reflect the traditional features of other southern regions. Abruzzo has enjoyed considerable capital investment in private industry; it has a significant presence of large, small and medium-sized industries; local entrepreneurs are well represented in the region's industrial class; unemployment is low; and the region has benefited from significant increases in personal income.

During the 1970s and 1980s the region's economy displayed levels of development that were uncommon in the Italian south. The quality of its infrastructure (roads, highways, electric power, water, hospitals, schools and so on) is among the best in the south and ranks well with that of the centre–north. Where the region is still weak in relation to its immediate northern neighbours is in the lack of an adequate supply of subcontractors and a qualified service base for industry.

The economic downturn of the early 1990s revealed the

weakness of the interaction between industrial production and related economic activities in Abruzzo. The region's system of subcontractors and its supply of specialised parts, components and services are still strongly dependent on sources outside of region, especially those concentrated in the north and centre.

The lack of an adequate development of regionally located support services has been attributed to a variety of factors that are internal as well as external to the region. The internally oriented explanations focus on the lack of coordination in the region's economic-development policies, which have proceeded in a fragmentary fashion and have not tackled in a clear and efficacious manner the structural defects of the region. In the past regional leaders have been unable to prioritise their selection of policies or create a system of economic incentives to attract suppliers and services to the region. Difficulties in the formulation of regional development plans and the region's Community Support Framework illustrate the problems that the region has had in promoting the creation of policy networks to bring together the regional governmental apparatus with representatives of industry, small and medium-sized enterprises, artisans, service suppliers, commercial groups and local chambers of commerce. Planning has reflected the political imperatives of electioneering (that is, the generation of resources for purposes of creating clientelistic links to mobilise voters on behalf of regional political leaders) rather than economic development focused on the exigencies of consolidating the structure of the regional economy, making its products competitive outside the region, and increasing its ability to respond to international economic cycles.

Another factor adding to the region's difficulty in adequately planning and being in a position to stimulate the adaptation of the economic structure to local and international opportunities is the challenge posed by the fragmentation of local sectoral representative institutions. In Abruzzo and the neighbouring region of Molise an inordinate number of sectoral associations are trying to represent the same pool of entrepreneurs. Each association has its own small membership base and individual political point of reference, but each is incapable of adequately representing or penetrating the multitude of firms operating in the region. Therefore the weakness of the link between the region and the representative associations is aggravated by the fragmentary nature of the association's own link to individual firms. The numerical and organisational weakness of the associations prevents them from adequately representing the interests of the sector in their contacts with the region. In turn the region, – even if it wanted to – is inhibited from being able to implement its economic development policies in cooperation with the associations and ensure that the incentives provided by the policies will find their way down to individual firms.[5]

Another explanation of the problems facing Abruzzo and the other southern Italian regions is offered by SVIMEZ (1991) in its report on the state of the southern Italian economy and public efforts to stimulate economic development. The lament of SVIMEZ echoes the traditional criticism voiced by specialists studying development in the south. SVIMEZ concludes that central economic development policies for the south have always been based on and developed in relation to the interests of large firms located in the north. The argument is that the northern firms have an inordinate amount of control over political power in the country and are therefore in a position to influence and compromise the central government's economic-development policy. Investments are planned with the needs of northern firms in mind rather than southern economic growth.

According to this interpretation, the Italian strategy to promote regional development can be divided into three phases: (1) the preindustrial phase of the 1950s, which emphasised the construction of infrastructure in the south through the use of northern firms and creating demand for materials supplied by the north; (2) the industrialisation phase of the 1960s, when northern firms were given incentives to transfer production to the south (usually involving the least efficient and most environmentally hazardous plants) while at the same time using state funds to modernise their plants in the north; and (3) the phase of 1970s and 1980s, when emphasis was placed on income support and increases in the level of consumption so that southerners could buy the consumer goods produced by the north. The end-result of these policies was an improvement in infrastructure, communication, transport links and levels of consumption in the south, but there was no subsequent general relocation of private capital from the north to the south, nor encouragement of endogenous entrepreneurship to fulfill the needs of southern consumers. The south remained subordinate to production and decision making concentrated in the north.

While one could take exception to the partisan nature of the SVIMEZ explanation, it is undeniable that development in the south has been very uneven. The government's southern development strategy focused on large private firms relocating in the south with the support of government subsidies, or the location there of large public enterprises serving the national market. State intervention in the south has always steered clear of small and medium-sized enterprises, and it has been effectively unable to deal with small economic entities.

Large private firms did relocate in the south, but the pattern shows that the principle of geographic contiguity did not win the day. Development did not seep into the south in the way envisaged by the growth-pole strategy espoused by Perroux and his Italian imitators. The growth-pole strategy hypothesised that growth and its spin-off effects would focus around concentrations of capital (that is, large industrial plants such as the Italsider plant in Taranto or the oil refineries along the Sicilian coasts). What we have seen instead is that growth is much more geographically determined than was previously expected.

THE FAILURE OF THE THIRD ECONOMIC MIRACLE: CONTIGUOUS GROWTH AND THE SOURCES OF UNDERDEVELOPMENT

The underdeveloped areas that have grown the fastest have been those that are contiguous to territories with a significant level of growth. This was the case in the 1960s in relation to the development of Umbria and the Marche, as it was in the 1970s vis-à-vis the exit of southern Lazio (the provinces of Latina and Frosinone) from the Fund for the South. In the 1980s development was particularly evident in the northern parts of Campania and in the Abruzzo and Molise regions. However the pace of this growth has not proved sufficient to reverse the generally negative trends registered by the other parts of the southern periphery.

Abruzzo proved to be one of the main beneficiaries of the transfer of northern plants to the south in order to take advantage of economic incentives. The region's industrialisation phase took off around the end of the 1960s, when large industries were established in the region for the production of motor vehicles, telecommunication equipment, and chemical and pharmaceutical products. This phase was preceded by the building of major public infrastructure that linked the region to the north along the Adriatic toll road and the highway to Rome, and to points north and south along the Mediterranean coast through the Pescara–Rome highway. This highway network allowed the region to link its mountainous areas (covering the provinces of Aquila and Avezzano, which are close to Lazio and Rome) to the bustling seaside cities and towns that were experiencing sudden growth in tourism and light industry. During the 1980s and 1990s the region saw not only the growth of Italian-owned factories but also of important foreign concerns. Among the major foreign manufacturers located in Abruzzo are Honda, with its motorcycle plant in Atessa, and the Texas Instruments plant in Avezzano.

Despite the dynamism displayed by the Abruzzo region, the spurt of significant industrialisation did not quickly trickle down to the other southern Italian regions. Molise has benefited from the developments in Abruzzo along the Adriatic coast corridor around Termoli, which has become the site of a significant concentration of small and medium-sized enterprises. Like Abruzzo, Molise is home to major food-processing concerns (pasta and olive oil) as well as industries in the textile and fashion sector.

The trickle down of growth and investment has, however, left other areas of Molise completely untouched (see Figure 5.2). This is also the case with large interior areas in other southern regions. The exception to this rule is the industrial activity around Naples and Salerno, Avellino, Bari, Lecce and Matera. But the momentum behind the encouragement of local entrepreneurs and the growth of industrial districts has not been sufficient to overcome the structural obstacles to growth in the south that are to be found in both civil society and the state.

Southern entrepreneurs have to deal with a cost structure that is not present in the other parts of the country. First of all,

No. of employees:

◉ More than 20000
■ Between 10000 and 20000
▪ Less than 10000

Figure 5.2   Industrial districts in Italy

the individual entrepreneur has to face not only the challenges of competition but also the challenge of criminal organisations whose activities (protection rackets, highjacking of shipments and disruption of informal contacts and agreements) increase the cost of production.

Secondly, the entrepreneur in the south cannot take advantage of the external economies of scale that have manifested themselves in the north through three means: social solidarity based on a common civic culture emphasising the advantage of collective action; flexibility of production through constant redefinition of the necessary phases and participation of internal as well as external forces; and the productivity of local and regional institutions in providing a basis for the creation of external economies of scale. In the south the dominant view has been that collective action is incapable of creating sufficient individual returns (Sabetti, 1984). Therefore it is difficult to generate the system of mutual interdependence and trust that is the hallmark of industrial districts. In a parallel fashion, the political institutions are geared toward generating individual returns (individual jobs, favours, handouts and influence) rather than the societal goods that produce returns only in the medium to long term, and then only if the system operates efficiently.

Thirdly, the state in the south has been one of the main supporters of consolidation of non-civic society (Putnam, Leonardi and Nanetti, 1993). As Walston (1988) has observed, one of the main problems in developing the south has been the pervasiveness of state patronage as an easy source of financial gain and social mobility. The availability of state patronage has greatly enhanced the development of personal, clientelistic linkages (Chubb, 1986) managed by politicians who have provided the vital link between the population and the political system. It is, after all, the public office holder who determines access to public resources. The desire to participate in clientelistic ties is not restricted to the dispossessed in society; the pervasiveness of the system and the availability of abundant resources have served to encourage the spread of clientelism throughout all classes, areas of public life and the economy.

Finally, the social-service network that is so vital to the productive structure of the centre and north is missing in the south. Local services (public transport, day-care centres, all-day school programmes, help for the elderly and so on) either do not exist or do not function efficiently. In turn, the regional government is incapable of supplying the services to production (industrial parks, market research, vocational training, diffusion of technology, experimental stations, sponsorship at international fairs and so on) that have been crucial in spurring development in the Third Italy.

The dysfunction of local institutions has prevented economic development beyond the limitations imposed by the growth-pole/mass-production Fordist model. In the south this model implies the perpetuation of state-owned enterprises (Trigilia, 1992). The impact of growing competition introduced by the Single Market and the need to reduce the nation's deficit have brought to an end the belief that the south can continue to be subjugated to an economic model that places emphasis on the role of the state, focuses on centralised administrative–political decision-making practices, and relies on the prospect of large factories founded and sustained on a constant diet of national subsidies being turned into profit-making ventures.

The readiness of the state to bail out failing industries and maintain loss-making public enterprises has served to undermine the existence of a market economy in the south. In the past, the ability to remain in business depended more on political connections and access to public funds than on making profits.

The relationship between the market and political institutions has not been regulated by a system of differentiated functions where every component of society has its role and autonomy from the rest. Rather, there has been a mixing and intermingling of private and public functions that has served to create a dependent relationship between the market and the state.

The absence of a true market economy in the south has had a devastating effect on the growth of private enterprise. From the beginning, Italy's southern development policy has placed into question the very existence of market forces. Recent surveys have shown that significant state provision and public subsidies made available through political intermediation have stimulated strong resentment among existing small and medium-sized private entrepreneurs (Leonardi, 1991). The latter report difficulties in meeting the competition from state enterprises or private companies benefiting from large-scale national subsidies, which are in a position to ignore the rules of competition. Losses are always compensated by large public subsidies, and the bigger the enterprise the more difficult it is for the public authorities to allow it to close.

The lack of a true market for investment and production has dampened individual as well as collective forms of enterpreneurship – such as, for example, cooperatives among producers or local political institutions in operating as important stimulators of investment policies and alternative development strategies. The consequences of state provision in the substitution of market competition have been noticeable in the decline in the relative competitiveness of southern regions, and in the south's growing inability to find markets in northern Italy and Europe for locally produced manufactured and agricultural goods (Monaco, 1994).

When compared with those for regions in other parts of Europe's southern periphery, the data for southern Italy demonstrate that unless the stranglehold of the Italian political class over economic activity in southern Italy is broken and market considerations are reintroduced into production and investment decisions, the area runs the risk of slipping behind resurgent regions in Spain, Portugal and the former East Germany.

On the whole, regional and local-government institutions have not been in a position to make full use of regional, national or EC development funds. In the case of the Integrated Mediterranean Programmes, regions such as Sicily, Campania and Calabria have lost a large part of their allocations to areas in France due to their inability (or unwillingness) to spend the money in the manner and time dictated by the EC. The track record of Italy's southern regions has also been poor in relation to their ability to spend their 1989–93 CSF allocations.

The difficulty encountered by the southern Italian regions in meeting the minimum administrative and planning requirements set out by the CSFs – prioritising investments, engaging in ex-ante and ex-post evaluations and actually spending the available resources – places into question the very fate of regional development projects in the south. With regional development funds increasingly becoming dependent on the cooperation and authorisation of the EU, it is difficult to see how the southern Italian regions can radically change in a short period of time their traditional approach to the administration and management of policies. The 1995 regional elections will have to face not only the task of recruiting a new regional political class, but also of reinventing the approach to policy making and administration that needs to be taken in the south.

What is needed is a radical reform that will change both the manner in which the region manages policies and the linkage patterns established between the region and outside political organs. First of all, there is a need to eliminate interference from national organs in regional affairs on the assumption that the 'centre knows best' and that the southern regions are not capable of autonomously organising their own development priorities and strategies. Instead the regions need to be fully autonomous, self-governing and capable of experimenting with their own policies. Otherwise they will never learn to act on their own initiative or learn from their mistakes. Accordingly, there must be a complete cessation of interference from national institutions that in the past have suffocated regional initiatives and expropriated the region's role as a policy-making structure – all power to decide development projects needs to be transferred to the regional level.

The Agency for the South may have been abolished, but the desire to perpetuate central control underlies planning, decision-making and administration demands made by such organs as the CNEL and the Interministerial Committee for Economic Planning (CIPE), who believe that they know better than local political leaders and citizens what is necessary to promote regional development.[6] Forty years of failure seem to have done little to change the minds of exponents of centralisation.

Secondly, a radical restructuring of the regional administrative apparatus needs to be undertaken. The present southern administrative system is elephantine, has a low level of professionalism and is politically compromised. For a long time the divide between administration and politics has been ignored, and the consequences have been devastating. An incestuous relationship has been allowed to develop between political activity and the administrative class, thereby permitting top regional administrators to also become regional and local leaders of the governing parties. Such a relationship reverses the traditional links between the political leadership and the administrative apparatus to the detriment of political control and accountability over the decision-making process and the role of the bureaucracy in the administration of regional policies. In the case of these southern regions, the top administrators are, de facto, also the top political leaders and are in a position to appoint and control public-office holders.

Italy can no longer afford to have almost half of the country operating according to economic and political principles that are in contrast with those that reign in the other half and in the rest of the EU. Southern Italy has to conform even more quickly than it has in the past with other European regions' principles of economic activity and standards of decision making. If these changes are not implemented, the result will be further stagnation and decline as the source of national funding dries up. The Italian state must reduce both its budget deficit and runaway spending on the automatic transfer payments that are built into the health and pension systems. Otherwise it will be marginalised in the run-up to EMU. The economic future of southern Italy depends on internalising the criteria for regional policy decided and implemented at EU level.

NOTES

1. Calculated using all the twelve EU member states, but excluding the newly incorporated East German Länder. See EUROSTAT, 1994.
2. The two Italian regions of Molise and Sardegna were able to qualify for Objective 1 status because of political bargaining among the member states. The compromise allowed for a change in the eligibility rules in order to permit not only Molise and Sardegna but also Northern Ireland, Corsica and Valencia to benefit from continued Objective 1 support, to say nothing of the change in the 'units of analysis' undertaken to permit Flevoland (NL), Hainaut (B), the Highlands and Islands (UK) and Merseyside (UK) to be awarded an Objective 1 designation (CEC, 1993).
3. The presence of southerners in Italy's public apparatus is well documented. See Cassese, 1977.
4. The recent economic difficulties encountered by the Abruzzo region have given rise to a significant literature. For the most recent works, see Alessandrini and Fazzi, 1993; IARES, 1993; Alessandrini, 1992 and Leonardi, 1991.
5. In 1992 the regional government of Abruzzo collapsed when almost the entire *giunta* was arrested for not having applied the required criteria when awarding EC funding to firms. The regional leaders adopted a non-prioritised and non-selective approach to the use of EC funds – that is, a general 'sprinkling' of funds to politically connected firms rather than to those deserving support based on the CSF programme criteria.
6. At the end of June 1992, the CNEL announced its willingness to assume the role of 'guiding the transition between the extraordinary

intervention and the ordinary one' and to become 'the depository and the guarantor of the ability of the South to plan on the basis off indications from Europe'. These are exactly the forms of interference by the centre over the formulation of regional development policies that have blocked rather than promoted economic and social development in the south.

REFERENCES

Alessandrini, S. (1992) *L'Abruzzo nel Mercato Unico Europeo* (Teramo: Demian Editore).

Alessandrini, S. and C. Fazzi (1993) *L'Abruzzo regione a meta' del guado* (Teramo: Demian Editore).

Amato, P. *et al.* (1979) *Compagne e movimento contadino nel mezzogiorno d'Italia: dal dopoguerra ad oggi*, vol. 1, Monografie regionali (Bari: De Donato).

Barucci, P. (1978) *Ricostruzione, pianificazione, Mezzogiorno* (Bologna: Il Mulino).

Cassese, S. (1977) *Questione amministrativa e questione meridionale* (Milan: Giuffre').

CEC (1993) *Community Structural Funds, 1994–99* (Luxembourg: Office of Official Publications of the European Communities).

Chubb, J. (1982) *Patronage, Power and Poverty in Southern Italy* (Cambridge: Cambridge University Press).

Conti, S. (1979) 'Industrialization in a backward region: the Italian Mezzogiorno', unpublished Ph.D dissertation, University of London.

D'Antonio, M. (1991) *Il Mezzogiorno nella struttura economica italiana* (Milan: Franco Angeli).

EUROSTAT (1993) *Basic Statistics of the Community*, 30th edition (Luxembourg: Office of Official Publications of the European Communities).

EUROSTAT (1994) *Rapid Reports: Regions*, no. 1.

IARES (1990) *Rapporto sulla situazione economic sociale e territoriale della regione Abruzzo* (Chieti: IARES).

ISTAT (1986) *Le regioni in cifre, Edizione 1986* (Rome: ISTAT).

ISTAT (1992) *Le regioni in cifre, Edizione 1992* (Rome: ISTAT).

King, R. (1973) *Land Reform: The Italian Experience* (London: Butterworth).

King, R. (1985) *Industrial Geography of Italy* (London: Croom Helm).

King, R. (1987) *Italy* (London: Harper & Row).

King, R. (1988) *Il ritorno in patria: Return migration to Italy in historical perspective* (Durham: University of Durham).

Leonardi, R. (1991) 'Riflessi della riduzione del sostegno comunitario sull'economia regionale, con particolare riguardo al sistema industriale', Presidenza della Regione Abruzzo, L'Aquila, Italy, November.

Monaco, T. (1994) 'European Integration and Regional Cohesion: The Economic Impact of the Single Market on Italian regional development', Occasional Papers of the Economic and Social Cohesion Laboratory, European Institute, London School of Economics, October.

Pobielski, G. (1974) *Italy: Development and Crisis in the Postwar Economy* (Oxford: Oxford University Press).

Putnam, R. D., R. Leonardi and R. Y. Nanetti (1993) *Making Democracy Work: Civic Traditions in Modern Italy* (Princeton: Princeton University Press).

Rodgers, A. (1979) *Economic Development in Retrospect* (Washington, DC: V.H. Winston).

Romano, A. (1988) *Mezzogiorno 1992: le nuove economie per lo sviluppo competitivo* (Milan: Franco Angeli).

Romero, F. (1993) 'Migration as an issue in European interdependence and integration: the case of Italy', in A. S. Milward (ed.), *The Frontier of National Sovereignty: History and Theory, 1945–1992* (London: Routledge), pp. 33–58.

Sabetti, F. (1984) *Political Authority in a Sicilan Village* (New Brunswick: Rutgers University Press).

Saville, L. (1964) *Regional Economic Development in Italy* (Durham: Duke University Press).

SVIMEZ (1991) *Rapporto 1991 sull'economia del mezzogiorno* (Bologna: Il Mulino).

SVIMEZ (1992) *Rapporto 1992 sui mezzogiorni d'Europa* (Bologna: Il Mulino).

SVIMEZ (1993) *Rapporto 1993 sull'economia del mezzogiorno* (Bologna: Il Mulino).

Tarrow, S. (1967) *Peasant Communism in Southern Italy* (New Haven: Yale University Press).

Trigilia, C. (1992) *Sviluppo senza autonomia: Effetti perversi delle politiche nel Mezzogiorno* (Bologna: Il Mulino).

Walston, J. (1988) *The Mafia and clientelism: roads to Rome in post-war Calabria* (London: Routledge).

Wolleb, E. and G. Wolleb (1990) *Divari regionali e dualismo economico* (Bologna: Il Mulino).

6 The Findings: Independent Variables

ECONOMIC CHANGE AND THE ROLE OF PLACE

Having traced the change in levels of productivity and social well-being over time, it is now necessary to turn to the search for variables that will explain the changes in regional development measured by the dependent variables in the regions covered by the nine member states of the EU. Of necessity, reference will also be made to the results of the independent-variable analysis concerning the three newer member states.

Given the nature of the current dataset, the search for independent variables was limited by the availability of data. Up to now, only four variables could be analysed to account for the change in both dependent variables. Data for a fifth variable – capital investment – was not consistent at the regional level for a number of countries, and therefore could not be used for longitudinal analysis.

The first independent variable constructed for analysis derives directly from the core–periphery divergence hypothesis. As illustrated above, the argument is that the closer a region is to the core, the higher its expectation for growth and development. Taking the regions of the 'golden triangle' as the 'core', the other regions were coded according to three concentric circles away from the core to form a 'distance from the core' measure. If the core–periphery hypothesis is correct, the expectation is that there is a positive correlation between changes in GDP and PPS for the core regions and negative growth for the peripheral regions – that is, higher levels of growth take place in core areas while peripheral areas experience lower rates of growth. If, however, the opposite is true, then the correlation will be negative. The peripheral-ascendancy hypothesis suggests that the peripheral areas are growing faster than the core regions. Therefore the correlation between the variables of growth and core status should be a significantly negative one.

The second independent variable is drawn from the

'industrial-cycle theory', which argues that industrialisation undergoes a cycle that starts from the birth of an industry in a region and eventually moves up to 'senescence' (IFO, 1990). To approximate different levels of industrialisation, the percentage of the workforce in industry in 1970 is taken as the basis for comparing changes in GDP and PPS through to the late 1980s.[1] This variable, of course, assumes that the relationship among the three economic sectors – industry, agriculture and services – remains constant over time and that it does not undergo a fundamental change with the restructuring of Fordist production, the decline in importance of the EC's energy supplies, and the emergence of small and medium-sized enterprises under a new configuration of production and services.[2]

The third variable is the change in harmonised unemployment rates in the 1980s to test whether the changes in the rates of unemployment account for the changes in GDP and PPS. Classical economic theory suggests that, given no change in labour-migration rates, as economic growth takes place unemployment rates should fall. The counterevidence against this intuitive generalisation is presented by the cases of southern Italy and Spain, where – despite growth – unemployment has remained steady or even risen. Nevertheless the main argument predicts that levels of unemployment will correlate negatively with changes in GDP and PPS. As unemployment decreases, positive changes in the two dependent variables will take place and vice versa. Harmonised levels of unemployment data are available for the period 1977–90 and cover the nine member states in a continuous and complete manner.

The last variable evaluates the potential relationship between the rate of European Investment Bank loans and EC financial contributions through the Structural Funds in the form of loans and grants to promote development.[3] The data for this variable were gathered from the REGIO datasets and cover the period 1980–7.[4]

It needs to be stated at the outset that the best predictor of levels of development in 1991 is how developed the regions were in 1970. However this variable is not perfect, and it tends to decay over time. The changes characterising the regions are slowly disassembling their relative standings and changing their comparative positions. The level of well-being (PPS) and GDP are changing rapidly in the EU as the reaction to market forces varies across the regions. As regions converge they also undergo changes in their relative positions in the ranking. This is particularly the case with ascendant peripheral regions undergoing industrialisation and tertiarisation of their economic bases, as well as in regions undergoing industrial decline in terms of manufacturing base or the wholesale disappearance of extractive industries, such as coal. The declining levels of correlation over time provide support for the thesis that regions are jockeying for position in an increasingly integrated European market.

THE SEARCH FOR EXPLANATORY VARIABLES

When the four independent variables are run against changes in the GDP and PPS index scores, the following results emerge.

Distance from the core

Distance represents the most significant predictor of change in PPS and GDP. The correlation between 'distance' and change in PPS and GDP index scores is strong and statistically significant: -0.4369 for PPS and -0.3684 for GDP. Both levels of correlation are significant at the 0.0001 level. There is a similar correlation between a region's distance from the core and growth in GDP (-0.4376). The implication of these findings is that regions distant from the core area are undergoing faster change than those in or close to the core, thereby reducing the amount of differentiation that previously characterised the core and periphery.

When the 'distance' analysis was conducted using the entire twelve-country sample for the shorter period of time, the correlations dropped significantly below those registered for the EC-9 over the twenty-one year period. The reasons for this are various. First of all, the analysis of Spain, Portugal and Greece covers a shorter period of time, thereby reflecting lower degrees of change. Change over a twenty-one-year period will undoubtedly be greater than change over an eleven-year period. Secondly, the economic conditions under which the regions in the EC-9 were operating vis-à-vis their new colleagues were radically different in the 1980s (a period of recession) than they were in the 1970s, when the boom was in full swing. The nine member states enjoyed the advantage of prolonged access to relatively more open markets and proactive, EC-sponsored programmes designed to stimulate regional development, but Greece did not gain access until 1981, and Spain and Portogal until 1986.

Thirdly, the three newer member states gained full advantage of EC membership after the post-1988 doubling of the Structural Funds and the entry of the peseta and escudo into the ERM in 1990. In both cases their economic development indicators witnessed significant growth as the impact of the new financing regime and openness of the markets started to impact on their domestic markets.

Another indicator of the changing nature of peripheral regional economies in the EC-9 is the correlation between distance and the percentage of the workforce employed in industry. In 1970 the correlation was −0.5023 while in 1977 it declined to −0.3339, and it continued to decline in the 1980s. This result may be accounted for by economic-convergence theories, such as those discussed above and more specifically by those advanced by Losch (theory of the maximum profit-location) and von Thunen and Weber (least-cost theory of location) (Richardson, 1969).

The problem with considering distance as a satisfactory explanatory variable for changes in GDP and PPS is that it does not tell us which growth factors (for example investment, wages, technological change and so on) are fuelling the change. At this point we only know that change *is taking place* and *where* it is taking place, but we do not have a clear indication of *why* the change is occurring or *how* integration is impacting on the regional economies in an empirical fashion. Answering these questions requires the existence of a more complete and sophisticated data base than the one currently available to researchers on European integration and convergence.

The level of industrialisation

The level of industrialisation in 1970 was not such a good predictor of changes in GDP and PPS. The percentage of the workforce in industry did correlate with changes in the index scores – at −0.21 for GDP but only −0.12 for PPS. The GDP correlation was significant at the 0.05 level, but the PPS correlation was not significant. Therefore the industrial cycle may account for some of the change, but it clearly does not account for all of it. One of the reasons why this may be the case is that regions and national governments did not investment equally in restructuring their ailing industries in the 1970s and 1980s. The EC's *Second Survey of State Aids in the European Community in the Manufacturing and Certain Other Sectors* (1990) reveals that in the period between 1981 and 1988 aid to manufacturing, excluding shipbuilding and steel, increased significantly in Italy and Germany but decreased substantially in the UK and Ireland. Thus, given the aid provided by national and regional governments, the industrial-restructuring cycle was shorter in Italy and Germany than in the UK where industry was allowed to decline as part of a sifting-out industrial policy designed to eliminate non-competitive firms and reduce government subsidies. Another reason for the change can be found in the growing tertiarisation of the economy in developed as well as less-developed economies. The rise of the service sector tends to blur the traditional dicotomy between agricultural versus industrialised economies. Thus the distinction between core and peripheral economies has become less obvious on the basis of the distinction between service and industrial employment. This is particularly the case when we consider the role played by research and services in modern manufacturing. They tend to be lumped together with other services, such as shops, restaurants and public administration, while their contribution to the modernisation of production is fundamental to maintaining competitive industries.

Unemployment levels

The use of unemployment levels as an explanatory variable fared slightly better than industrial stages for the EC-9 sample. This variable correlated negatively with both GDP (−0.25) and PPS (−0.22) and both correlations were significant at the 0.01 and 0.03 levels, but were less strong than the correlation produced by the distance variable. A reduction in unemployment rates is an important indicator of increased productivity and well-being, but it is not satisfactory in and of itself. The rise of the welfare state, the increase in public bureaucracies and the payment of unemployment benefits have reduced, on the one hand, the negative impact of unemployment on well-being, while on the other hand they have reduced labour mobility – that is, the incentive to seek employment in areas experiencing relative labour shortages – as was the case in the 1950s and 1960s (Jones, 1993; Flora, 1986).

High levels of unemployment may, in fact, be a corollary to seasonal employment – that is, where seasonal employment in, for example, tourism is an important component in the regional economy there is a high incidence of off-season unemployment and this is reflected in the annual unemployment figures. High unemployment rates in areas with diversified economies and a high service component may mask the existence of seasonal labour patterns. In these areas levels of productivity and well-being may rise but unemployment will continue to persist at very high levels. As a consequence the area displays significant increases in productivity and well-being but it continues to register high levels of official unemployment.

EC spending

Another potential explanatory variable is the level of EC spending in the regions through various financial instruments, ranging from ERDF grants to EIB loans. Taking into account the composite size of EC contributions to individual EC-9 regions, the analysis shows that over time there was an increasing correlation between EC contributions to individual regions and changes in regional GDP and PPS indexes. During the period for which data are available, the relationship between the two variables increased and achieved a level of significance of above 0.05. We find that after 1988, with the reform and doubling of the Structural Funds, EC contributions had an increased impact on levels of growth and well-being in the less-developed areas. Expressed in a different way, the data suggest that *the increase in Community grants made a real contribution to economic and social cohesion and was probably one of the major factors in fuelling an acceleration in the rate of that cohesion.*

This expectation is particularly applicable for the three Objective 1 member states (Ireland, Greece and Portugal). If we consider that Structural Fund contributions by the end of

1993 accounted on the average for 3 per cent of GDP for the three smallest peripheral states, it is not surprising that the EU is seen as important to the economic development of the peripheral member states. In the particular case of Portugal, over the five-year period covered by the CSFs EC-funded investments provided 21.5 per cent of overall economic investment, 60 per cent of the annual Investment Plan of central government and 40 per cent of municipal-government investments (Madureira-Pires, 1992; Piampão, 1994).

This aspect of European financing will increase in importance with the implementation of the Delors II funding package, which once again doubles Structural Funds contributions. The combination of EU funding plus private-sector funding will play a substantial role in regional growth and in adapting peripheral economies to the challenges of increased competition and an integrated market.[5]

Investment

The role of differing rates of investment has been a common explanatory variable in accounting for different rates of growth in regional economies. However the fragmentary nature of the data does not allow us to use this variable to explain changes in GDP and PPS. Data are consistently missing over the years for France, Belgium and the UK, and they are spotty for Ireland and Denmark. Thus we are not in a position to ascertain whether different rates of investment are or are not correlated with change in our index scores. However studies of convergence in the US have focused on the important role played by higher levels of investment in the southern, southwest and western states in the 1960s. Casetti (1985) showed that the productivity of land, labour and capital in the southern states surpassed those of the midwest in 1967. Roger Stough (1993) has argued that slower rates of growth in the Rustbelt 'served to "push" economic activity to the periphery or alternatively, greater rates of growth in the periphery served to "pull" economic activity to the periphery'. The data presented in Chapter 5 showed that Greece lagged behind the other Objective 1 countries in using Structural Fund financing to attract foreign and domestic investment. Structural Fund payments are more important than foreign direct investment in Greece. In Spain foreign direct investment was already seven times higher than EC contributions during Spain's first year of membership (1986), and it has maintained a strong position ever since. Portugal and Ireland, in turn, have experienced a greater balance between the two types of investment, but as the CSFs came on line there was a dramatic upswing in private foreign investment in the two smaller countries.

Taken as a whole, the four independent variables discussed above provide valuable insights into the possible elements that are associated with variations in the dependent variables. The best predictor of change in the dependent variable is distance from the core, and the rate of EC expenditure seems to be increasingly associated with rates of growth. Unemployment levels and position in the industrialisation cycle display a lower capacity to explain change. The weakness of the two latter variables may be due to the changing structure of industrialised economies (that is, a shift away from large industrial enterprises and economies of scale to more flexible production cycles based on small units of production and a mix of technological services) and the characteristics of economies that are highly dependent on seasonal activities and employment. Nevertheless, taken together, the analysis of the dependent and independent variables points to one unequivocal conclusion: the basis for Structural Fund strategies and the means by which increased expenditure can be justified needs to be changed. It is no longer necessary to maintain the myth that the expenditure of large sums from the EU budget is justified on the basis that the poor regions are declining in relation to the core, nor that past expenditure has not led to a reduction of the cohesion gap. On the contrary, the present study shows that EU expenditure has played a fundamental part in aiding underdeveloped regions and opening the way to greater participation and competition in the Single Market.

THE CONSEQUENCES OF COHESION ON POLICY MAKING

The conclusions that can be drawn from the above analysis are quite clear. During the last forty-one years both economic and social cohesion have been improving in the EU. Levels of productivity and social well-being have increased, and the gap between the poorer and richer regions has decreased. To a certain extent, the expectations written into the preamble of the 1957 Treaty and emphasised in the Single European Act and the Maastricht Treaty have been promoted by economic integration. The expectation is that, as further integration takes place through consolidation of the single market and monetary union, the prospects for the weaker EU regions will improve.

This surprising finding may have some very simple economic explanations. In turn, the policy implications are clear and unequivocal.

First of all, a number of predictions made by the economic convergence theories seem to be supported by the data. It is advisable to begin to think of the EU's economic space as an increasingly integrated whole, a move that has already been made by business, sectoral associations and economic-development agencies but which has not yet completely penetrated academic disciplines dealing with the EU.

Scholars still view the state and individual national markets as the dominant frames of reference. Little attention has been given to analysing what has been happening within the nation-states and how investment decisions and competitive strategies developed by firms, associations, entrepreneurs and individual citizens have expanded to take into account the new competitive and economic reality of the EU.

The EU, for its part, has assumed a clearer, European-wide focus in its economic and social policy making. Moves in this direction are noticeable in the emphasis given by the EU, in its networking programmes, to the creation of a European-wide economic-policy decision-making structure and to monitoring the implementation of investment projects.

The forces of economic convergence and the EU's own policies favouring economic integration (that is, the creation of the Single Market and movement toward EMU) will tend to reduce even further the differences between core and periphery in the scope and pace at which economic shocks ripple out across EU markets. Therefore, as part of the integration process the EU needs to develop the capacity to use taxation and economic-transfer powers to ease economic shocks and alleviate their negative impact on local peripheral economies, but the goal of economic integration should not be conceived as antithetical to regional growth. Structural Fund grants are not *compensation* for participation in EMU, rather they are *stimulators* and even *accelerators* of growth in the context of the economic and social opportunities provided by EMU.

Accordingly, the rationale behind doubling Structural Fund allocations and creating the Cohesion Fund are to be found in the acceleration of growth in peripheral areas as part of the goal to reduce the gap between developed and underdeveloped regions to acceptable margins in the medium term. Just what 'acceptable' margins are still has to be debated and agreed upon, but it is now clear that cohesion is no longer an abstract and impossible goal.

Second, the basis for competition within the EU has changed radically with the emergence of alternative development strategies that focus not only on traditional economic infrastructure but also on institutional and social infrastructure. Regional and local governments and semi-public authorities are partners in development and vital links in the economic chain that spurs economic development in core as well as peripheral areas.

Comparisons of growth patterns show that at lower levels of economic growth and maturity centralised state systems are in a position to make a significant contribution to economies of scale and the efficient use of resources. However, as economies mature, centralised administrative structures tend to stifle local initiative and hinder the search for market niches to be occupied by local economies. Centralised systems may be necessary for economic take-off and to bring to bear on local conditions exogenous factors such as capital, technology and infrastructure, but decentralised forms of government are vital to maintain mature levels of economic performance and fine-tune local economies to make maximum use of endogenous forms of development. Thus, in order to maximise the impact of European-level funding, the EU needs to partner its programmes for economic development and investment in capital, skills and infrastructure with ones focusing on the stimulation of endogenous factors of production, such as decentralising decision making and policy implementation in the peripheral regions and allowing local programmes to be structured by local needs and competitive possibilities.

This is of particular importance in the three smaller states – Ireland, Portugal and Greece – where centrally directed growth has clearly reached saturation point. The benefits of decentralisation in providing a stimulus to endogenous economic growth far outweigh any of the shortcomings associated with additional expenditure to create a new level of administration or employ additional administrative personnel at the regional level. Decentralisation also helps to develop the local supply of 'social capital' that is such an important attribute of regions and localities that have undergone spontaneous forms of development (Nanetti, 1989). However, it is not sufficient to merely create representative regional and local government institutions. These institutions must have the power to decide on local economic and social priorities and be in a position to take initiatives to implement these decisions. Thus, subnational units of government need to have decision-making powers in planning and development of social and economic policies, and to be directly involved in the implmentation of these policies. On this basis, subnational governments can become active and constructive partners in the development process in cooperation with national and EU authorities.

Third, the ability of the EU to intervene in support of peripheral ascendancy has increased enormously due to the Structural Fund reforms undertaken in 1988 and 1993, the prospect offered by the new European Economic Area agreement, the decision to double Structural Fund allocations after 1993, and the creation of a Cohesion Fund to finance environmental and transportation projects affecting the least-developed regions. The discussion presently underway on the configuration of the Structural Funds provides the EU with an ever stronger role in influencing regional economic and social outcomes. European-level intervention does make a difference, and it will become increasingly important given the need to reduce national funding for development projects in the lagging regions and states. EU intervention would make an even greater difference if the Structural Funds and networking policy were to be based on a clearer understanding of the evolving situation and the relationship between EU financing and the spurring of local and foreign investment in targeted areas. Market forces do play a role, but there is a need for an incentive structure to encourage firms to site their production facilities in peripheral regions rather than outside the EU.[6]

Fourth, in order to maintain control over future

development, the EU not only needs to refine its instruments of control and supervision in the allocation and use of Structural Funds, it must also improve its ability to follow developments at the regional level by rationalising and improving the collection of regional-level data. Up until now this responsibility has remained in the hands of the national authorities. In order properly to oversee economic conditions and developments throughout its territory, the EU needs to upgrade its data on a yearly or quarterly basis.

The completion of the Single Market and the fall of national borders as barriers to cross-border economic interaction suggest that the EU needs to create a 'seamless' database for the territory of the union at the regional and even communal levels. With the introduction of Geographical Information System (GIS) technology in the field of regional and urban planning, the existence of a coherent and complete database for the EU becomes a fundamental tool for the monitoring economic impacts and the planning of future economic and social policies for Europe's regions and localities.

Fifth, the EU needs to develop models to evaluate investment programmes at both regional and local level. At the present time the regulations concerning the Cohesion Fund and the three Structural Funds speak eloquently of ex-ante and ex-post evaluations of specific projects. The reality is, however, that these evaluations are not carried out because (1) an adequate EU-wide data base does not exist at the subnational level[7] and (2) emphasis has not been placed on finalising the development of models that are capable of carrying out this evaluation. Without such evaluations, the exact output of EU-funded projects remains uncertain and this lays the EU open to attack by those who would rather use the resources for other purposes.

The EU needs to create a common methodology for the conduct of evaluation of investment policies undertaken by the Structural Funds, Cohesion Fund, and national and regional/local authorities if investment projects are not to be treated as only one-off attempts to stimulate jobs and expenditures. At the present time, regional and national authorities use – in the best of circumstances – a variety of instruments, that is, cost-benefit analysis and input-output tables, to measure the economic impact of policies, and, in the worst case, no ex-ante or ex-post evaluation is carried out despite the fact that such an evaluation is explicity called for in the regulations.

Sixth, the data and analysis presented here suggest that reduction of the gap between developed and less developed regions is still on target. Cohesion is a realistic goal for the medium to long term, and the rate of achieving that goal can be significantly influenced by full consolidation of the Single Market. This generalisation is based on the assumption that realisation of the Single Market will be accompanied by a policy aimed at reducing the gap between core and periphery in the current level of economic and institutional infrastructure through legislative provision as well as making available economic resources to stimulate economic development in the less favoured regions. The EU needs to adopt an increasingly proactive policy stance that builds on the partnership principle – bringing together the EU, member states and regions – initiated in the IMP programmes and consolidated in the CSFs. Much more still needs to be done to rationalise the system and make it fully responsive to the needs of economic development, but the performance of the EU in reducing past disparities bodes well for the future.

NOTES

1. This variable was closely correlated in 1970 in a negative direction with the level of the agricultural workforce. The two indicators tended not to remain as direct opposites in the 1980s due to the rapid rise of the service sector.
2. On the emergence of the service sector as an important component in the adaptation of industrial districts to new forms of production, see Sforzi, 1994.
3. The financial data taken into account concern the amount of aid received by the regions from the EC through the ERDF, EAGGF-Guidance, ESF grants and EIB loans.
4. In subsequent reports on the data, the EIB loans to the regions are missing.
5. See the analysis of the second Community Support Frameworks for Ireland, Portugal, Spain and Greece discussed in Nanetti, 1994.
6. The choice facing entrepreneurs in the EU when relocating new productive capacity is often not between different parts of the EU but

rather between EU countries and those outside. Thus the EU must be careful to reduce the incentives for domestic producers to locate their production facilities outside Europe, as took place in the US in the 1960s and 1970s when factories moved out of the older industrial belts in the midwest and on the east coast to settle not in the south or west but outside US national borders.

7.   The situation is particularly acute in the four peripheral EU countries, given that the EUROSTATE NUTS designation does not in all cases correspond to the traditional subdivisions of the four nation-states involved.

REFERENCES

Casetti, E. (1985) 'Manufacturing Productivity and Snowbelt-Sunbelt Shifts', *Economic Geography* (May–June), pp. 313–24.

EC (1990) *Second Survey on State Aids in the European Community in the Manufacturing and Certain Other Sector* (Luxembourg: Office of Official Publications of the European Communities).

Flora, P. (1986) *Growth to Limits: The Western European Welfare States since World Wae II* (Berlin: De Gruyter).

IFO (1990) *An Empirical Assessment of Factors Shaping Regional Competitiveness in Problem Regions* (Luxembourg: Office of Official Publications of the European Communities).

Jones, C. (ed.) (1993) *New Perspectives on the Welfare State in Europe* (London: Routledge).

Madureira-Pires, L. (1992) 'European Community Development Policies: The Case of Portugal', paper presented at the European Research Seminar, London School of Economics, European Institute, 28 February.

Nanetti, R. Y. (1989) *Growth and Territorial Policies: The Italian Model of Social Capitalism* (London: Pinter Publishers).

Nanetti, R. Y. (1994) *The Rise of the Periphery: Development Planning in the Regions of the European Community* (London: Frank Cass).

Pimpão, A. (1994) 'Analysis of Regional Convergence in Portugal', paper delivered at the Second Meeting of the Network on Economic and Social Cohesion, Florence, Italy, 3–4 June.

Richardson, H. W. (1969) *Elements of Regional Economics* (London: Penguin).

Sforzi, F. (1994) 'The Tuscan model: an interpretation in light of recent trends', in R. Leonardi and R. Y. Nanetti (eds), *Regional Development in a Modern European Market: The case of Tuscany* (London: Pinter Publishers), pp. 86–115.

Stough, R. (1993) 'Rise of the Southern Periphery in the United States: Understanding the Fortbelt-Sunbelt Shift', in R. Leonardi, *The State of Ecomic and Social Cohesion in the Community Prior to the Creation of the Single Market: The View from the Bottom-Up* (Brussels: Commission of the European Communities), Chapter 2.

7 The Convergence Model of European Integration

INTEGRATION AND CONVERGENCE IN THE EUROPEAN UNION

To understand fully the consequences of the social and economic convergence analysed in the previous chapters, we need to reexamine the manner in which European integration is conceptualised and the way that nation-states have responded to the transfer of policy areas from the national to the European level. The convergence model of European integration proposed in this chapter posits the argument that integration can be seen as a multitier phenomenon affecting not only different levels of government (national, regional and local) but also various sectors of society, such as the economic, political and social systems. Integration, on the one hand, creates supranational institutions. On the other hand, when it is combined with convergence it has a profound effect on the structure, decision-making processes and implementation procedures adopted by national and subnational governments in regulating economic and social behaviour.

This chapter will also present the argument that the nation-state has been bombarded by a variety of forces internal to Europe, as well as external ones manifesting themselves in the world economy. The combined impact of these forces has been to change the ability of the state to control particular policy areas and processes. As the EU has consolidated its role, increased its statutory powers and accumulated increasingly larger resources for redistribution to individuals, companies and localities in the twelve member states, the loci of decision making and implementation of sectoral policies have changed significantly.

A review of nation-state structures from the early 1970s to the early 1990s shows that control of certain policy areas moved upward to the European level, some decisions moved downward to lower levels of government, and other activities previously carried out by government have been moved laterally from the public to the private sector. The combined impact of these three types of 'off-loading' have served to reverse the tendency manifested during the course of the first thirty years of the post-Second-World-War period, in which the nation-state accumulated tasks and functions. The shedding of powers and responsibilities has, up until now, been treated as specific to certain countries and as a byproduct of the deregulation, liberalisation, privatisation and cost-cutting tendencies of individual leaders. Recently, national governments have undertaken to dismantle not only inefficient companies in the public sector but also natural monopolies controlling public transport, telecommunications, energy and utilities. The argument presented here is that the slimming down of the traditional European welfare state is not only attributable to the programmes and goals of individual leaders, but to a more system-wide phenomenon that is taking place in Europe and that is intimately linked to the process of integration and convergence.[1]

Another important transformation that is visible at the nation-state level is the change in the traditional relationship between government and society. Centres of national power no longer carry out governmental functions as before. Since the Second World War there has been considerable change in (1) *who* (that is, which organs of government, administration and private-sector interests) is involved in decision making in specific areas of policy; (2) *how* policies are decided, in that there is a growing multiplicity of loci for decision making and implementation that no longer correspond to the formal institutions involved in public decision-making organs; and (3) *what* can be and is decided (that is, the specific content of decisions affecting specific policy areas) at various levels of the political system.

The literature on policy analysis has attempted to account for these changes with a variety of explanatory models – from pluralism to neocorporatism and from intergovernmentalism to the study of community power structures and the emergence of policy communities – but in all cases the study of policy-making structures has had to deviate from the previous notions of state dominance and the exercise of the upper hand by governmental representatives in all interactions with societal

forces. Even in continental European countries with strong
state dirigiste traditions, the growing pluralist nature of policy
making and implementation has been accepted as a given.[2]
Before discussing in detail the shape of state restructuring in
the European context, we need to clarify the use of a number
of key concepts.

The hypothesis advanced in this chapter is that the off-
loading process, the realignment of state–society linkages and
the changing mix of relevant participants in policy making are
all part of the dynamic generated by integration and convergence. Convergence is a longitudinal process through which
formal as well as informal behaviour and values become increasingly similar because of a variety of domestic and international factors. Colin Bennett (1993) has argued that
convergence is a process that emphasizes the dynamic rather
than static qualities of change. What is important in being able
to empirically establish the existence of convergence is whether
the characteristics of the units of analysis being compared
become more similar over time (i.e., converge) or whether
they become more dissimilar (i.e., diverge). Figure 7.1 presents
a breakdown of the four different types of convergence dynamic that can be observed in modern European nation-state
systems, and how these dynamics manifest themselves in the
three main components of society: the economic system, the
political system and the social system.[3] The argument presented
here is that convergence provides one of the important preconditions for integration: as the policy-making and policy-
implementation structures of countries converge it becomes
easier and more feasible to formulate integration strategies by
creating new institutions to manage policies in the economic,
political and social spheres.[4]

Integration, on the other hand, is a quite separate concept
and condition from the state of partial or complete convergence. In the above discussion on regional disparities, complete convergence is defined as representing a state of cohesion:
the various component parts of the system operate as one.
Factors of production within each system can operate on a
completely equal basis and are free to flow from one part of
the system to another. In, for example, a cohesive, European-
wide administrative system one would find administrators in

CONVERGENCE OF:

SYSTEM	GOVERNMENTAL POLICIES	DECISION-MAKING & IMPLEMENTATION STRUCTURES	ELITE AND MASS BEHAVIOUR	ELITE AND MASS VALUES
Economic	Agriculture, monetary, industrial etc.	Role of R&D, size of sectors, structure of industry etc.	Levels and structure of consumption, entrepreneurship, competition, cooperation	Attitudes on cooperation and competition, lending, savings, investment
Political	Foreign, EC, welfare-state market, monetary fiscal etc.	Administration, political party system; intergovernmental relations, judicial review etc.	Elections, party competition, career structures, professionalism	Norms on common good, unwritten rules for behaviour in public office, civic norms
Social	Education, housing, welfare, health etc.	Class structure, race structure/distribution, elite–mass relations, cultural institutions	Class and race relations, spatial location of residences, social mobility	Attitudes on class, race, opportunity, equality, cooperation and conflict

Figure 7.1 Convergence in Europe

different national settings operating according to the same informal norms, formal rules, goals, career structures, recruitment patterns, management styles and so on as their counterparts in other national bureaucracies (Wessels, 1991). Administrators operating in cohesive but separate administrative structures are able to come together to work in common structures without an extensive period of retraining or readjustment.[5]

Integration, on the other hand, as formulated by the original neofunctionalist theorists and proposed here, is posited on the creation of new supranational institutions to govern the systems that are converging. In the political sphere integration requires:

1. The strengthening and consolidation of existing European political institutions (that is, Commission, European Court, European Parliament), the incorporation of other institutions into the EU structure (for example EPC and WEU), and the growth in power of the European-wide political-party grouping over their national components (to date European elections have been conducted as national elections in a European disguise).
2. A further 'rooting' of European political institutions in the consciousness and political awareness of European citizens through the creation of a strong European loyalty and identity among elites as well as the general public.[6]

For economic integration to exist, steps must be taken to create institutions with the ability to decide and manage economic policies – such as a central bank structure, a monetary system and so on – as well as allocating decision making and implementation of monetary and fiscal policies to European executives and legislative branches of government. Until now economic integration has been created in a piecemeal fashion in Europe.[7] The ECSC Treaty created the High Authority for Coal and Steel and the Rome Treaty the Commission. With the implementation of the Maastricht Treaty, the EU will be endowed with eleven new institutions. The Frankfurt-based European Monetary Institute will operate as the precursor of a European central-bank system.[8]

Socially, integration will have been achieved when interest

groups and voluntary associations organise themselves at the European level, and when institutions at the supranational level become independent of their associated national organisations in the making and enforcement of their own decisions. Economic interest groups have formed more quickly at the European level than have other voluntary groups. Business and labour groups (UNICDE, CES and CEEP) are now solidly entrenched in Brussels and other sites where European institutions are located (Greenwood, Grote and Ronit, 1992). Other voluntary groups representing gender, class and place have taken longer to become established and operational at the European level. Social integration on a more normative basis is harder to operationalize. While convergence can be measured by the change in cultural norms and attitudes displayed by mass publics in each member state, it is more difficult to conceive what characteristics normative social integration would assume. One alternative is to operationalize normative integration as the extent to which European public adopt a European identity (i.e., identifying themselves as citizens of Europe and supporting the creation, strengthening and activities of European level institutions).[9]

As is illustrated in Box 7.1, complete convergence (cohesion) in an economic system occurs when factor prices in different markets are equalised, so that operations taking place in the single, unified market face no internal barriers to the free and open circulation of information, goods, services, capital and persons. Integration, on the other hand, is realised when supranational economic institutions are empowered to take decisions that are binding on all members of the community. The bottom part of Box 7.1 suggests that the same rule applies to political and social systems. As is the case with economic cohesion, social cohesion is based on a vigorous process of convergence.

Political union is seen as the culminating stage of integration – that is, the point when supranational institutions are underpinned by the widespread allegiance of the citizenry. At this stage the supranational institutions operate independently of their national counterparts, the balance of power between the supranational and national centres of power being spelled out in formal and legal terms, and intergovernmental interactions representing a common element in the interactions

Box 7.1 Comparisons between complete convergence and integration

---

Complete convergence takes place when cohesion is achieved:

1. Economically – there is an equalisation of factor prices in the various sectors that operate within a single, unified market where there are no internal limitations to the circulation of information, goods, services, capital and persons.
2. Politically – transnational parties are created to take charge of candidate selection, political campaigns and coordination of legislative behaviour in European-wide elections, and intergovernmentalism is the standard form of decision-making in public administration and policy making.
3. Socially – the national societies operate as one cultural market, share common social values, and operate their social institutions in a coordinated and parallel fashion.

Integration takes place when union is achieved:

1. Economically – supranational institutions are created to manage the unified market, such as a central bank, a securities and exchange commission and so on.
2. Politically – supranational institutions are created to manage decision making and implementation, such as a commission, a parliament, a court of justice and a court of accounts.
3. Socially – supranational institutions are created to govern social activities such trade unions, employers organisations, voluntary organisations and so on.

---

between the European core institutions and the peripheral national bodies vying for resources and influence.

Divergence and disintegration

The considerations discussed above imply the theoretical existence of the reverse dynamic and end-product of convergence and integration: divergence and disintegration.[10] Disintegration is not only a theoretical possibility; it is also an empirical reality that manifested itself in Europe on the heels of the collapse of Communism and after the end of the First World

War. Willem Molle describes the consequences of the First World War on economic conditions in Europe as one of economic disintegration:

> With the outbreak of the First World War, a process of disintegration was set in motion. During the war, every country emphasized the need for autarky: to depend economically on foreign countries makes a country vulnerable in military terms. The result was a steep drop in international trade. Not only did free trade suffer from the war, the movement of production factors was also more and more curtailed. Under the pressure of conscription, among other things, the free movement of persons collapsed completely. Capital was more and more contained within national borders by a multitude of national rules (Molle, 1990, p. 45).

Figure 7.2 presents a matrix that places integration–disintegration and convergence–divergence along two separate axes, thereby creating a two-by-two table. By empirically operationalising the two dimensions, one can trace over time the evolution of nation-state systems (group of states) in Western or Eastern Europe, or even single countries, along the two separate and distinct axes. Our original hypothesis is that changes in nation-state systems have an impact on the structure of individual states.

Through the use of the matrix the dynamics of a nation-state system can be plotted with time-series data on the extent of its convergence and on the level of integration achieved among its component parts. We would argue that each cell has its own logic and dynamic. Thus the usual course of a system along the two axes takes place within a defined cell. However in extreme circumstances individual countries or nation-state systems can move from one cell to another through major institutional or political crises – for example following 'watershed events' (such as the fall of the Berlin Wall in 1989) that change the linkages between state and society, the relationships among various parts of the state, the legitimacy of existing state institutions and processes, and the relationships among the nation-states in the wider international system. The position assumed by a nation-state system in Time 1 vis-à-vis Time 2 would place it on a precise spot in the matrix and reflect the level and direction of convergence–divergence and integration–

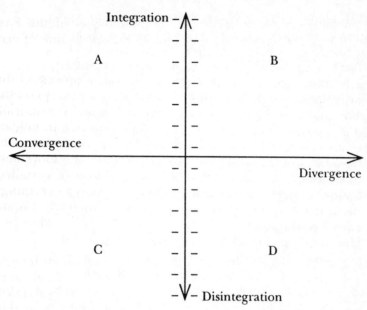

Examples of cell dynamics:

Cell A: Convergence and integration dynamic operating within the EU through voluntary adherence and participation. Integration regulated by legal system.

Cell D: Divergence and disintegration dynamic operating within former Yugoslavia and Soviet Union. Reversal of trends only through the use of force by centralizing internal power.

Cell B: Integration and divergence dynamic as hypothesised by centre–periphery theory. Integration through force and the consequent economic divergence manifesting itself in the periphery. Central organs then attempt to reverse divergence trends through direct intervention.

Cell C: Convergence and disintegration dynamic as exemplified by transitional regimes. Change brought about by a convergence of values and behaviour through cultural penetration via electronic and other media. Penetration sets off political disintegration and thereby opens the way for political and economic transformation. If disintegration is not blocked, it can lead to an undermining of convergence.

Figure 7.2   Convergence–divergence and integration–distintegration matrix

disintegration achieved by the constituent member states in a nation-state system, or by the component parts of one state if it is undergoing substantial transformation.

Two examples of the dynamic taking place in Cells A and D immediately come to mind. In the former we would place the trend displayed by EU member states, while in the latter we could easily identify the dynamic of divergence–disintegration that manifested itself in Yugoslavia, where a previously federal state broke up into a number of smaller states. In both cases the eventual outcome of the dynamic is the creation of new state structures. In Cell A the result is the creation of a new and more complex institutional entity (the European Union) while in the lower right-hand cell the end-product is a multiplicity of new states.[11]

The matrix in Figure 7.3 can also be used to study the dynamics operating in the economic as well as the political and social systems. As with integration, disintegration is not complete until the 'overarching' institutions governing a previously integrated society are dissolved through mutual consent or destroyed by civil war.[12] Politically, disintegration takes place when territories in previously federal or even unitary nation-states break-away to form new political entities.

In the economic sphere disintegration is evident when new political regimes set up separate customs offices, currencies, central banks and all the other structures necessary to manage their new national markets. Economic disintegration usually has a negative impact on outside economic links by disrupting established trade channels, the circulation of productive factors, and the diffusion of technologies and know-how. As a consequence production declines, as do levels of consumption (Bookman, 1993).

The signs of social disintegration are probably the most evident in the short run, and they are characterised by the organisation of separate 'national' (that is, ethnic) communities in areas where previously multi-ethnic societies and social institutions existed.[13] For example, all kinds of voluntary groups and sectoral interest-group associations break up to form separate, ethnically defined organisations.

Once disintegration is underway there is no telling how far it will proceed. Its final resting point depends on the depth of animosity unleashed by the divergence process. The rate and depth of divergence can break through ethnic bonds as well as the language and religious barriers that had previously served to delineate the borders of self-defined communities.

So far discussion of the matrix has concentrated on Cells A and D, in which the dynamics along the two axes are 'coherent' – that is, where convergence lines up with integration and divergence is combined with disintegration. Is it possible to find systems in which the dynamic is 'contradictory', as hypothesised in Cells B and C? In Cell B the move toward divergence is combined with integration, while in Cell C convergence is associated with disintegration. To identify cases that will fit into these two cells, we need to mix and match different types of societal system – for example there may be integration in the political system but divergence in the economic system. On this basis numerous examples come to mind.

To begin with, the dynamic in Cell B is a familiar one to regional economists and students of centre–periphery relations. It reflects the economic consequences for peripheral areas of political integration through force as implemented by national elites in the creation of nation-state systems. In Chapter 2 we discussed in detail centre–periphery relations as analysed by political scientists and economists, where the emphasis was on the use of state power to subjugate and exploit the periphery.[14] Cell B also reflects much of the theorising that has gone into formulating economic divergence approaches to regional development, or more precisely, regional economic decline as discussed in Chapters 2 and 3. In these cases integration is not voluntary. It is carried out by the sword, and the consequences of integration are not distributed evenly throughout society. In the process central elites and institutions gain while the periphery loses in relative as well as absolute terms, and it is the very process of economic divergence that provides the state with the rationale to intervene extensively in the economy.[15]

The dynamic operating in Cell C is the most problematic from the point of view of finding relative cases. The most likely examples of the Cell C dynamic can be found where there is a convergence of value structures with points of reference in systems outside and antagonistic to the existing internal system, which attempts to resist change. Examples of these kinds of rift between the values adopted by citizens and the lack of significant congruence in the form and processes of the existing political institutions is provided by the democratic transformation of former authoritarian systems in Europe (for example Portugal, Greece and Spain, and Eastern Europe as a whole). One could argue that, in these societies and nation-state systems, the collapse of the established political institutions was preceded by the convergence of elite and mass values with the political norms of the democratic countries of Western Europe. As a consequence, the former institutions disintegrated and were replaced by new systems through peaceful transition.

In the case of the transition of the three Western European countries from authoritarianism to democracy, the forces of disintegration were checked through the rapid consolidation of democratic institutions and processes. It can also be argued that in the three Western European examples of peaceful transition the halt and reversal of the disintegration forces was significantly helped by the quick and effective incorporation of these countries into the EC. In fact Laurence Whitehead has argued that the transition from authoritarian to democratic systems in southern Europe was profoundly influenced by the existence of functioning and prosperous European-wide supranational institutions:

> the Southern European experience indicates that a significant shift of international orientation (perhaps even of perceptions of national identity) is likely to accompany any major regime change from authoritarian rule to liberal democracy. The European Community has acted as a powerful catalyst both of democratisation and of national redefinition in contemporary Southern Europe. It has achieved this influence not through military occupations, but by offering an elaborate structure of economic and social incentives for changes in group and national behavior (Whitehead, 1991, p. 45).

Since the late 1980s the situation in Eastern Europe has developed along different lines. Political institutions, practices and values have still not been consolidated beyond a minimal basis and political and social divergence still threaten the body politic. From the perspective of the current members of the EU, the incorporation of some or all of the Eastern European countries has to be predicated not only on the existing convergence of values, but even more on the convergence of economic, legal and social systems toward the European norm. The upheavals in the former Soviet Union demonstrate that legal norms, institutions and procedures supportive of market economies and democratic political institutions have still not been thoroughly internalised as the fundamental rules of the game. Not only is the international military and political stance of the former Soviet states still unresolved, but also the very boundaries and composition of the states remain in question. Without a clear and permanent resolution of these fundamental questions it is difficult to imagine how these new states could assume an equal and full role in European affairs, where the member states participate in the determination of common policies in political, economic, social and security matters. Only when as the Eastern states clearly demonstrate an overall convergence dynamic with their Western neighbours will they be able to join the move toward integration.

Necessary and sufficient conditions for integration

In a similar fashion to the unlimited potential of divergence, the convergence dynamic can bring together different political communities. A review of the history of the EU and attempts to create regional communities in other parts of the world shows that the convergence of national systems is a necessary but not sufficient condition for integration. At the same time, the creation of supranational institutions will not guarantee the convergence of national systems. Without the preexistence of convergence in broad areas of policy making, political and economic integration will not be feasible in the short to medium term. Formal attempts to create integration within a pattern of wide divergences will face the prospect of remaining ephemeral or even collapsing. Moves toward integration that are not preceded by extensive convergence have little meaning in the daily lives of individual citizens and little effect on group behaviour in society. The new institutions founder and collapse before they are able properly to function and make effective inroads into restructuring policy making and encouraging further convergence.[16]

The existence of convergence makes integration possible,

but it does not make it inevitable. Nor can convergence be conceived as a viable substitute for integration. It is argued here that convergence provides an important condition for integration and serves as a crucial phase of transition in the latter, but it is not the same thing. Integration is the process by which existing institutions, communities, policies and values are brought together to form new political, economic and social entities, such as the European-level policy-making structures and processes activated by the EU. As a goal, integration is only possible when elites and mass publics feel that they have more to gain from integration than from remaining exclusively within the confines of the nation-state – that is, the will to break out of the confines of the nation-state must be greater than the will to remain within the parameters dictated by the nation-state. Such cost–benefit calculations are based on economic self-interest as well as on the future and immediate real gains to be made if domestic political and economic actors are able to influence political and economic outcomes at higher levels of aggregation and conceive the outcomes of bargaining arrangements as positive-sum rather than zero-sum games (Wessels, 1991).

The necessary relationship between convergence and integration raises a number of questions. The first concerns the strategy of the integration process: should economic integration precede political integration or should the opposite be the case? Undoubtedly the choice of the founding fathers of the EC was one favouring economic integration as the fundamental building block of eventual political integration. In contrast, European federalists believed at the beginning of the postwar period that the creation of European institutions was the first goal to be achieved, while the pursuit of economic integration as a precondition for political integration constituted a loss of precious time and effort.

The events during the first decade of the postwar period showed that the revival of the European state system would make it difficult to follow a federalist approach when moving toward political integration. The UK was unwilling to commit itself to European union, and in 1954, through its rejection of the European Defence Community, the French National Assembly brought to a halt any further consideration of political integration. As a consequence the supporters of integration had to content themselves with the limited form of integration allowed by the sectoral economic approach adopted in the Paris and Rome treaties, involving the coal and steel industries and agriculture.

The second question is whether the dynamic of convergence and the integration process can operate at various levels and sectors – that is, does each process have to develop in a parallel fashion in all sectors of activity? Developments in Western Europe have shown that convergence and integration can develop at different paces, levels and sectors. Integration of military systems (NATO) took place in Europe long before similar moves were made in the economic and political spheres, and the dynamics of economic convergence significantly preceded signs of political convergence (Urwin, 1993).

We would argue that, as part of postwar socioeconomic development and the modernisation of Western European society as well as the common struggle against the Soviet Union, Europe underwent a process of political, economic and social convergence based on a common identity, purpose and interest. The existence of a common enemy certainly aided this process, but it was not its exclusive component. Support for integration came from the need to rebuild economic, political and social structures destroyed by the war and to build an alternative to the nation-state system that had dominated the prewar years (Taylor, 1983; Haas, 1958, 1964).

A final question that can be asked concerning the relationship between convergence and integration is whether integration can take place before convergence. Our reading of the European experience suggests that integration can take place before convergence becomes manifest in all spheres and levels of activity, but some convergence must precede integration. During the 1950s sectoral integration was undertaken under conditions of partial or limited convergence. A convergence of views was present in crucial decision-making centres – that is, centres of power controlled by elites whose values and behaviour converged significantly on key procedures and objectives. This was the case during the 1950s in foreign ministries and prime ministers' offices (for example the Plevan Plan) in France, Germany, Italy and the Benelux countries.

Integration through convergence as proposed here posits the view that integration is possible only when perceptions of interests and values have converged in a significant manner. At a minimum, elite strategies and perceptions must converge before plans for integration can be operationalised.[17]

The question of the lag between the convergence of elite and mass values is an interesting and important one in light of the new emphasis on integration through referendum that has swept over Europe during the course of the debate on the Maastricht Treaty, and in the procedures that will be followed by the countries lining up to enter the EU. Although nation-states have not adopted the same means of ratifying European treaties, their commitment to European integration is not in question. Long before the European ideal was given substance, national governments entered into binding agreements with other countries without ever submitting these agreements to public referenda.

Using the four dynamics of convergence shown in Figure 7.1, it is probable that in 1950 – at the time of the Schuman Declaration, or even during the drafting of the European Defense Community Treaty in May 1952 and the European Political Community Treaty in March 1953 – little had converged in European nation-states other than the agreement of key political elites on the need to forge new political relationships and find supranational solutions to the structural problems that were afflicting postwar European societies and political systems. How much these elite views were supported by the mass public in the individual nation-states is still open to question, but it is undeniable that political elites in the immediate postwar period had a public mandate to search within the democratic context and the geographical confines of the Western European security alliance for solutions to the serious domestic economic and social problems. Prior to the creation of the first institutionalised forms of European integration, concrete steps had been taken to integrate Europe's defence strategies and establishments through the creation of the North Atlantic Treaty Organization, and even before that significant inroads had been made into nation-state economic autarky with the setting up of the Organization of European Economic Cooperation, the Congress of Europe and the Benelux Customs Union.

Once the more serious economic problems had been resolved, the success of the mixed convergence and integration strategy reinforced the legitimacy of existing domestic political and institutional arrangements. The choice of market economies found growing and broadly based support, as was the case with internal democratic institutions and procedures. As a result of their success in rebuilding their national economies in a more open and converging manner, national political systems were consolidated, and the integration of institutions at the EC level began to assume a more definitive and important role in European as well as domestic politics.

The convergence of views and values operating at both elite and mass levels is still important in order to support the consolidation of supranational institutions, but it does not need to be (nor can it remain) as open-ended as before. In fact the delegation of authority to national governments to make decisions at the European level has been significantly reduced to make way for a more direct relationship between European institutions and the general public, and to provide democratic oversight over the implementation of decisions. The present delegation of authority tends to be more selective, given that convergence has in the meantime also manifested itself in other governmental policies, in decision-making and implementation structures and in both elite and mass behaviour. The public are much more aware than before that decisions taken at the European level have a direct impact on the daily lives and well-being of citizens.

It is argued here that, once established, supranational institutions can be a factor in accelerating the convergence process and in prescribing how particular policies should be implemented and certain decisions made. Instructive in the first case are the numerous attempts by the Commission, the European Court and the Court of Auditors to encourage national governments to comply with EU regulations and directives in carrying out national and EU policies, and thereby converging on how policies are viewed and implemented. Convergence in these cases is encouraged by the existence of a supranational authority that oversees, guides and, if necessary, imposes sanctions against non-compliance in relation to the rules of state behaviour required by the European level of authority.

The broader European experience since the early 1970s shows that the phenomenon of convergence is not limited in its effect to those countries participating in the EU. In fact the creation and operationalisation of European-level institutions has had a profound impact on surrounding countries, and most of all on the members of EFTA – the alternative European model of market reorganisation.

The steady erosion of EFTA demonstrates the difficulties inherent in free-trade areas and the attractiveness of integrating political communities. The current members of EFTA have voluntarily converged toward the economic and administrative policies and structures that exist within the EU as a conscious bridge-building process toward eventual EU membership. In other words, convergence is seen by outside states as a precondition for membership and as a means of preparing themselves to join a powerful economic and political entity. The growing similarities in policy processes between members of the EU and EFTA are the product of learning, imitation and adaptation to the changing exigencies of national governments so that they can link their decision-making processes to the deliberations of the EU. A case in point is offered by the actions of the Austrian government in voluntarily adopting EU regulations and directives to regulate its external and internal activities which has paved the way for its entry into the Union.

THE THEORETICAL STRUCTURE OF THE EUROPEAN END-STATE

A question that has been raised in the past regarding the European integration process is: what will be the contours of the end-state that emerges from the dual convergence–integration dynamic? The answer supplied by neofunctionalists is that European integration is a process rather than an ideal. There is, as argued in the past by Haas (1971) and more recently by Schmitter (1991), no ideal end-state or goal in the European integration process, though certain forms of federal or confederal systems seem to be favoured by the direction assumed by integration.[18] What is, however, inevitable in the neofunctionalist formulations of the end-product of integration is the creation of a new state structure.

After thirty-five years of European integration are we any closer to being able to define with greater accuracy what that end-state will be? The evolution of the EU has not moved in the manner that has been common in the past. In the US and other federal systems, the fleshing out of the federal components and the relationship among institutions at the national level and between the federation and its constituent parts took time to develop, and in most cases this development took the form of interpreting and modifying the existing constitution through the appeal process (Sbragia, 1992). The EU, however, does not have a formal constitution. It has the Rome Treaty and its two modifications, which have been taken up by the European Court of Justice (ECJ) as the functional equivalents of a protoconstitution. The ECJ has proceeded to interpret cases and set judicial precedents on the basis of Treaty principles.

In the light of the protoconstitutional nature of the Treaty and the gradualist approach adopted by the ECJ and other European-level institutions in defining their powers vis-à-vis the nation state, it is our contention that no one country in Europe or one current model of government encapsulates all of the political ideals. The EU is clearly not proceeding down the road of creating a federal administrative structure such as the one that has evolved over time in the US. However this does not mean that the European institution-building process is devoid of political ideals or purpose. On the contrary, certain political norms and practices have become generally accepted on a broad basis in Europe and are reflected in changes taking place in supranational-level institutions.

The construction of supranational institutions in the EU is governed by a constant series of compromises among the member states and various organs of the EU. It is the creation of institutions through compromise that highlights the importance of the convergence process on the choice of institutional reform: the closer the reforms are to the emerging consensus or similarities in processes and norms already present in the European state system, the less difficult and controversial are the changes.

In a similar fashion, parliamentary democracy, free and open elections and the rule of law are widely accepted as the norm for political behaviour and serve as the self-defining characteristics of European political institutions. It should be remembered, though, that these norms have only been broadly accepted by all national governments during the course of the last two decades. At the beginning of the 1970s three of the twelve current members of the EU did not have democratic regimes, pluralistic political structures, or free and competitive elections. Even in the parliamentary democracies the principle of open elections without state interference was not accepted by all the governing or opposition parties operating within the system.

The ideals behind European integration have come to symbolise the democratic norms and practices that are part of institution building in the EU, and these ideals have served as a beacon for the developing democratic regimes in Eastern Europe. Europe is emerging not only as an economic and political reality on the world stage; it also represents an ideal of a political system endowed with democratic procedures and institutions, and a social and economic system that reflects an active social conscience.

The structure of the political system being constructed at the European level is quite different from the ones we find at the nation-state level. As the result of choice as well as necessity, the EU has developed into a polycephalic entity in which the centres of political decision making, economic activity and cultural expression have been consciously scattered throughout its territory, and its institutional structure is more reminiscent of a confederal rather than a unitary state structure. EU member states range from highly centralised states to federal ones, and there are a wide variety of institutional structures and practices. Therefore it is difficult to conceive of an institutional structure at the European level that will faithfully reflect all the existing differences among its constituent states.

At the present time the institutional model that is most appropriate for the EU is one that allows the greatest amount of differentiation at the national level, such as a loose confederation of semi-sovereign states. In this form of state structure the authority exercised by the central institutions is derived from the constituent governments. Accordingly the members of the European central executive (that is, the Commission) display two essential characteristics of a confederal state in the making: they are weak and they are appointed to the body by the constituent national political entities. Despite the changes contained in the Maastricht Treaty (the terms of the members of the Commission run parallel with those of the European Parliament and the Parliament provides a vote of confidence for the Commission), the EU continues to resemble a loose confederation that still has a long way to go before (or if ever) the balance of power is tipped in favour of the central institutions vis-à-vis the constituent states.

Another important point to be remembered is that the qualitative leap between convergence and integration can only be undertaken if new, additional institutions are created. Integration is not concerned with the mixing and intermingling of existing national institutions through various forms of shared sovereignty, compromise and bargaining. It is rather the process by which old institutions are changed as well as new institutions created in response to the changing needs and goals of the wider European political system. What the European-level institutions lack at the present time is the instrumentation for implementing decisions. Up until now EU decisions have been implemented through the compliance of member states and the willingness to accept EU decisions and law as binding on member-state behaviour. Member-state compliance with EU decisions weakens the need to create a separate EU bureaucracy. That function can be easily handled by the national and subnational administrative systems that are already in place and operating in compliance with EU decisions.

Figure 7.3 presents a model containing five components of the European institution-building processes as they manifest themselves in the EU's economic, political and social systems. The figure seeks to depict the process of convergence in terms of the bringing together of central and peripheral states, with divergent systems gradually moving closer together to form a more harmonious and integrated unit.

Box 7.2 goes on to suggest how convergence in these areas is being furthered and consolidated through the formulation of EU programmes and institutions.[19] The European-level institutions produced by integration represent the value-added or supranational (upgrading common interests through mutual compromises) component in European decision making that is not possible to achieve through country-by-country, individualistic decision-making processes, even under the conditions of convergence.[20]

Institution building in the EU is seen in the context of the

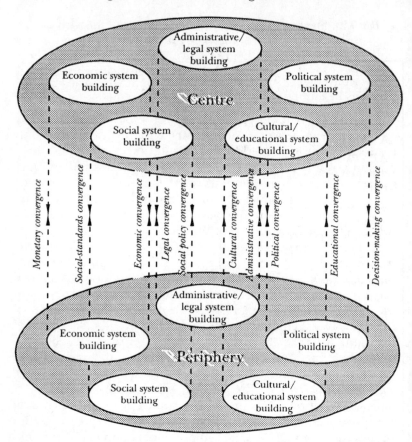

Figure 7.3　Centre–periphery convergence model

dynamic of convergence-leading-to-integration, a process that cannot be accounted for by the concept of intergovern-mentalism or adequately described by international-regime theory.[21] New institutions and policy-making and implementa-tion processes are the product of collective forms of decision making involving nation-states in combination with other in-dependent political entities – such as the Commission, the European Parliament and the European Court of Justice – which in most cases do not merely reflect the cumulative impact of current or past identifications of national interest, but instead the calculation of future gains to be achieved in the common decision-making process. Policies are not only

Box 7.2   Measurement of convergence and the integration
response

How convergence can be measured among countries and
regions in Europe, and the EU integration response in terms
of new programmes and institutions

A   Physical convergence

A1   Physical distance: the time necessary to bridge physical
distance between the periphery and the centre by air, rail and
road.

Response: EU programmes to promote transport networks on
a European-wide basis in order to reduce travel time – for
example the European TGV network, Eurotunnel and so on.

A2   'Electronic' distance: the use of electronic communication
systems to eliminate the gap between core and periphery and
between metropolitan and non-metropolitan areas within nation-
states.

Response: EU telecommunications programmes designed to
create common standards and provide access to the full range
of existing telecommunications technology throughout the EU.

B   Economic convergence

B1   Production and investment differences: levels of productivity,
increase in GDP, levels of manufacturing, levels of trade, levels
of investment and so on.

Response: stimulate the process of convergence through total
elimination of tariff and non-tariff barriers to trade.

B2   Monetary differences: interest rates, exchange rates, size of
public deficit, savings rates.

Response: creation of European monetary union based on a
common currency, institutions to regulate fiscal and monetary
policies and common budgetary discipline.

C   Political convergence

C1   Differences in political systems: political party programmes and
campaigns, election rules, political parties contesting elections,
electoral outcomes and so on.

Response: convergence and coordination of political
programmes for European parliamentary elections and creation
of European-wide political-party groupings endowed with

decision-making powers and procedures to resolve internal conflicts.

C2   Differences in decision-making practices: majority versus coalition government, role of consensus and compromise, role of opposition and so on.

Response: greater sharing of ideas and experiences through periodic meetings of political-party groups and decision-making institutions.

C3   Administrative differences: administrative structures and practices, recruitment and promotion of elites, linkages with subnational structures, coordination across ministries and so on.

Response: cooperative experiences in COREPER and expert committees, regulations and directives of EU; decisions by European Court; evaluations by the Court of Auditors on implementation of EU policies.

C4   Legal standards and practices: legal structures and practices, appeal process, role of ECJ and EU law.

Response: impact of ECJ rulings and the penetration of EU law on legal procedures and rulings in member states.

D   Social and cultural convergence

D1   Social policy: levels of provisions by public sector, unemployment, elderly, youth, pre-school and so on.

Response: Social Fund programmes, Social Charter, Social Chapter in Maastricht Treaty.

D2   Social standards: levels of well-being, levels of consumption, life expectancy, causes of death, crime rates and so on.

Response: EU programmes to reduce regional and social disparities, rulings by the ECJ and actions by the European Parliament on sexual and racial discrimination.

D3   Educational practices and standards: level of illiteracy, structure of higher education, curriculum in required public education, peak research institutions.

Response: EU programmes such as ERASMUS but also activities to promote a convergence in curriculum and standards in European universities as spelled out in 9.93 Green Paper.

D4   Cultural values and attitudes: artistic and musical preferences, social attitudes, values.

capable of spilling over into other sectors and levels of the policy process, they also spill out of the institutional framework. The impact of decisions may not be governable in the manner and direction desired by national or even supranational political leaderships.

The developments that have taken place in the implementation of the Single European Act and the ratification of the Maastricht Treaty show that countries and their political elites are in a position to make strategic choices at particular junctures in the European integration process. But there are no guarantees that once those decisions are made the masses or organised interest groups will follow. We have seen over the last few years that European integration is capable of developments not foreseen in previous theoretical formulations of the process. A case in point is offered by the implementation of the 1992 programme, which by the beginning of the 1990s had gone far beyond what Margaret Thatcher had intended when she and her cabinet sponsored the initial integrated market ideal of market deregulation and guided the ratification of the Single European Act through the House of Commons.

Another important example of how the European integration process can slip out of the hands of national elites is provided by the ramifications throughout the EC of a slim majority of Danes voting against the Maastricht Treaty. Forty-nine thousand negative votes in the 1992 Danish referendum forced the holding of a second referendum in Denmark, and the organisation of a referendum in France almost exploded in the face of the Socialist government. Both contributed to the unravelling of the EMS and the subsequent divergence of monetary policies. These events demonstrate that European integration is now much more than the result of elite politics, intergovernmental bargaining and the mere implementation of nation-state interests. The reality is much more complex and the number of relevant actors much greater than before.

THE IMPACT OF CONVERGENCE AND INTEGRATION ON NATION-STATES

European integration and the current trend in convergence are not only concerned with the creation of supranational institutions; they are part of the process involved in the re-structuring of nation-states. Watts (1981) has argued that we are witnessing in the EU the evolution of a two-fold process in which, on the one hand, there is an explicitly expressed desire for economic benefits, political power and security in moving modern societies and political systems toward greater inter-dependence and rationalisation of functions through the for-mation of larger political units. On the other hand, there is what may seem at first sight a contradictory movement toward the search for identity – that is, 'the desire for smaller, self-governing political units more responsive to the individual citizen and the desire to give expression to primary group attachments . . . which provide the distinctive basis for a com-munity's sense of identity and yearning for self-determination' (Watts, 1981, p. 3).

Convergence theory helps us to understand how political systems can accommodate these parallel and at times contra-dictory pressures on modern nation-state structures. The con-vergence model of integration, as applied to EU member states, postulates that there has been an upward, outward and down-ward redistribution of policy responsibilities.

The policies that have moved upward to the European level mainly concern macro issues involving industrialised econo-mies. These include the determination of external commer-cial relations, competition rules and procedures, industrial policies, the financing of research and development, and the achievement of socioeconomic cohesion. The nature of inter-national competition in industrial goods demonstrates that national markets and resources are no longer sufficient to maintain modern, technologically advanced productive systems and governmental policy structures. The EU structure pro-vides a more appropriate institutional and market context in achieving economies of scale in both the production and dis-tribution of goods as well as in governmental decision making and implementation. The formulation of a national industrial policy for the UK and France, to say nothing of Denmark or Ireland, is no longer sufficient to guarantee the well-being of workers and entrepreneurs or to provide national companies with the ability to compete in open national, European or world markets.

As part of this gradual withdrawal of nation-states from the governing of economic markets, there is a parallel move to remove the state from the direct management of economic enterprises. Liberalisation and privatisation are seen not only as a means of increasing the efficiency of the enterprises concerned, but are also viewed as realistic instruments for reducing budget deficits by no longer making the state responsible for the losses incurred by public enterprises. Liberalisation and deregulation have tended to weaken the link between the public sector and the economy by redefining the state's role as one of overseer rather than active participant in the initiation and management of economic activity. Through privatisation the risks of management are passed from the public to the private sector. Privatisation also eliminates the possible political manipulation of industrial activity and selection and promotion patterns within the public firm for narrow party electoral purposes. As a consequence, privatisation reduces the amount of resources that are at the disposal of national political elites.

Devolution of responsibilities in service delivery and decision making in particular economic areas also serves to reduce the political resources at the disposal of national elites. Since the early 1970s we have seen a general reform of political and administrative structures in the former Napoleonic state systems and the four Scandinavian countries.[22] Decision making and administrative responsibilities have been transferred to subnational governmental units. Even in policy areas where the EU is active, we have seen an increase in the role and participation of subnational governmental structures in implementation. This rise in power of subnational elites has been most conspicuous in regional policy, vocational education, tourism, territorial planning and so on. These changes in administrative responsibilities are part of the operationalisation of the EU principles of partnership (cooperation among different levels of government in the implementation of common policies), additionality (summation of investments from different governmental bodies) and subsidiarity (allocating responsibility to the administrative/political level closest to the problem), which have moved the focus and control of regional policies from the national to the European level.

The operationalisation of these principles has been particularly important in relation to the provision and delivery of services impacting on the quality of life of individual citizens. Since the early 1970s most nation-states in Europe have delegated service-delivery functions to lower levels of government that are in a better position to fine-tune to local needs the content and type of service delivery. In a similar manner, the EU has moved the locus of its regional development policies away from the national level to the regional one in order to interact with local officials, who are both closest to the immediate needs of the people and in a better position than national officials to tailor-make a solution that meets local exigencies.

With the ratification of the Maastricht Treaty, the role of subnational institutions in European policy making has been consolidated through the creation of the advisory Committee of Regions, which parallels the consultative role of the Economic and Social Committee. Though the Treaty does not give the Committee of Regions decision-making powers, for the first time it formally recognises the role that sublevels of government can play in the EU policy process, along with national governments (the Council), interest groups (the Economic and Social Committee) and directly elected members of the European Parliament. Such a development would not have been possible had the nation-state structures of some of the larger European states (Italy, Spain and France), along with those of the smaller countries (Belgium and Portugal), not converged – through the creation of regional governments and federal communities – toward the preexisting German federal model of autonomy in socioeconomic affairs. Regionalisation and federalisation are part of the general phenomenon of decentralisation that has characterised large as well as small nation-states in Europe.

Convergence theory also hypothesises that the processes by which common European-level policies are decided and implemented in member states have converged. The growing plurality of institutions involved in policy making and implementation in the EU has served to change the policy processes in some of its fundamental characteristics:

1. The monopoly of the nation-state has been eroded because other institutions are now involved and the established hierarchical relationship among institutional levels

does not always find the nation-state in the strongest position.

2. The need to adopt cross-national criteria to define and implement policies has become important due to the differentiated sources of financing and the need to coordinate the activities of a multiplicity of institutional and socioeconomic actors.

3. The adjudication of conflicts among the various actors in issues involving EU action is conducted within the confines of EU and not national law.

The impact of the above characteristics on national policy making and implementation can be studied by analysing the patterns of interactions between states and between individual states and the EU. Keohane and Hoffmann have suggested that the appropriate framework for analysing the EU structure is network theory, in which 'individual units are defined not by themselves but in relation to other units' (Keohane and Hoffman, 1991, p. 13). The current network structure operating in the EU goes well beyond the exchange of information or preference of interactions. It involves the creation of explicit policy implementation structures that flesh out the methods and procedures for consolidating the presence of the EU in civil society without creating a centralised, European-wide bureaucracy. State building in the EU is not following the path traced by the emergence of nation-states in Europe through a top-down process emphasising taxation, conscription and bureaucratisation. Instead the process is voluntary in nature and it displays a number of bottom-up features. European union can only come about through mass identity and loyalty given freely by individual citizens, groups of citizens and constituent territories to the supranational entity, and that prospect still lies in the far distant future.

The present study started as an attempt to measure social and economic cohesion as part of the development of a broader conception of centre–periphery relations and the dynamics of European convergence. It has now moved toward a reformulation of integration theory as applied to the EU. The exact contours of the final end-state may not be clear, but the outlines of an evolving confederation are beginning to emerge in the formation of the European state structure. In the following two chapters we will try to identify the organisational logic of the EU's evolving institutional architecture by looking at its component parts and networking strategy as they manifest themselves in the transfer of decision-making powers in crucial economic sectors from the national to the European level.

NOTES

1. How the link with European integration and convergence can be established will be discussed in greater detail below, but it is important to note here that convergence as a concept is missing entirely in the neofunctionalist literature and it is only tangentially present in intergovernmentalist approaches to integration. See Chapter 10 on this point. On the current trend in privatisation, see Wright (1994).
2. A case in point was the French government's difficulty in deciding what position to take on the GATT negotiations, faced as it was with an inflexible position on the part of the farmers and growing frustration on the part of industrial interests.
3. The major discussion of policy convergence is contained in Bennett (1991). A useful discussion of economic convergence is presented by Iain Begg and David Mayes in (European Parliament, 1991: p. 29), and political party convergence is analyzed in Richard Katz and Peter Mair (1993).
4. The literature on policy convergence recognizes that policy making and implementation structures and policy contents may be converging for other reasons than being part of an integration process. Bennett (1993: p. 215) has identified four possible causes of convergence – emulation, elite networking, harmonization and penetration – without explicitly citing integration. The type of policy convergence taking place within the EU can be traced to all four of the processes cited by Bennett, but in contrast to other industrialized nation-states the members of the Union have undergone an additional pressure for convergence tied to the European level state-building process underway in the Union. Convergence as a result of state-building encourages the component parts of the new political entity to conform to developing Union norms and procedures in trying to maximize individual and national returns. On harmonization in the EU, see Hurwitz (1983).
5. See the interesting argument presented by J. Burnham and M. Maor (1993) on the measurement of convergence in administrative style and behaviour within member states of the EU.
6. This type of rooting may entail the emergence of 'anti-integrationist' parties during European Parliament campaigns. Such an eventuality is

not unlikely given the animosity toward Europe expressed by the British Eurosceptics and other nationalist forces in Europe. European union has become for them the major political cleavage in the European and national political systems.

7. It is interesting to note that Haas' (1958, p. 12) definition of economic integration contained four of the five elements that would be considered here as part of economic convergence (that is, 'elimination of tariffs, quotas and exchange controls on trade among member states'; 'abandonment of the right to restore trade restrictions on a unilateral basis'; 'harmonisation of national policies that affect price structures and the allocation of resources'; and 'free ... movement of capital and labour'. The only element to be considered here as an example of economic integration would be his 'joint action to deal with problems resulting from the removal of trade barriers within the community and to promote more efficient utilisation of the resources of the area'.

8. The Maastricht phase of European integration has brought into existence a wide variety of new institutions. At the end of October 1993, during a special meeting of the European Council, the member states engaged in a strenuous bargaining process to assure their countries a maximum number of institutions. See the 30 October 1993 issue of the *Financial Times* for the allocation of these new EC institutions to member states.

9. On the issue of social convergence and integration see, in general, the book edited by Garcia (1993) and, more specifically, the chapter on a comparison of European, national and local identities by European mass publics in Reif (1993).

10. The word 'disintegration' is used to refer to the dissolution of overarching institutions as economic, political and social systems diverge.

11. After the First World War disintegration took place in the Austro-Hungarian and Russian Empires.

12. These overarching institutions may have been supranational, federal or even unitary in nature, as is suggested by the pace and pattern of dissolution of political institutions and communities in Eastern Europe and the former Soviet Union. When the overarching institutions are dissolved and the civil war continues between former constituent parts, now organised in to separate state systems, the war assumes an interstate character.

13. Social disintegration raises the problem of minority rights (that is, the rights of those who do not belong to the dominant ethnic community but who were equal members of the previous multi-ethnic community). Given that social disintegration is also accompanied by political disintegration, the protection of minority rights by the dominant ethnic group is, at best, problematic. If it is not addressed by the political elites, then it leads to further disintegration and divergence in all areas.

14. Centre–periphery relations reflect the early history of nation-states, when national governments tended to be more rapacious than

redistributive in orientation (that is, emphasising taxation and conscription rather than redistribution in national policies).

15.   This form of reasoning may explain the off-loading state operations engaged in by the nation-state as part of European integration – that is, the creation of a new institutional entity at the supranational level is not posited on the basis of continued or renewed interference in the economy because of the economic convergence process that is underway.

16.   By the mid-1970s almost all of the regional communities developed in the Third World to emulate the European Common Market during the 1960s had collapsed. The failure of other regional communities can be attributed to the fact that domestic systems were diverging rather than converging and that the creation of supranational organs proved to be practically impossible (Haas, 1975).

17.   It is interesting to note that Haas' (1958, p. 16) major indicator of political integration is the reorientation of the values of the elites and mass public in relation to the supranational European institutions: 'Political integration is a process whereby political actors in several distinct national settings are persuaded to shift their loyalties, expectations and political activities toward a new centre, whose institutions posses or demand jurisdiction over the pre-existing national states'.

18.   On the federal goal of integration, see Mayne, Pinder and Roberts (1990).

19.   Molle (1990, pp. 472–7) presented an initial attempt to quantify European convergence and integration using economic and policy indicators.

20.   Up until now, the supranational component of European institutions has been subordinated to the national government decision-making process due to the dominant role of the Council of Ministers in the passage of regulations and directives. As is argued by Mancini (1991) and Shapiro (1992), only the European Court of Justice has been able from the beginning to incarnate a complete supranational spirit, identity and role. That role is now being shared with the European Parliament, which has been strengthened by the Maastricht Treaty.

21.   This point is adequately illustrated by the track record of European Political Cooperation (EPC). Despite the claims of its supporters, it has not led to integration (Wallace, 1983) and will not lead to integration until it is brought fully within the existing EU institutional structure.

22.   See the discussion of the devolution of powers from national governments to subnational entities in the Napoleonic states in R. Leonardi and R. Y. Nanetti (1990), and Rose (1989) in the four Nordic countries.

REFERENCES

Bennett, C. J. 'What is Policy Convergence and What Causes It?', (1991) *British Journal of Political Science*, 21, pp. 215–233.

Bookman, M. J. (1993) *The Economics of Secession* (New York: St. Martin's Press).

Burnham, R. and M. Maor (1993) 'Converging Administrative Systems: Recruitment and Training in EC Member-States', paper presented at the Annual Conference of EGPA, ENA, Strasbourg, 7–10 September.

European Parliament (1991) *A New Strategy for Social and Economic Cohesion After 1992* (Luxembourg: Office of Official Publications of the European Communities).

Garcia S. (ed.) (1993) *European Identity and the Search for Legitimacy* (London: Pinter Publishers).

Greenwood, J., J. R. Grote and K. Ronit (1992) *Organised Interests and the European Community* (London: Sage).

Haas, E. B. (1958) *The Uniting of Europe: Political, Social and Economical Forces, 1950–1957* (London: Stevens & Sons).

Haas, E. B. (1964) *Beyond the Nation-State* (Palo Alto: Stanford University Press).

Haas, E. B. (1971) 'The Study of Regional Integration: Reflections on the Joy and Anguish of Pretheorizing', in L. Lindberg and S. Scheingold (eds), *Regional Integration: Theory and Research* (Cambridge, MA: Harvard University Press), pp. 3–42.

Kastendiek, H. (1990) 'Convergence or a Persistent Diversity of National Politics?', in C. Crouch and D. Marquand (eds), *The Politics of 1992: Beyond the Single European Market* (Oxford: Basil Blackwell), pp. 68–84.

Katz, R. S. and P. Mair (1993) 'Varieties of Convergence and Patterns of Incorporation in West European Party Systems', paper presented at the Workshop on 'Inter-Party Relationships in National and European Parliamentary Arenas', ECPR Joint Sessions, University of Leyden, 2–7 April.

Keohane, R. O. and S. Hoffmann (1991) 'Institutional Change in Europe in the 1980s', in R. O. Keohane and S. Hoffmann (eds), *The New European Community: Decisionmaking and Institutional Change* (Boulder: West View Press), pp. 1–39.

Leonardi, R. and R. Y. Nanetti (1990) 'Emilia-Romagna and Europe: a case study of regional transformation in preparation for the Single Market', in R. Leonardi and R. Y. Nanetti (eds), *The Regions and European Integration: The Case of Emilia-Romagna* (London: Pinter Publishers), pp. 1–12.

Mancini, F. (1991) 'The Making of a Constitution for Europe', in R. O. Keohane and S. Hoffmann (eds), *The New European Community: Decisionmaking and Institutional Change* (Boulder: West View Press), pp. 177–94.

Mayne, R., J. Pinder and J. Roberts (1990) *Federal Union: The Pioneers* (New York: St. Martin's Press).

Molle, W. T. M. (1990) *The Economics of European Integration: Theory, Practice, Policy* (Aldershot: Dartmouth).

Moon, F. (1985) *European Integration in British Politics 1950–1963: A Study of Issue Change* (Aldershot: Gower).

Reif, K. (1993) 'Cultural Convergence and Cultural Diversity as Factors in European Identity' in S. Garcia (ed.) *European Identity and the Search for Legitimacy* (London: Pinter Publishers), pp. 131–153.

Pinder, J. (1993) 'The Single Market: a step toward union', in J. Lodge, (ed.), *The European Community and the Challenge of the Future*, second edition (London: Pinter), pp. 51–68.

Rose, L. (1989) *Nordic Experiments with Liberated Government: Increased Autonomy or Continued Central Control?* (Oslo: NIBR).

Sbragia, A. (1992) 'Thinking About the European Future: The Uses of Comparison', in A. Sbragia (ed.), *Europe-Politics: Institutions and Policymaking in the 'New' European Community* (Washington, DC: Brookings Institution), pp. 257–92.

Schmitter, P. (1991) 'The European Community as an Emergent and Novel Form of Political Domination', Estudio/Working Paper, 26 (Madrid: Juan March Institute).

Shapiro, M. (1992) 'The European Court of Justice', in A. Sbragia (ed.), *Euro-Politics: Institutions and Policymaking in the 'New' European Community* (Washington, DC: Brookings Institution), pp. 123–51.

Taylor, P. (1983) *The Limits of European Integration* (London: Croom Helm).

Urwin, D. W. (1993) *The Community of Europe: A History of European Integration since 1945* (London: Longman).

Wallace, W. (1983) 'Political Cooperation: Integration through Intergovernmentalism', in H. Wallace, W. Wallace and C. Webb, (eds), *Policy-Making in the European Community*, second edition, (New York: John Wiley), pp. 373–402.

Watts, R. L. (1981) 'Federalism, Regionalism, and Political Integration', in D. Cameron (ed.), *Regionalism and Supranationalism: Challenges and Alternatives to the Nation-State in Canada and Europe* (Montreal: Montreal Institute for Research on Public Policy), pp. 3–19.

Wessels, W. (1991) 'Administrative Interaction', in W. Wallace (ed.), *The Dynamics of European Integration* (London: Pinter), pp. 229–241.

Whitehead, L. (1991) 'Democracy by convergence and Southern Europe: a comparative politics perspective', in G. Pridham *Encouraging Democracy: The International Context of Regime Transition in Southern Europe* (London: Leicester University Press), pp. 45–61.

Wright, V. (ed.), (1994) *Privatisation in Western Europe: Programmes and Problems* (London: Pinter Publishers).

8 Networks and Networking in the European Union

NETWORKS AND NETWORKING STRATEGIES

The impact of integration and convergence on the EU's institutional architecture has been significant in the aftermath of the Single Market and the Maastricht Treaty. Starting in 1987 the EC needed to manage the new market within a greater European-wide rather than a national context. The implementation of the Single European Act witnessed a steady movement of decision making in crucial economic and social policy sectors to the European level in the search for rationalisation, scale and efficiency to compete on a world scale (Hufbauer, 1990). These changes in the structure of decision making and the new terms of reference for the economies of member states have stimulated the need to rethink the structure and nature of European policy-making institutions so that the pursuit of economic and social objectives can remain grounded on the foundations of representative government (that is, policy-making organs are subject to scrutiny by representatives directly elected by the people) and law (the legal foundations for the organs making decisions must be grounded in Treaty provisions or regulations passed by the Council).

The second pressure for change is the one originating from the grass roots. The very existence of the EU and the commitment of member states to the Single Market has already fundamentally affected individual decisions made by citizens and entrepreneurs in taking advantage of the opportunities provided by the integration process. As argued in the previous chapter, integration is no longer only a top-down process; it has assumed an increasingly clear bottom-up characteristic that is challenging traditional notions and expectations concerning the pace and nature of institutional adaptation. Taken

217

together, these dual pressures for economic and political reforms have wide implications for the EU's institutional structure and the role played by subnational governments at the European level (Adonis and Jones, 1991). This chapter will look at the role that networks and networking strategies have begun to play in the formulation of an innovative approach to the problem of policy implementation in the EU. The impact that integration and convergence have had on the nation-state structure requires the EU to look for alternative forms of instrumentation for the implementation of policies that does not depend on the creation of hierarchical bureaucratic structures (Peters, 1992). Given the presence of existing national bureaucracies, from the beginning the strategy has to be more informal and horizontal in nature, and these are the very characteristics of networks now developing in the regions.

With the 1988 reform of the Structural Funds and the formulation of the first round of Community Support Frameworks, local and regional authorities became quite active in establishing their presence in Brussels and interacting with the offices of the Commission. In 1988 the Council on European Regions and Localities was created to maintain official contact with DG XVI, the Directorate General responsible for the administration of the Regional Fund. The provisions of the Maastricht Treaty have gone further in the direction of institutionalising the presence of subnational bodies at the European level through the creation of the Committee of Regions.

The overall impact of these initiatives has been to change the nature of the linkage system that brings together the Commission with subnational governments and socioeconomic groups at the local level. Since 1989 the combination of a greater organisational presence of the regions in Brussels and the partnership established between the Commission, national governments and the regions in the implementation of the CSFs has given a new meaning and imperative to the maintaining of viable ties between the EU and the regions.

With the CSFs and the other initiatives taken in preparing for the Single Market, the role of subnational authorities has changed substantially. This trend accelerated with the implementation of the Single Market and the negotiation of the second round of CSFs. The institutional imperatives of the original reform of the Structural Funds and the Single Market have now been joined by a new reality: the pursuit of economic and social convergence as an intra-EU rather than an inter-state exercise.

The existence of cohesion as an explicit and widely shared goal of the EU has significantly changed the prospect for and the daily reality of the role and function of regional and local governments at the European level. The recent changes in the EU's programmes and rules for the operation of the Single Market has had a strong impact on the horizontal and vertical linkages created on a European-wide basis to bring together subnational institutions into a more effective and efficient policy-making and implementation structure. Subnational governments now enjoy much greater leeway in contacting their counterparts in other countries and establishing direct contacts with the Commission (Vickerman, 1990).

With the elimination of national boundaries as barriers to the free flow of goods, services, individuals and capital, national frontiers have declined as impediments to intergovernmental cooperation among member institutions. What has been considered in the past by national governments as 'foreign-policy' initiatives (that is, contacts among subnational units geographically located in different nation-states) have now been transformed into 'internal' policy, given that national boundaries have been eliminated as impediments to economic interaction and policy making.[1]

The implications of such a change is to enable subnational governmental units to cooperate not only along an expanded vertical linkage track (national government-to-region) but also along a horizontal one (region-to-region) (Leonardi and Nanetti, 1990). The opportunity of conducting horizontal operations is actively pursued by the Commission in its experimentation with pilot projects within and outside the CSFs. The primary objective of these projects is to define a new mode of behaviour and orientation that stresses the importance of EU-wide rather than individual national market orientation and target as the necessary reference points for the planning of firm investment, production and marketing strategies.

The shift from a national to an EU frame of reference for economic and social policy making by public as well as private institutions has been a basic component of European policy making since the initiation of the 1992 programme (Grahl and Teague, 1990; Crouch and Marquand, 1990; Cutler *et al.*, 1989). What has yet to be understood fully is that the change in perspective and opportunities introduced by the Single Market requires new policy instruments and structures. The Maastricht Treaty has tried to answer some of the macro political and institutional exigencies raised by the Single Market, but the other institutional requirements of the Single Market – the micro- and meso-level responses – have been formulated only on an ad hoc basis through the adoption of a network approach to policy making and implementation.

The need to reformulate our thinking according to the new premises of European union is particularly necessary if the goal of economic and social cohesion is to be pursued with conviction and the dynamics of convergence sustained by adequate policies. The realisation of the internal market permits, first of all, the EU to devise regional development policies that provide additionality to national regional-development efforts. Secondly, it creates the basis for European-wide interactions by individuals, enterprises, development agencies and subnational governments in the implementation of economic and social policies.[2] Thirdly, it allows new economic markets to emerge. Regions in contiguous geographic areas are now free to formulate and administer policies together, aid the forging of contacts between entrepreneurs and sectoral associations operating in the same sector but in different national and regional contexts, and increase the capacity of local and regional authorities concerned with economic development to evolve new policy responses to economic challenges emerging from within as well as from outside the EU.[3]

An essential part in determining the success of subnational institutions' response to the demand for new linkages and approaches to policy making will be based on the nature of the current linkage networks existing at the intra- and interregional level, bringing together subnational institutions with private groups and interests present in society.

Based on previous work carried out on the links between regional institutions and economic development,[4] the present analysis is based on five assumptions. The first is that regional forms of collective action (for example political institutions, administrative structures, and trade and voluntary associations) *do* have a role to play in the promotion of positive economic outcomes (North, 1991). Research on regional institutional performance in Italy has shown that subnational governments, social organisations and economic associations are important in mobilising autonomous and self-sustaining forces for local development.

The second assumption is that institutions can learn from their previous successes or failures in developing responses to new problems – that is, that there is an institutional learning process or feedback mechanism that allows lessons to be learned from pilot schemes. What is learned from the policy experiments can be fed into a new policy process that is capable of correcting the approaches, structures and content of previous policies. Evidence supporting this assumption is provided by longitudinal case studies on how regions in Italy – for example Friuli–Venezia Giulia, Emilia–Romagna, Tuscany and Sicily – have responded to policy and institutional challenges originating from within and outside the region and how these lessons have been transmitted to other regions facing similar problems.[5]

The third assumption is that regions have the capacity to react to problems and can seek solutions at appropriate institutional levels. In the case of post-1992 Europe, the appropriate level for the resolution of problems is increasingly identified as the EU.[6] Cross-frontier and transregional cooperation constitutes a new prospect for EU activity, and a number of projects focusing on the forging of cross-border links are now underway (Cappellin, 1993; CEC, 1989).

The fourth assumption is that a successful creation of transregional networks will be enhanced if regions already have operational network systems at the subregional level. The link between formal and voluntary institutions on the one hand, and regional and subregional networks on the other, is part of an overall conceptualisation of development that considers functional governmental institutions as a form of 'institutional infrastructure', or 'institutional capital', and an important element in determining economic and social outcomes.

The final assumption is that the greater the density (number) and differentiation (variety) of networks, the greater the capacity of the regional socioeconomic system to respond to crisis and develop alternative policy responses. Networks in this conception operate as facilitators of policy making and, especially, policy implementation. The more networks there are, the more individual actors are linked up to the policy-making and implementation process.

The argument behind the last two assumptions is that, just as a basic necessity of economic development is the existence of a well-developed infrastructure to facilitate economic interaction – roads, telecommunications, waterways and so on – the development of diffused forms of small and medium-sized enterprises and entrepreneurship requires the existence of a well-developed institutional infrastructure.[7] 'Institutional infrastructure' can be conceived as a series of interlocking institutions, ad hoc structures, relationships and agreements for collective action. One of the essential elements in the scheme is the existence of effective regional and local government authorities (in other words, in both their political and administrative manifestations) with the capacity to stimulate the development of informal and formal structures – that is, networks – for collective action in the pursuit of development goals.

NETWORKS AND INSTITUTIONAL INFRASTRUCTURE

The concept of network is used here to differentiate the notion of institutional infrastructure from that of formal organisations. The existence of formal organisations at various levels of decision making and policy implementation is an essential part of creating a functioning network system at the local level. But formal organisations do not exhaust the requirements for the existence of networks. Formal subnational institutions represent one but not necessarily all of the conditions required for the mobilisation of diffused forms of growth and the proliferation of differentiated and dense network structures.

For adequate institutional infrastructures to exist as a motor for local and regional economic development beyond the stage of economic take-off, formal subnational governmental organisations need to be supplemented by a series of less formal arrangements – ranging from ad hoc, temporary agreements to more structured alliances that continue over time – for the purposes of organising collective action.[8] The concept of network allows us to discuss collective action conducted through various levels of formal and informal organisations.

Existing regional networks serve as the basis for interactions in policy making and implementation between private social and economic groups and associations for the purpose of creating policy-making and implementation networks. The nurturing and consolidation of such networking systems is seen as increasingly important in the face of the substantial growth in the role of 'micro' (employing 0 to 9 workers) and small and medium-sized (from 10 to 499 workers) enterprises in accounting for the increases in new entrepreneurship and employment. According to the EC's survey of enterprises (CEC, 1990a), in 1986 micro and small to medium-sized companies accounted, respectively, for 27 per cent and 45 per cent – or an overall total of 72 per cent – of EC employment and an overwhelming 99.9 per cent of all enterprises in the EC. Under these circumstances it is vital that these micro, small and medium-sized enterprises participate in a networking system in order to overcome the limitations imposed by their lack of size, resources and geographic position in making full use of the potentials provided by the internal market.[9]

Our conception of subregional networks is based on the view that learning from experiences with networks is transitive in nature – that is, what is learned at one level or one network system can be applied in another network or level of interaction. For example networks can (and do) exist and operate at the *intraregional* as well as *interregional* and *transregional* levels. Intraregional (within one region) networks are common in consolidated regional systems, while interregional (within one national territory) networks are less common given the relatively recent history of regionalised nation-states where the state–region relationship has continued to dominate the region-to-region one.

What is a completely new phenomenon is the existence of transregional networks founded on the basis of agreements among entities located in diverse nation-states. The territorial scope of the network (that is, whether it remains within national borders or not) does not change its nature or structure. Networks can vary in size and in the level at which they operate. Basically networks are flexible systems permitting the interaction of discrete institutions, groups and individuals to achieve a common goal.

The flexibility of networks constitutes the basis for our argument that previous experience with subregional networks greatly facilitates the task of creating, participating in and sustaining new transregional networks. Experience of and success in networking at one level can be used by political institutions and organised groups in society as a resource base to engage in networking at other levels. From this perspective, networks constitute more than formal agreements to cooperate. They also represent a general outlook and a propensity to act in a particular manner to achieve a collective good.

Networks are based on the existence of fundamental equality among the participants, and they are inherently voluntary in nature. Participation in networks cannot be decreed, nor can it be based on force. The will to participate must come from a basic entrepreneurial approach by the regional government toward economic development problems and the shared conception that network schemes serve as a useful tool in achieving economic and institutional goals.

In existing network systems studied at the intraregional level, the interaction between public institutions and the private sector is seen by the participants as a two-way relationship in which the region is not only the mediator for the payment of governmental subsidies and the administrator of transfer payments, but also the initiator of development policies in supplementing or filling in where national (and increasingly EU) initiatives are not forthcoming or are inadequate in relation to local exigencies. The concept of the region as an institutional 'entrepreneur' participating in a proactive manner in regional socioeconomic development has yet to be fully taken into account by EU regional and sectoral policy makers, even though the Commission has constantly reiterated its support for mixed public–private initiatives. Taking a proactive stance on the issue of development is one example of voluntary action by the region that some might argue is beyond its statutory responsibilities and an invasion of the realm that should be left exclusively to the private sector. We would argue, however, that in post-industrial economies the lines separating the public and private sector and the responsibilities of public authorities for economic and social outcomes have become blurred and need to be redefined in light of pragmatic exigencies rather than legal or philosophical tracts.

The concept of the region as entrepreneur is based on the *a priori* existence of a private–public partnership and an ethic for the pursuit of economic and social development as a common good that is definable and can be acted upon at the regional level. According to the notion of regional development as a product of conscious public policy, the role of the private sector is to concentrate on the productive and distributive phases of the economic process, while that of the public sector is to mobilise collective goods – such as social services, investment projects and policy planning. In addition, both sides of the institutional divide are interested in developing and maintaining the national and international competitive edge of local production units through public policies that aid in the continuous reexamination of products, markets and productive structure.

We would hypothesise that where public–private networks and common-good orientations are missing, balanced and diffused forms of economic development have difficulty in materialising. There is, instead, growth of alternative forms and models of economic development. In many cases we have seen growth in dependence on strategies that have been determined outside the immediate regional territory. In the past this has meant that development schemes have been formulated, financed and administered by central state authorities. The logic of the centralised model emphasises centralised sources of capital investment, economic infrastructure projects, industrial plants with high levels of capital investment, and public administration as the primary sources of non-agricultural employment, with centralised transfer payments as the primary method of maintaining standards of living and employment. Another way of expressing this relationship is in terms of the 'distance' between policy-making centres in the system. The existence of networks is based on policy-making bodies achieving 'institutional autonomy', which permits policy initiatives to surface from the subnational level. Institutions that are not able to sustain the creation of networks must, by definition, seek to remain close to or dependent on their source of vital resources, such as finance, legal adjudication and the political power provided by central government elites, administration and policy-making structures.[10]

Dependence on central government for economic policy and transfer payments is one of the major differences separating larger from smaller member-states in Objective 1 areas. The latter still depend to a great extent on centralised administrative structures while the former have moved to more decentralised forms of decision making and administration. We are not arguing that the role of centralised authorities may be counterproductive to development in underdeveloped areas. Rather we are postulating the possibility that the decentralisation of decision making power and resources to the subnational level may make a positive contribution to local development above and beyond what is added in terms of expenditure on running a new tier of government. The encouragement of local and regional government initiatives in favour of the local economy helps to stimulate the evolution of a regional networking pattern capable of making an additional contribution to sustaining and even accelerating regional economic development.

Institutional decentralisation and policy-making autonomy are two of the necessary components in launching an intensive system of regional networking. First of all, it is much easier to mobilise a region's socioeconomic forces through decentralised political structures. In centralised systems the mobilisation imperative is left to members of the public administration or to private political forces such as political parties and semi-public interest groups and sectoral associations, as is illustrated by the cases of Greece, Ireland and Portugal. In decentralised systems there is a greater chance of interplay between public institutions and private groups on the basis of functional specialisation and mutual interest. The cases of France, Germany, Italy and Spain demonstrate that the role played by public officials operating within autonomous political institutions is quite important in forging links between institutions and socioeconomic forces for the pursuit of collective interests in a planned and transparent manner.

The current system of networking that links regional institutions and social and economic groups in the EU's more developed regions is not based on the subordination of either the groups to the institutions or the public institutions to the groups. It is, instead, based on an autonomous and mutually reinforcing relationship where the different but complementary needs of the participants in the network are met. From the regional perspective, the regional government achieves a much greater penetration of the socioeconomic fabric of society and higher levels of political mobilisation by operating through its networks with socioeconomic groups. The groups are, in turn, given access on an organised and predictable basis to public decision making and resource allocation. Thus it is in the interest of all the participants to consolidate, perpetuate and even expand the network.[11]

While the mutual advantages of an intraregional network bringing together regional governments and interest groups are readily apparent, what are the advantages of interregional and transregional networks? The advantages accruing from inter- and transregional networks are similar in nature. Networks in both cases allow regions to achieve certain goals that could not be achieved if they were to act on their own. Cappellin (1993) has argued that regional cooperation permits regions, as geographic and economic expressions, to achieve six distinct goals. Three of these goals apply equally to inter- and transregional cooperation as we have defined the concept in this report. The three advantages are: (1) the achievement of economies of scale not possible through the development on an individual basis of infrastructures, research, development, services and so on in order to overcome size thresholds; (2) the joint use of common resources (for example rivers, sea, forests and so on) in order to avoid the creation of external diseconomies such as air and water pollution; and (3) the common use and development of geo-economic systems in order to build higher levels of interaction among regions sharing a common border or geographic territory.

The other three advantages initially apply to more explicitly transregional cooperation networks that attempt to overcome the limitations imposed by national borders as traditional barriers to the free flow of goods, services, capital and people between regions existing within different nation-states. These three advantages are: (1) a reduction in 'transaction costs', which in the past have raised the cost of doing business across national frontiers; (2) avoidance of economic conflict and retaliatory measures that limit the size and scope of mutual development; and (3) an increase in regional decision-making autonomy from national authorities. All six goals provide a positive stimulus from the region's point of view in the planning and realisation of networks at the transregional level.

Having established the advantages of networking from the regions' point of view, why should the EU, a European-wide institution, be interested in promoting transregional networks? The current debate on political union demonstrates that the building of European institutions through reinforcement and consolidation of the legislative (providing legislative powers to the European Parliament) and executive (extending the scope and powers of the Commission) powers will take a long time. As discussed in Chapter 1, the process of institution building has been a gradual one, and the evolution of adequate administrative structures to handle the growing responsibilities for sectoral policies is still under discussion. It seems quite reasonable to predict that the creation of an extensive European bureaucracy will be a long-term rather than a short-term endeavour. Therefore the Commission faces the problem of administering policies devoid of a territorially based administrative apparatus.

The use of networks solves part of this problem by making EU policies as self-administering as possible. Managing policies through networks:

1. Requires a minimal amount of administrative input by the Commission.
2. Takes advantage of networks that reach down to the grassroots level without requiring the intermediation of national administrative structures.
3. Provides direct contact with the 'active socioeconomic forces' operating at the local level.
4. Allows operation on a Union-wide basis.
5. Allows expansion in response to increased demands for participation from new areas and sectors.
6. Provides the possibility of monitoring the progress of programmes on a continuous and efficacious basis.
7. Does not threaten any of the institutional actors present at the national or local level.
8. Provides a positive stimulus to reorient the views and frames of reference of local actors away from local and national perspectives to a more European perspective.
9. Allows flexibility by adding on to the network structure additional responsibilities and/or a greater complexity of procedures and structures in policy making and implementation as required.

In sum, networks are the ideal instrument for a gradual, piecemeal approach to the creation of a European policy-making community given the lack of a territorial administrative structure.

What, however, does the entrepreneur gain by operating through a network system? The answer is provided by identifying what is transmitted through the linkage structure in the simplest kind of intraregional network. First of all, a linkage system provides information on the regional economy by identifying where skills are located, where complementary productive capacity can be organised, where credit can be accessed and under what kinds of advantageous conditions, and what the overall plans of the governmental organs are regarding the development of infrastructure, investments and productive capacity. Secondly, a network system provides services that are valuable not only for the management of an enterprise but also in keeping up with market and technological trends. Thirdly, a network system provides intermediation at the political level to enter new markets, broader horizons and establish new ventures. As discussed above, participation in a network and taking advantage of the opportunities it offers to disseminate information on markets, opportunities, skills, specialisations and so on provides the entrepreneur with the opportunity to specialise his output for a particular market niche and achieve an external economy of scale through the operations of the network. In a modern economy operating in a highly competitive market, networks can become indispensable mechanisms for the organisation of information, production, and distribution, and be important in determining the success and survival of the enterprise in a competitive environment.

THE OPERATIONALISATION OF NETWORKS

Having described the reason why networks exist and the positive contribution they can make to policy making and implementation in the EU, we must now define networks and analyze how they have been operationalised in the past. What we need to know is how to distinguish empirically between the different types of network that exist in the real world – that is, within the EU, within nation-states and within regions. Our consideration of networking within the EU is based on a definition of network that contains at least some minimal criteria.[12]

The minimum elements for a network to exist, as expressed in graph theory, are the presence of 'objects' or 'nodes' in the system – for example points on a graph – and 'relationships' – for example lines joining those points. Networks exist when more than two points are connected, and the points must be fairly equal in nature. Hierarchical institutions or relationships existing within formal administrative structures would not constitute networks in the manner being used here. In our most obvious case of transregional networking, the objects being networked are regional or other local-government institutions operating on an equal basis, and the relationships consist of formal agreements to cooperate in the pursuit of common policy objectives.

The type of policy networks that are of interest here are those that can provide a potential contribution to the Commission's policy-planning and implementation process, and these in our opinion must contain six basic elements:

1. Public institutions and private firms to serve as the basis for the network system.
2. The content or interactive form of the linkage connecting the objects in the network should be provided by a specific policy.
3. The policy area covered or the environment within which the network operates should use resources made available through a Commission initiative.
4. The territory over which the network operates should cover the regions and member states.
5. The timespan over which the network remains operative should be defined in the programmes that set up the network.
6. A shared, repeated, routinised and predictable set of behaviour among members over time.

Putting these elements together, we can define a policy network within the EU as an agreement for collective action based on a common set of objectives, resources and instruments for the purpose of planning and managing a service, product or sector within a defined territorial space.

From this perspective, transregional networks are an agreement operationalised through a series of relationships that permits the subjects (for example regional institutions) to take action and be involved in determining decisions and implementing policies outside their immediate territorial jurisdiction. Thus, if a network is to become operative and institutionalised on a European-wide basis, it is important to determine: (a) its level of institutionalisation (is it just a temporary agreement to act in unison or a contract and institution created to decide and implement action over time?); (b) its territorial presence (how many regions are involved and how are they connected to other levels of government?); and (c) its reach (is it a mono- or multi-sectoral in nature?) In the post-1992 EU context regional networks can operate throughout the territory of the twelve member states, but in practice the territorial presence of the network will be defined by its membership, scope and capacity to undertake effective policy making and implementation.

The second important element to be considered in discussing networks is the potential pool of members or actors capable of being effectively involved in the operation of a particular network. If we look at the existing ad hoc network systems that have sprung up spontaneously in the EU to deal with the co-ordination of law-enforcement issues or the cooperation among national air pilots associations, businesses and trade unions – we see that networks can be created to involve a wide variety of subjects, ranging from individuals and firms to voluntary groups and governmental units.

Despite the large number of potential areas where networks can provide a positive input into the policy-making and implementation process, they are still limited in number. Existing EU programmes such as Europartnership, BC-NET, LEDA and others already constitute explicit network systems linking individuals and entities throughout the EU. However these networks are limited in a number of other dimensions. The density and variety of subjects involved are low in comparison with the potential pool of actors present in the twelve member states, and the spread of territory effectively covered by the programmes is still restricted (CEC, 1990c).

In addition to being sparse, current EU networks are not yet sufficiently diverse in terms of function or level of operation to meet the policy implementation needs of the EU. Each network tends to operate at one level, sector or type of participant, and the impact that it has on effectively reorienting individual and institutional decisions and plans is still low. In fact the present approach to networking relegates the Commission-initiated networks mainly to the role of supplying information, creating communication links and bringing entrepreneurs together. The dynamic generated by the operation of the Single Market requires the Commission to reconsider its role in the management of economic policy at the European level and take a more active and direct part in the operation of networks.

The third element characterising networks is the nature of the interaction. This interaction can be limited to exchange of information or can extend all the way up to the joint management of important policy sectors.

The US and Canada supply a number of examples of multiregional agencies for the management of services and resources and are involved in complex activities covering both private and public sector. One of the more interesting aspects of comparative work on subnational institutions inside and outside Europe is the extraordinary similarities in the pattern of responses to social-welfare and economic-growth policies formulated by local and regional governments. In a number of cases, what one observes taking place in Europe is also underway in federal political institutions in other decentralised institutional and political settings in North America and Asia. Take, for example, the two most striking innovations experienced by subnational government in Europe from the early 1970s: institution building and local government as a vital economic actor. Today we see European subnational governments facing a changing reality that closely parallels developments noted by scholars of Canadian federalism in the 1960s: growth in the size, power and scope of provincial governments in response to the exigencies associated with the evolution of the Canadian welfare state and the growing involvement of provincial governments with issues of economic development (Black and Caims, 1966). The concept was labelled by Canadian scholars as 'province building'.

In a survey of the literature, Young, Faucher and Blois (1984) discuss the process of province building in a manner that closely resembles what happened at the subnational level in Europe in the 1970s and 1980s. The authors write:

Provincial bureaucracies have grown enormously in size and competence; not only are they essential tools of provincial politicians, but their own interests also favor expanded, activist states. Increased revenues and new capabilities of policy-making and co-ordination have enabled surer management of socioeconomic change. Hence, provincial states have grown in capacity to serve provincial interests – or to shape them (p. 784).

Networking in Europe can be seen as a first informal step toward the creation of formal, institutionalised arrangements in the form of European agencies and institutions capable of tackling economic and social problems from an EU perspective. Accordingly, networks organised on a transregional basis would be in a position to assume policy initiatives, formulate programmes for intervention, mobilise resources, administer programmes, and conduct programme supervision and verification on an EU-wide basis and as an alternative to the creation of separate national agencies.

Finally, networks can be designed to resolve specific problems not capable of being managed by hierarchical, centralised institutions and structures. Once the initial problem is resolved, the network can, in fact, move on to cover other spheres of activity. This was the case with the Tennessee Valley Authority, which went from its initial task of land reclamation and flood control to the production of atomic energy. As a consequence networks can be seen as flexible policy-making and administration structures that evolve over time in response to the shifting needs of the participants and territory in which they operate.

In the changing institutional structure of the post-Maastricht EU, networks can also be seen as 'pre-institutions' or stepping stones on the way to reassembling institutions above and beyond the present boundaries drawn by the nation-state. One of the rationales behind the Commission's present experimentation with area-wide networks is that regional networks will help fill the institutional vacuum that will develop once nation-states lose their exclusive rights over the activities of subnational political, economic and social institutions. The next chapter will look at how networks can be classified and how they have been operationalised in the EU.

NOTES

1. At the end of 1993 the Italian government informed the regions that they no longer needed to request permission to organise visits to Brussels, nor when contacting other regions in the EU and in 1994 the regions were given permission to set up their own offices in Brussels. With the creation of the Committee of Regions formal as well as informal contacts among EU regions and local authorities have become institutionalised and part of the day-to-day business of the Committee.

2. A case in point here is the need to go beyond the nationally oriented networking arrangements found in national vocational programmes, such as the JET network in France, and in new EU-oriented networks such as PETRA. See CEC (1990b) and CEC (1991).

3. Although we do accept the notion advanced by the Cecchini Report (1988) that the creation of the Single Market will represent a net economic benefit for citizens as well as entrepreneurs, we are not completely convinced that the main benefit of the internal market will be derived from the encouragement of economies of scale *within* the corporation and greater access to information (Siebert, 1989). The position advanced in this chapter is that the realisation of the Single Market, coupled with an active programme of networking, will help achieve economies of scale *external* to the enterprise but internal to the network that becomes the crucial determinant in the production and information network to which the enterprise belongs (Owen, 1983).

4. See Leonardi and Garmise, 1993; Putnam, Leonardi and Nanetti, 1985; Leonardi and Nanetti, 1994.

5. See Bartole and Agnelli, 1989; Leonardi and Nanetti, 1990, 1994; Regione Siciliana, 1990.

6. See the results of the EUI conference (1989) and Cappellin and Batey (1993).

7. See the model developed by Nanetti (1988). Past studies (for example PA Cambridge Economic Consultants, 1989) have shown that lack of adequate economic infrastructure operates as a constraint on the realisation of competitiveness (reduction of costs to a minimum), access to outside markets, expansion in the levels of production and employment, and maximisation of profit margins. The argument presented by Becattini (1994) and Dei Ottati (1994) is that the creation and functioning of industrial districts in Tuscany is based on the sum of functioning formal and informal networks.

8. For a discussion of the theoretical elements of collective action, see Putnam, Leonardi and Nanetti, 1993, pp. 163–7.

9. The EC study shows that large enterprises with over 500 employees account for a majority of employment in the three sectors dominated by public utilities and state enterprises: energy and water (73 per cent), mineral and chemical (57 per cent) and transport and communication (51 per cent). In metal manufacture and other manufacturing sectors the percentage of employees working in large industries is respectively 49 per cent and 30 per cent (CEC, 1990a, Table 3.3). Size and availability of resources provide large corporations with the ability

to develop their own industrial networks outside the institutional contexts provided by local and regional governments.

10. See Putnam, Leonardi, Nanetti and Pavoncello, 1984; Israel, 1987.
11. Neocorporate arrangements cannot be considered a type of network
    because the relationship is hierarchical and depends on the role of
    the state to codify the resulting decisions and implement them through
    the existing legal and administrative structures.
12. For a preliminary discussion of network theory in the study of social
    and political phenomena, see Berkowitz, 1982, and Knoke, 1990.

REFERENCES

Adonis, A. and S. Jones (1991) 'Subsidiarity and the Community's Constitutional Future', Discussion Paper No. 2, Centre for European Studies,
Nuffield College, Oxford.

Bartole, A. and A. Agnelli (eds) (1989) *Friuli-Venezia Giulia: Vent'anni di
regionalismo* (Bologna, Il Mulino).

Becattini, G. (1994) 'The development of light industry in Tuscany: an interpretation' in R. Leonardi and R. Y. Nanetti (eds) *Regional Development
in a Modern European Economy: The Case of Tuscany* (London: Pinter),
pp. 69–85.

Bellini, N., M. G. Giordani and F. Pasquini (1990) 'The Industrial Policy of
Emilia-Romagna: The Business Service Centres', in R. Leonardi and R. Y.
Nanetti (eds), *The Regions and European Integration: The Case of Emilia-
Romagna* (London, Pinter), pp. 171–86.

Berkowitz, S. D. (1982) *An Introduction to Structural Analysis: The Network
Approach to Social Research* (Toronto: Butterworths).

Black, E. R. and A. C. Caims (1966) 'A Different Perspective on Canadian
Federalism', *Canadian Public Administration*, vol. 9, pp. 27–47.

Cappellin, R. (1993) 'Patterns and Policies of Regional Economic Development and Cohesion among the Regions of the European Community' in
R. Leonardi *The State of Economic and Social Cohesion in the Community Prior
to the Creation of the Single Market: The View from the Bottom-Up* (Brussels:
Commission of the European Communities), chapter 3.

Cappellin, R. and P. W. Batey (eds) (1993) *Regional Networks, Border Regions
and European Integration* (London: Pion Limited).

CEC (1989) *Guide to the Reform of the Structural Funds* (Luxembourg: Office
for Official Publications of the European Communities).

CEC (1991) 'COMETT I: Final Report of the Commission (1986–1990),
SEC(91) 1016 final, Brussels, 7 June.

CEC (1990a) 'Enterprises in the European Community' (Luxembourg,
Office for Official Publications of the European Communities).

CEC (1990b) 'BC-NET Activity Report: Results and assessment of the experimental phase', COM (90) 476 final, Brussels, 18 October.

CEC (1990c) *EC Research Funding*, 2nd edition (Luxembourg: Office for
Official Publications of the European Communities).

Cecchini, P. (1988) *1992: The European Challenge* (Aldershot: Gower).

Corradi, S. (1991) *Erasmus, Comett, Lingua, Tempus: Educazione permanente e formazione universitaria internazionale* (Milan, Franco Angeli).

Crouch, C. and D. Marquand (eds) (1990) *The Politics of 1992: Beyond the Single European Market* (Oxford: Basil Blackwell).

Cutler, T. *et al.* (1989) *1992 – The Struggle for Europe* (Oxford: Berg).

Dei Ottati, G. (1994) 'Prato and its evolution in a European context' in R. Leonardi and R. Y. Nanetti (eds) *Regional Development in a Modern European Economy: The case of Tuscany* (London: Pinter), pp. 116–44.

EUI (1989) 'Trans-Border Cooperation in Europe', Conference held at the European University Institute, Florence, 4–5 June.

Grahl, J. and P. Teague (1990) *1992 The Big Market: The Future of the European Community* (London, Lawrence & Wishart).

Hufbauer, G. C. (ed.) (1990) *Europe 1992* (Washington, DC: Brookings Institution).

IFAPLAN (1990) 'PETRA Yearbook 1990' (Brussels, July).

Israel, A. (1987) *Institutional Development: Incentives to Performance* (Baltimore: Johns Hopkins University Press).

Knoke, D. (1990) *Political Networks: The Structural Perspective* (Cambridge: Cambridge University Press).

Leonardi, R. and S. Garmise (1993) 'Conclusions: Subnational Elites and the European Community' in R. Leonardi (ed.), *The Regions and the European Community: The Regional Response to the Single Market in the Underdeveloped Areas* (London: Frank Cass), pp. 247–74.

Leonardi, R. and R. Y. Nanetti (eds) (1990) *The Regions and European Integration: The Case of Emilia-Romagna* (London: Pinter).

Leonardi, R. and R. Y. Nanetti (eds) (1994) *Regional Development in a Modern European Economy: The Case of Tuscany* (London: Pinter).

Nanetti, R. Y. (1988) *Growth and Territorial Policies: The Italian Model of Social Capitalism* (London: Pinter).

North, D. C. (1991) *Institutions, Institutional Change and Economic Performance* (Cambridge: Cambridge University Press).

Owen, N. (1983) *Economies of Scale, Competition and Trade Patterns within the EC* (Oxford: Clarendon Press).

PA Cambridge Economic Consultants (1989) 'The Efficiency of Regional Policy in Member Countries of the European Community', mimeo, Cambridge.

Peters, G. (1992) 'Politics and Institutions in the EC', in A. Sgragia (ed.), *Euro-Politics: Institutions and Policymaking in the 'New' European Community* (Washington, DC: Brookings Institution), pp. 75–122.

Putnam, R. D., R. Leonardi and R. Y. Nanetti (1985) *La pianta e le radici: Il radicamento delle regioni nel sistema politico italiano* (Bologna: Il Mulino).

Putnam, R. D., R. Leonardi and R. Y. Nanetti (1993) *Making Democracy Work: Civic Traditions in Modern Italy* (Princeton: Princeton University Press).

Putnam, R. D., R. Leonardi, R. Y. Nanetti and F. Pavoncello (1984) 'Explaining Institutional Success: The Case of Italian Regional Government', *American Political Science Review* (March), pp. 55–74.

Regione Sicilia (1990) 'Quadro strategico di sviluppo', Palermo, mimeo.

Siebert, H. (ed.) (1989) 'The Completion of the Internal Market: Symposium 1989', mimeo, Kiel Institute of World Economics, Kiel, Germany.

Young, R. A., P. Faucher and A. Blois (1984) 'The Concept of Province Building: A Critique', *Canadian Journal of Political Science*, vol. 23, pp. 783–818.

Vickerman, R. (1990) 'Regional Implications of the Single Market', *Built Environment*, pp. 5–10.

9 Network Engineering in the European Union

FORMS OF LINKAGE NETWORKS

As defined in the previous chapter, networks are interactive systems that create relationships and constitute the basis for collective action across a variety of institutional levels and economic sectors. One of the fundamental aspects of our discussion of the change in the post-1992 institutional structure is the role played by networks in bringing together network actors (individuals, institutions, associations and so on) who find themselves in different geographic, sectoral and institutional settings. The territorial scope of the network is of fundamental importance because the potential for networking on an EU-wide basis is considerably enhanced by the creation of the Single Market. In this chapter we will discuss the outlines of the models that can be used to analyse the scope and content of European networks, and the chapter will conclude with a classification of existing network systems and the role that they can assume in the Maastricht phase of European development.

Figure 9.1 and Box 9.1 present the three (intra-, inter- and transregional) network systems discussed at length in Chapter 8. At the present time, extensive networking systems can be found at the intraregional and interregional levels, but the ones existing at the transregional level are dependent on decisive EU action, and this has been present only since 1990. The three systems of networking require different levels of commitment and sophistication, and the ability to network is unevenly distributed among regions and local governments within the EU.

Figure 9.1 describes the component parts of the regional structure that can be linked into the three network systems. The figure is composed of columns and rows defining the essential parts of the regional system. The three vertical columns define the legal status, organisational level and nature of network activity. The horizontal rows represent the different levels of complexity of the network: from the individual to the

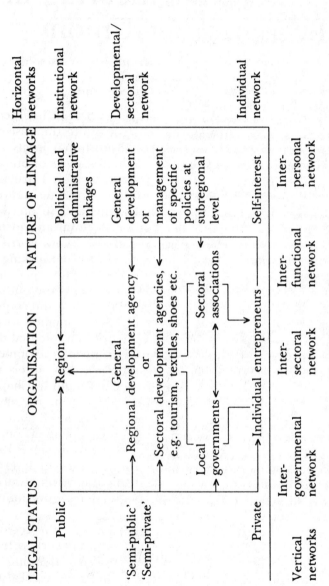

Figure 9.1 Component parts of the intraregional network systems

Box 9.1   Distinction between vertical and horizontal networks;
and definition of regional networks

Definition of vertical networks

1. *Intergovernmental networks* – governmental institutions at various levels of the regional system.
2. *Intersectoral networks* – interest groups and associations operating at various levels.
3. *Interfunctional networks* – governments, sectors, development agencies, and individuals at all levels of the system.
4. *Interpersonal networks* – individuals of diverse organisational, economic and social status.

Definition of horizontal networks

1. *Governmental networks* – governments at same institutional level, but operating in a different geographical space.
2. *Sectoral networks* – interest groups and associations at the same organisational level but in a different geographic space.
3. *Individual networks* – individuals operating at the micro level on the basis of interpersonal relationships.

Definition of regional networks developing in the EU

1. *Intraregional networks* – based on the existence of policy-making structures at the regional level, demands to participate on the part of socioeconomic groups, and the conception of policy making as 'governance' on the part of those participating.
2. *Interregional networks* – based on an intergovernmental policy-making and implementation process bringing together national and regional governments.
3. *Transregional networks* – based on the existence of a single market and the underpinning of EU policies with the principles of subsidiarity, and social and economic cohesion.

---

semi-public/semi-private level and all the way up to the regional government level. Box 9.1, on the other hand, presents the three basic types of horizontal and vertical linkages that can be established by linking the component parts presented in Figure 9.1.

The left-hand column in Figure 9.1 distinguishes between the legal bases of the operating structure (that is, between public and private law). In most cases, apart from those in regional and local government institutions, the actors engaged in networking operate under the provisions of private law. In the second column the items listed differentiate the different types of organisation involved in the network structure. Where regional governments exist, they operate as the overall umbrella organisation that assumes responsibility, in accordance with constitutional and legal provisions, for the formulation and implementation of development policies.

From the perspective of networking as well as from day-to-day experience, regional governments operate both as initiators of networks in penetrating the surrounding socioeconomic fabric and as the target of networking by interest groups and individuals interested in accessing the public policy-making process and gaining influence over the distribution of public resources. We have seen in the case of the three small and centralised member states of Ireland, Portugal and Greece that where regional governments are absent the networking system has a weak intraregional character and is structured on a more national basis. This local–central link is in many ways characteristic of the classical centre–periphery relationship, in strong centralised states.

The lack of regional governments instils a greater focus on national systems in which the distance (expressed in territorial and institutional terms) between the network nodes is much greater, the density of network systems at the subnational level is lower, and there is a lower level of interaction among the subnational network nodes. Networks therefore not only facilitate the interaction of nodes located in different territorial space, but may in fact also promote the interaction of nodes operating in the same territory.

In centralised states the emphasis of the linkage system is on the importance of vertical rather than horizontal linkages. Consequently the dynamic of the centre–periphery model is focused more on an unequal one-to-one relationship (a local actor interacting with a central one) than on a more equal all-to-one (a multiplicity of local actors interacting with one central actor) or an all-to-all (local actors interacting with each other with a minimal awareness of the central actor) relationship. The EU's choice of the latter (all-to-all, and to a limited extent all-to-one) structure as the basis of its networking strategy services move it clearly away from the confines of the unequal one-to-one, centralised model that is prevalent in centre–periphery relationships.

The existence of regional development agencies is encouraged when governments at the national, regional and local levels are in a position to assume political responsibility for economic and social development. However, apart from the management of administrative functions, governments in Europe have not been willing to delegate the promotion of economic development to regional officials or administrations. Instead the task has been allocated to formalised or ad hoc regional and local development agencies, sectoral associations and territorial organs responsible for overseeing economic enterprises in a specific geographic location, such as chambers of commerce, tourism agencies and so on. In most instances these agencies are created by the public sector with support from the private sector (Yuill, 1982).

Development agencies with multiple functions (for example chambers of commerce) tend to emphasise representation as their primary function, while single-function agencies (for example tourism agencies) develop a greater market orientation. It is the latter type of agency that is likely to establish ties with associations and firms operating in the sector and become the catalyst in the creation of new ventures, ideas, products and services that are functional to the sector. The role of sectoral associations and local governments is important because they represent the intermediate level in the networking system that is capable of maintaining contact with the micro level (that is, the individual entrepreneur/citizen who operates as the 'nucleus' or the grass-roots operator of the regional linkage system) on the one hand, and institutional representatives responsible for the management of public policies on the other.

The row and column components of Figure 9.1 suggest that theoretically there are two basic components of networking. The first is the *horizontal* networking link, bringing together actors operating at the same level of the system, while the second is the *vertical* variety that connects nodes at different institutional/political levels. The former network system operates to link geographically equivalent organisations, individual firms, regional governments and sectoral associations residing in different geographic areas. The latter brings together organisations operating at different institutional levels, in different organisations, and even in different geographic areas but not in the same organisational/institutional structure. It is, in fact, this variety of networking that is very important in formulating networks as a method for organising productive sectors across local, regional and national boundaries.

TYPES OF NETWORK SYSTEM

Figure 9.1 lists four different types of vertical networking system that are found within regions: intergovernmental, intersectoral, interfunctional and interpersonal. Intergovernmental networks bring together various levels of the institutional structure, such as regions, provinces and communes, in order that they may coordinate their activities to achieve a common goal; this outside an hierarchical relationship by which lower-level institutions are subordinate in practical as well as legal terms to higher-level institutions. A case in point was the level of coordination built into the IMP programmes in Italy, France and, to a certain extent, Greece, which brought together the Commission, national governments and regional governments in an equal relationship for the purposes of implementing the programmes and specific measures at the local level.

Intersectoral networking is a common phenomenon among political parties and interest groups operating within one region. Farmers' groups meeting on a regular basis at various levels and in different locations with representatives of industry to coordinate their lobbying activities on, for example, the use of pesticides and chemical fertilisers is an example of intersectoral networking designed to maximise the impact of both groups on public decision making. Such lobbying has also become common at EU level in relation to R&D programmes, and in specific policy areas such as telecommunications.

Interfunctional networking brings together actors from various levels in the system to tackle common problems, for example regional governments, sectoral associations and individual actors. The IMP programmes and the CSFs have followed this course by assigning the task of administering the programmes at the regional level to coordination or administrative committees that meet formally every month but also keep in touch on a regular basis to resolve day-to-day issues arising from the implementation of the measures contained in the subprogrammes.

Interpersonal networks flourish where individuals are able to maximise their personal gains through joint action outside an established hierarchical procedure. Often the purpose of the network is to gain access to resources controlled by formal organisations such as governmental bodies. This is the nature of informal cliques and factions within highly structured organisations as well as interfirm agreements to pool resources to increase growth and profits.

While vertical networks bring together actors at different levels, horizontal networks represent the interaction of actors at the same level – be this institutional or sectoral. The networks at all three levels forge links between governments, sectors and individuals occupying the same organisational level but operating in different territorial spaces.

Having identified the general component parts of networks (and in particular those of intraregional networks), we can now turn to a consideration of the types of network that can evolve at the inter- and transregional levels through the interaction of vertical and horizontal networks. In the real world the two forms of network are not separate and distinct entities – they interconnect in a mutually self-sustaining manner.

It could be argued that horizontal networks are easier to establish and maintain than vertical ones. Interregional, horizontal networks are quite common in states with extensive experience of regional government. The best examples of interregional networks are provided by federal states such as Canada, the US and Germany, but they have also become a growing phenomenon in Italy and Spain. Adding a vertical component to networks tends to introduce hierarchy and bureaucratisation. Such a move can be counterproductive unless significant material incentives and procedures are introduced to guarantee the circulation of information, demands and decisions throughout the system.

Based on the ad hoc networking that has taken place so far

VERTICAL NETWORKS

HORIZONTAL NETWORKS	Inter-governmental	Inter-functional	Inter-sectoral	Inter-personal
Governmental	Macro	Macro	Macro	Micro
Sectoral	Macro	Meso	Meso	Micro
Individual	Micro	Micro	Micro	Micro

Governmental networks: 4 macro and 2 meso
Individual networks: 6 micro

Figure 9.2   Types of transregional networks

in federal and regionalist systems, we can identify three basic types of transregional networking that are evolving in the EU in response to the exigencies of the Single Market. The theoretical possibilities of meshing together vertical and horizontal networks is illustrated in Figure 9.2.

The first form of transregional system can be called 'macro' networking, whereby regional institutions are involved in formal relationships with institutionalised bodies at the regional level in other areas (that is, in other parts of the country or in other countries, such as regular consultative bodies bringing together regional officials). The Assembly of European Regions, which operated between 1988 and 1993 as an institutionalised macro transregional network in the same manner as the Governors' Conference in the US and the Conference of Regional Presidents in Italy, served to bring together subnational executives to discuss similar problems. Macro networks would also have a role to paly if the EU were to encourage the development of transregional authorities on the model of the New York Port Authority of the TVA, by combining intergovernmental, interfunctional and intersectoral networks and functions that link up with horizontal governmental and sectoral networks.[1]

The second type of transregional networking can be described as 'meso' networking, bringing together interest groups and associational organisations that share common goals and strategies and possess the ability to transform these into formal, institutionalised commitments. Moves in this direction have become increasingly common at the European level with the establishment of European groupings and associations so as more effectively to lobby the Commission and Council of Ministers. These networks have only an indirect governmental component through interfunctional networks. The emphasis here is obviously at the interest-group and sectoral-association level.

The last type of transregional networking can be labelled a 'micro' network. It is represented by interpersonal relationships where the bond among the participants is not their institutional or group affiliations but rather their personal ties and interests. Individuals participating in micro networks operate predominantly as isolated entities, even when they have an institutional role in governments or sectoral associations. Once the individuals who make up the network are removed, the network collapses or is subordinated to other individual interests. Micro networks are the easiest to create and may at times constitute the nucleus of future meso and macro networks. This is, in fact, the dominant characteristic of the present generation of networks in the EU.

THE ETHICS OF NETWORKS

The characteristics of transregional networks highlight the importance of the ethic that underpins the creation and operation of the network. Two forms of public-policy approaches can be distinguished: 'public oriented' and 'private oriented'. The former can be regarded as an approach oriented toward achieving broader, longer-term public goods while the latter is oriented toward more individualistic, short-term gains. Using this distinction to differentiate the dynamics of network systems, we have posited the association of the 'governance' ethic with macro and meso networks. Macro/meso networks originate from the initiative of regional governments and the predominant characteristic of the network is the importance of the relationship between governments and organised interests (development agencies and sectoral associations). The goals of governance networks correspond to 'collective objectives', such as regional development or optimising the use of public resources to benefit regional society. Thus the governance motivation is expected to emerge as the predominant one in macro and meso networks, which, according to the cells in Figure 9.2, correspond to six different mixes of networking systems.

The alternative ethical underpinning of networks emphasises the individualistic component of the network, which also accounts for six cells in Figure 9.2. What drives the individualistically oriented network is the calculation of individual gain and personal ties. Micro networks represent the interaction between the interpersonal, vertical networks and the horizontal, individual networks. These types of network tend to be quite common in societies and organisations where there is a large discrepancy between the elite at the top and the masses at the bottom of the hierarchical ladder, where regional institutions are not well institutionalised, and where subnational governments and sectoral associations are not independent of centralised sources of power and resources.[2]

In regions where the governance form of network persists, we have found that public officials emphasise their ties with organised groups and associations (frequent, policy-oriented meetings with group representatives) and exhibit a much lower interest in meeting individual citizens to distribute individual favours. Members of the governance-oriented networks tend to judge their success by policy outputs that meet stated organisational goals. In the individualistically oriented network system, success is judged by the extent to which the network assumes the outlines of a clientelistic apparatus founded on a dyadic relationship between the central actor – the patron – and the peripheral participants – the clients. Thus, in regions where individualistic networking predominates, regional officials report a sustained level of one-to-one contact and the need to constantly service individual requests to the detriment of group and collective-good-oriented requests. In the latter context, it is the individualistic network rather than the governance network that provides the greatest return to the participant, and the network tends to favour individual gains rather than group, institutional or collective goals.

Studies have shown that regions with strong political and institutional infrastructures possess a robust and active governance networking system, which links the regional level with interest groups operating at equivalent or lower levels (Dei Ottati, 1994; Putnam, Leonardi and Nanetti, 1993). In weak regions, on the other hand, there is a preponderance of clientelistic networks linking individuals to the institutions in the system. Evidence shows that there is a strong link between extensive, governance-oriented internal networks and high levels of institutional performance. In turn the latter is correlated with the traditional presence of strong mass organisations operating in the economic and social spheres. In fact the data strongly support the thesis that the presence of extensive intraregional networks is a prerequisite for public institutions to perform at high levels of efficiency and effectiveness in the production and distribution of public goods and services.

Piore and Sabel (1984) were among the first to understand that the industrial districts in the northern and central part of Italy are, in effect, linkage networks bringing together not only different manufacturers based on a horizontal division of labour, but also networks growing out of a partnership between local entrepreneurs and local and regional governments. In this regional configuration of networking, local governments provide industrial parks, social infrastructure (all-day schools, nurseries and day-care centres) and public infrastructure (roads, electrical hook-ups and so on), while regional governments provide the economically targeted professional education programmes, access to credit, and support services that are necessary for a diffused model of enterprise. In other words, diffused forms of enterprise based on small and medium-sized companies may arise or thrive where macro and meso networking exist across a variety of institutions and groups – that is, private as well as public institutions, groups and actors. From this perspective, the existence of regionally based and functioning macro and meso networks can be seen as prerequisites for the creation of territorially diffused, EU-wide network systems oriented toward promoting and consolidating small and medium-sized enterprise.

EU NETWORKS

Since the late 1980s the Commission has emphasised the role of networks in the implementation of its policies and programmes at the European level. These experiments have largely been focused on small and medium-sized enterprises, research and development, information and communication technologies, industrial technologies, biotechnologies, Structural Funds, and vocational and university-level education. Table 9.1 presents a non-exhaustive list of current EU-initiated networks according to date of initiation, the DG responsible, entities participating, the purpose of the programmes and the type (micro, meso, macro) of network created. The purpose here is to evaluate the trend in networking in the EU and to determine whether the EU is developing more complex forms in tackling the new problems and issues that arise.

The entries in Table 9.1 show that since 1989 there has been an explosion of EU activity in the field of networking, mostly involving DG XII, DG XIII, DG V, DG XVI and DG XXIII. Though it is clear that the EU has been active in spinning out network systems, the scarcity of data on the number of participants makes it difficult to estimate the density of these networks or the intensity of their interactions at the local level.[3] It has been reported by participants in technological innovation networks that companies tend to participate in more than one network. Thus, there may be different networks (SPRINT, COMETT, RACE and so on), but the companies participating in them are always the same. A similar pattern is found in the participation of universities in educational networks such as ERASMUS, TEMPUS, COMETT and so on. This phenomenon of single entities participating in multiple networks is also found among small and medium-sized enterprises and their supporting agencies. Euro Info Centres and Business and Innovation Centres are already participating in a variety of separate networks designed to promote the networking of SMEs in the EU.

The model of networking advanced by the EU emphasises the grass-roots or 'bottom-up' approach. Commission formulations of networks have emphasised the horizontal sectoral and individual networks containing a minimal vertical component. The EU has also stressed in the majority of its initiatives the bringing together of micro-level actors – individuals, firms, universities, local action groups, local governments and so on – to exchange information and share experiences in order to improve their individual performance and the forging of horizontal, one-to-one contractual arrangements. Networking in these contexts is conceived by the Commission as predominantly

Table 9.1 European Union Networks

Name	Mana-ging DG	Year Started	Area of Activity	Subjects Interacting	Network Objectives	Type of Network
BC-NET	XXIII	1988	SMEs	Advisers through BRE comm. system	Firm cooperation	Micro
Euro-partnership	XXIII	1988	SMEs	Business through meeting	Firm cooperation in targeted areas	Micro
EBN	XXIII	1990	SNEs	EBICs	Improve marketing of serviced firms	Micro
SPRINT	XII	1986	Technical cooperation	Advisers, firms, development agencies	Industrial and technical cooperation	Micro
VALUE	XII	1989	Technical cooperation	Firms	Disseminate EU R&D information to firms	Micro
RACE	XIII	1988	Technical cooperation	Firms	R&D work in IBC telecommunication	Micro
ESPRIT II	XIII	1988	Technical cooperation	Firms	In precompetitive R&D in information technology	Micro
COMETT I/II	XII	1986	Technical training, education in EU framework	Firms, universities, UTEPs	Establishment of industry–university consortia	Micro
DELTA	XII	1988	Technological training	Firms, universities	Technology support for learning and training at a distance	Micro

BRITE/ EURAM	XII	1989	Basic R&D in new materials	Firms	Micro
THERMIE	XVII	1989	Technical cooperation	Firms	Micro
GENOME ANALYSIS	XII	1989	Improve study of human genome	Firms	Micro
RADIATION PROTEC- TION	XII	1989	Improve radiation protection	Firms	Micro
STEP/ EPOCH	XII	1989	Environmental protection	Firms	Micro
DRIVE	XIII	1988	Improve road Transport	Firms	Micro
AIM	XIII	1988	Advanced informatics in medicine	Hospitals	Micro
EURET	VII	1989	Transport	Firms	Micro
FOREST	XII	1989	Forestry	Firms	Micro
REWARD	XII	1989	Recycling of waste	Firms	Micro
B.C.R.	XII	1988	Applied metrology	Firms	Micro
BRIDGE	XII	1989	Biotechnology	Firms	Micro

Pooling of research resources and findings

Application of new energy technology

Improvement of human genetic map, training

Research and training in radiation protection

Scientific and technical support for EU environmental policy

Information technologies for transport efficiency and road safety

Information technologies in health care

Development of EU transport network

Renewable raw materials forestry and wood products

Recycling technologies, energy from waste

Improve reliability of chemical analysis

Research and training

Table 9.1 (Cont.)

Name	Mana-ging DG	Year Started	Area of Activity	Subjects Interacting	Network Objectives	Type of Network
ECLAIR	XII	1989	Agro–industrial	Firms	Develop ag. products for industrial use	Micro
FLAIR	XII	1989	Food technologies	Firms	Improve food safety and quality	Micro
TELEMAN	XII	1989	Hazardous materials	Firms	Developing remote systems	Micro
JOULE	XII	1989	Non-nuclear energies	Firms	Develop energy technologies	Micro
MAST	XII	1989	Marine science and technology	Firms	Improve knowledge of marine environment	Micro
FAR	XIV	1987	Fisheries and aquaculture research	Firms	Develop aquaculture	Micro
SCIENCE	XII	1988	Scientific and technical Coop.	Universities	Promote training through research	Micro
SPES	XII	1989	Economists	Individuals	Develop cooperation networks	Micro
MONITOR*	XII	1989	Strategic analysis	Universities, Firms	Improve evaluation of R&D programmes	Micro
DOSES	XIII	1989	Statistical data	Universities, Firms	Promote use of advanced statistical techniques	Micro

VALUE	XIII	1989	R&D research results	SMEs	Dissemination of R&D results	Micro
INSIS	XIII	1982	Information exchange	Member states	Information exchange among member states	Micro
LEDA	V		Human resources	Local govt officials	Information and sharing of job-creation information	Micro
ERASMUS	V	1987	Human resources	University students and staff	Education mobility and cross-fertilisation	Micro
LINGUA	V	1989	Human resources	Students, workers, businessmen, teachers	Learning of other EU languages	Micro
TEMPUS	V	1990	Human resources	University firms in E. Europe with EU counterparts	Promotion of cooperation of EU and E. European universities, firms, students, staff	Micro
PETRA	V	1988	Human resources	European resources network of training partnerships	Support and upgrade national vocational education programmes	Micro
IRIS	V	1989	Human resources	Firms	Vocational training for women	Micro
FORCE	V	1990	Human resources	Firms	Encourage investment in and dissemination of innovations in vocational education	Micro
EURO-TECHNET	XII V	1985	Technology human resources	Firms, schools	Demonstration projects in information technology and vocational training	Micro

254

Table 9.1 (Cont.)

Name	Mana-ging DG	Year Started	Area of Activity	Subjects Interacting	Network Objectives	Type of Network
STRIDE	XVI	1990	Structural funds	Firms	Technological transfer less developed regions	Micro
RECITE	XVI	1991	Structural funds	Regions and cities	Joint pilot projects	Macro
ENVIREG	XI	1990	Structural funds	Firms and local govts	Environmental pilot projects	Meso
TELEMA-	XVI	1991	Structural funds	Objective 1 regions, firms	Exchange of technical information	Meso
EUROFORM	V	1991	Structural funds	Objective 1 regions, local govts, firms	Joint vocational education programmes	Meso
NOW	V	1991	Structural funds	Objective 1 regions, local govts, firms	Pilot projects for women	Meso
HORIZON	V	1991	Structural funds	Objective 1 regions, local govts, firms	Pilot projects for handicapped	Meso
LEADER	VI	1991	Structural funds	Objective 5b areas, firms	Rural development programmes	Meso
INTERREG	XVI	1990	Structural funds	Border areas	Promote economic integration	Meso

* MONITOR is further subdivided into three programmes: SAST, Strategic Analysis in Science and Technology; FAST, Forecasting and Assessment in Science and Technology; and SPEAR, Support Programme for Evaluation Activities in Research.

a technical link – such as the BRE communications system linking advisers and users of BC-NET or the ones being promoted in TELEMATIQUE, LEADER and EUROFORM programmes – but also as an aid to promoting mutually beneficial contacts between individuals and firms that previously were not connected. In the first instance, the Commission supplies the hardware and software that make the links possible, and in the latter the Commission operates as an 'incubator' for micro interpersonal networks to become established and to flourish.

The networks managed by DG XXIII and some of those promoted by the Structural Funds and the Framework Programmes are directed at facilitating contacts and developing opportunities for cooperation on a transregional basis between individuals and companies who would otherwise not be able to search for partners outside their immediate vicinity (CEC, 1990d). In these cases, networking operates to compensate for the lack of a 'vertical dimension' in SMEs – an advantage enjoyed by large, multinational corporations capable of establishing a presence in a variety of national settings – thereby facilitating exchanges between various national branches of the company and between the company and other enterprises in the pursuit of common interests. A current example is the differentiation taking place in IBM's organisational structure and research and development strategies. IBM is moving towards a far more decentralised and 'networked' model of internal and external interaction.

Thus in the EU network systems the vertical component, or central unit, is kept to a minimum. For example the BC-NET system is basically an office that manages the hardware and software of the system and helps users of the system to make contact with each other or search for more information; LEDA and PETRA are run from small coordinating offices in, respectively, London and Brussels; and COMETT is run by a committee comprising two representatives from each member state. A minimal amount of secretarial service is provided by the Commission.

In May 1990 BC-NET, currently the most advanced network in the EU, processed over 20 000 'cooperation profiles' – that is, requests for partnerships – and a substantial number of cooperative agreements had been worked out.[4] Europartnership, a cooperative arrangement between DG XXIII and DG XVI, networks in a different manner. Once again, the participants in the network are individual entrepreneurs, but rather than being put in touch with each other through a communications system, they are brought into personal contact at annual conferences (Ireland in 1989, Andalucia in 1990 and Wales in 1991). Once introduced, the expectation is that they will continue their contact through formalised agreements and joint ventures – that is, instigate contractual arrangements between their individual companies. Therefore the programme does not operate as a standing, physical network. Rather it functions as a go-between to bring companies together. Once the partnerships are formed, they operate on their own initiative and resources without further assistance. A similar approach is adopted by the COMETT programme – once agreements have been established between firms and universities they are rotated out of the system in order to make way for the 'coupling' of new participants.

All three programmes emphasise the role of networks in bringing together entities to form what in most instances is a dyadic, micro network, rather than acting as a manager of all-to-one or more institutionalised network systems that concentrate on the management of policy rather than on individual partnerships. In other words, once dyadic relationships are formed they are spun-off into formal contractual arrangements among the participants to make room for potential partners to meet and forge new links. At the present time, many of the Commission's micro networks are oriented toward the production of dyadic relationships.

A similar, if not exactly the same, approach has been used by the LEDA and FORCE programmes for the exchange of information on successful policies and experiments in tackling unemployment problems on the part of local government and economic/social development officials. These two programmes bring together officials who can benefit from an exchange of experiences in moulding their individual policies and programmes.[5]

The informality of the LEDA programme has been partially set aside in formulating the guidelines of the new generation of networks spawned by the reform of the Structural Funds and the implementation of programmes beyond 1992 in the new setting of the Single Market. LEADER, OUVERTURE,

EUROFORM, NOW, TELEMATIQUE and HORIZON foresee a much greater role for networks in bringing together regional and other governmental bodies and development agencies in Objective 1 and 5b areas. These five programmes, in fact, posit their networking system on the existence of a common communications link in the joint management of pilot projects and activities. Of necessity, the communication link will have to be supplemented by periodic meetings or seminars, where a more systematic exchange of information and brainstorming to solve common problems can take place. Thus the ongoing operationalisation of the Structural Funds is increasingly looking toward the establishment of joint information systems, data bases and management techniques that can be used across a variety of regions to standardise policy outputs and increase administrative efficiency in the field of human resources and regional development programmes receiving Commission funding. These types of initiative have the ingredients to develope into all-to-one networks where the regions share an interest in devising a common strategy for their interactions with the EU. The EU will decide how resources are to be allocated and managed and carry out ex-post evaluations of the programmes.

STRUCTURAL FUNDS NETWORKS

The new generation of Structural Funds networks, experimented with during the first phase of the Community Support Frameworks, represent a shift in focus away from the micro and toward the meso and macro forms of networking described in Figure 9.2 as they espouse the establishment of intersectoral, interfunctional and intergovernmental networks. Along these lines, DG XVI, the directorate general responsible for regional policy, has operationalised Article 10 of the ERDF regulation 4254/88 on the promotion of pilot projects among regions and cities by launching the RECITE programme. This is aimed at stimulating cooperation among subnational administrative entities in their pursuit of common objectives, such as improving administrative efficiency, achieving economies of scale by sharing the costs of common programmes, transferring know-how between the less and more developed parts of Europe, and improving the overall economic performance of less favoured regions.

The RECITE network consists of participants in cofinanced projects, but the emphasis remains, once again, on the horizontal component of the link. The only vertical aspect of the network is conceived as the periodic exchange of information between the Commission and the 'contact person' representing the pilot project. The minimum size necessary for the establishment of a RECITE cooperation scheme is two participants from different member-states, while the maximum number can be extended to ten. While the participation of two parties in our view does not constitute a network, the programme has started with modest goals in order to stimulate regions' and localities' awareness of the full potential of the approach. Though the funds available are limited, what is of great interest in the RECITE programme is that it is one of the first European network programmes to make the jump to the third level of horizontal networking in Figure 9.2 – that is, the networking of governmental bodies at the subnational level. In fact one of the prerequisites for participation is that the members of the authority have to be 'elected by universal suffrage'.

It is still too early to tell whether RECITE will encourage regions and cities to link up over a variety of policy areas, whether it will stick to its initial sector-by-sector approach, or whether the project-specific networks will be encouraged to link up with each other. The 1991 call for proposals suggested that a broader view could be applied. Pilot projects to be funded by the programme had to be concerned with economic development and improving the administrative efficiency of regional and local governments.

Conceivably, after an initial experimental phase, the programme could venture toward the creation of transregional networks with the objective of jointly managing policy programmes, but that is still far off in terms of the EUs ability to conceptualise and operationalise such entities. In most cases these programmes are geared toward the transition to the Single Market and the decision on how to organise the Structural Funds after 1993. The current orientation of the Commission is to open the way to greater and more intense intraregional networking (CEC, 1994).

Other Structural Funds programmes also hold out the prospect of evolving more complex networks. A case in point is the LEADER programme, which posits two networking tasks. Its first goal is to network rural areas through local action groups financed by the programme. It is intended to bring together various types of enterprises – agricultural, service and industrial – to coordinate development strategies and make use of common services such as marketing, market research, telecommunications systems, information on development opportunities and so on. Second, the LEADER programme envisions an overall network of various LEADER groups throughout national and EU territory so that they may share information, strategies and even markets in order to develop fully their prospects for growth.

Despite these innovations in Structural Funds programmes, there has been a counterattack on the part of nation states to protect their interests and initiatives vis-à-vis subnational entities. The best case in point is the creation of the Cohesion Fund, which has no role in the preparation and supervision of projects for the regions. However, with projects at the subnational level there is always a need for a local partner. The national government, through its transport and public-works ministries, is able to carry out necessary infrastructural work, but it is in a very difficult position to do so with regard to environmental projects. Here the natural partner is the city or town where the water-treatment plant, sewage disposal or and incinerators are located. Even if the Cohesion Fund does not explicitly foresee the possibility of sharing its findings and experimental programmes with other localities, this will become first a necessity and then a reality given the already extensive networks that link city governments and regions in the EU.

NOTES

1.   This is the line being pursued by the Mediterranean regions within the Committee of Regions in the MEDPLUS programme financed by the Commission.
2.   This is the classical form of clientelistic structure, described by

      students of politics, in representative systems with low levels of economic and social cohesion (Schmidt, Scott, Landse' and Guasti, 1977). It also describes well the networking system sustaining such organisations as the Mafia (Hess, 1973).

3.   Analysis of the density and intensity of participation would be possible with access to the list of all participants, or 'nodes', and their level of participation (that is, how many agreements or on-going programmes for cooperation do they participate in at the EU level?) in all EU-sponsored network systems.

4.   See CEC 'BC-NET Activity Report' (1990b).

5.   The VALUE and THERMIE programmes are designed to promote, respectively, the dissemination of research findings on technological innovation and energy conservation.

REFERENCES

CEC (1989) *Guide to The Reform of the Structural Funds* (Luxembourg: Office for Official Publications of the European Communities).

CEC (1990a) 'Enterprises in the European Community' (Luxembourg: Office for Official Publications of the European Communities).

CEC (1990b) 'BC-NET Activity Report: Results and assessment of the experimental phase', COM (90) 476 final, Brussels, 18 October.

CEC (1990c) 'European Economy: One Market, One Money', no. 44, October.

CEC (1990d) *EC Research Funding*, 2nd edition (Luxembourg: Office for Official Publications of the European Communities).

CEC (1991) 'COMETT I: Final Report of the Commission (1986–1990)', SEC (91) 1016 final, Brussels, 7 June.

CEC (1994) *The Future of Community Initiatives under the Structural Funds*, COM (94) 46, Brussels, 25 March.

Corradi, S. (1991) *Erasmus, Comett, Lingua, Tempus: Educazione permanente e formazione universitaria internazionale* (Milan: Franco Angeli).

Dei Ottati, G. (1994) 'Prato and its evolution in the European context' in R. Leonardi and R. Y. Nanetti (eds) *Regional Development in a Modern European Economy: The case of Tuscany* (London: Pinter), pp. 116–144.

Hess, H. (1973) *Mafia and Mafiosi: The Structure of Power* (Leyington, MA: D.C. Heath).

IFAPLAN (1990) 'PETRA Yearbook 1990' (Brussels: July).

Piore, M. and C. Sabel (1984) *The Second Industrial Divide: Possibilities for Prosperity* (New York: Basic Books).

Putnam, R. D., R. Leonardi and R. Y. Nanetti (1993) *Making Democracy Work: Civic Traditions in Modern Italy* (Princeton: Princeton University Press).

Schmidt, S. W., J. C. Scott, C. Lande' and L. Guasti (1977) *Friends, Followers, and Factions: A Reader in Political Clientelism* (Berkeley: University of California Press).

Yuill, D. (ed.) (1982) *Regional Development Agencies in Europe* (London: Gower).

10 Conclusions

THE EUROPEAN UNION AFTER MAASTRICHT

With the ratification in 1993 of the Maastricht Treaty by the British House of Commons and the dismissal of the challenge to the treaty mounted in the German constitutional court (Riechenberg, 1994), the process of deepening and widening the EU was back on track. What concerned the member states in the post-Maastricht context was the need to define the territorial parameters and political goals to be achieved by the end of this century. Thus, the first order of business was to bring to a conclusion the negotiations with the four EFTA applicants (Austria, Finland, Sweden and Norway) that were initiated in 1992.

The discussions with these applicants proceeded more expeditiously than was the case with the first expansion (that is, the accession of the UK, Ireland and Denmark) and with the last three southern European entrants (Greece, Portugal and Spain). The rate of progress in the negotiations was significantly aided by the work that had already gone into harmonising and converging policies, standards and decision-making approaches during the formation of the EEA (European Economic Area). But there were still significant issues to be hammered out, such as those involving the Common Agricultural Policy, regional funding, fisheries policy, state energy monopolies and so on.

During the negotiations it became clear that the expansion of the EU to sixteen members was reaching (or had already reached) the limits that could be achieved within the existing institutional structure and rules. Expansion was proving to be more difficult to achieve than proponents had suggested. Widening as well as deepening the EU was forcing member states to reevaluate the institutional underpinnings and overall political goals of the EU. The addition of the three Nordic countries and Austria means that all future members will be located outside the West European confines originally envisaged. Applicants include former Eastern European countries (for example Poland, Hungary and the Czech Republic), new political entities created after the collapse of Yugoslavia and the Soviet Union (for example Slovinia and the Baltic states), countries on the fringes of Europe (for example Turkey and Cyprus) and micro states within the European borders (Malta). The further expansion of the EU to include such countries would place into question the fundamental assumptions concerning the common cultural heritage and political destiny that had underpinned the Paris and Rome treaties.

Even revision of the decision-making rules necessary to incorporate the four most recent members led to brief outbursts of disagreement as to the relative weight of large and small member states when determining EU policies and the principles behind majority voting. The current compromise to maintain the momentum toward EU expansion and the automatic upgrading of decision-making rules is intended to remain valid only until the 1996 intergovernmental conference. In 1996 the EU will have to face a number of issues that were only partially addressed during the Maastricht debate. These revolve around a number of fundamental questions concerning:

1. The basic direction of the EU. Where is it headed? Will it become a complete pan-European institution or will it maintain its original Western European characteristics?
2. The institutional character of the EU. Is it an overblown, intergovernmental, international regime or will it emphasise its confederal/federal components?
3. The composition and role of European-level institutions. Will the EU continue toward Monetary Union? Will a European Federal Bank emerge from the European Monetary Institute? Will the Committee of Regions be given deliberative powers in relation to policies affecting the regions and local authorities? Will the Commission gradually become an executive body that is linked to the will of the European Parliament?
4. The balance between European institutions. Will decision-making powers remain balanced between the Council of Ministers and the European Parliament? Will national parliaments be brought into the deliberation of European-level policies? What is the Commission's future role to be?
5. The constitutionalisation of the treaties. Will the ECJ begin more formally to assume the role of a supreme court?

6. The fate of the nation-state. How will national decision-making and implementation adjust to the increasing Europeanisation of policies? What will be the impact of evolution on the nation-state and on the way nation-states are internally organised and structured?
7. The autonomy of subnational representative and governmental entities. How will the EU and nation-states respond to the increased activism of regional and local authorities in pursing their own economic and social agendas in response to increased competition and the globalisation of markets and business strategies?

The above questions will need to be addressed (though, not necessarily, thoroughly and clearly resolved) during discussions within the European institutions and during the bargaining process between member states as they work toward a mutually acceptable solution, given the current structure of available choices and solutions. Experience with the course of events and decision-making practices in the EU have made observers wary of expecting definitive answers and final solutions to such enquiries. What is most probable is that the 1996 intergovernmental conference will produce, once again, not final clarification, but piecemeal responses to the issues presented above, and the suggestion that final resolution of complex problems be postponed until the next intergovernmental conference.

The evolution of the EU has belied the expectations of, on the one hand, current federalists and former neofunctionalists, who expected full and rapid consolidation of the role and power of supranational European institutions over member states and, on the other hand, state-sovereignty advocates, who argue that the nation-state continues to reign supreme and has not lost any of its power and sovereignty to the evolving EU. Despite the avowed goals of both approaches, the models and paradigms that have dominated the study of European integration do not provide us with a clear prediction of what will happen in the near future, or of how the EU will devise answers to the current list of issues to be resolved.

The lack of guidance in predicting the future of the EU is to a great extent due to the less than adequate formulation and testing of hypotheses concerning the nature of integration, especially during the last two decades, which have witnessed an acceleration of European integration and also the abandonment of empirical studies on the direction and content of the EU. The reasons for these shortcomings can be traced to the evolution of research on European integration.

FEDERALISM AND FUNCTIONALISM

The federalist approach to European integration has never been primarily analytical in nature. Rather it has been prescriptive. The European federalists have been interested in advocating European unification (Dutheil de la Rochere, 1992; Burgess, 1989) as a means of responding to the limitations of the nation-state in the postwar period.

From an intellectual perspective, the federalists were the first to establish the difference between intergovernmentalism and supranationalism. For the federalists, the ECSC and EEC were the building blocks of an integrated Europe, whose goal it was to create a viable supranational system: the original goal was federal while the means was intergovernmental, given the existing institutional limitations (Spinelli, 1957).[1]

Federalists viewed the nation-state as incapable of (1) providing solutions to structural problems or forming adequate economic policies to meet the challenges of the globalized economy, (2) forging a common approach to military security and foreign policy, and (3) uniting the European people to assume their proper political role in world affairs. In 1957 Hans Nord, secretary general of the Netherlands Council of the European Movement, voiced the need to overcome the traditional parameters of the nation-state in finding solutions to Europe's postwar problems:

> we find that in the exercise of three most fundamental tasks of our national communities, namely the pursuit of prosperity, defense, and foreign policy, our national sovereignty has become largely fictitious. We are hampered and checked by the very frontiers which, in an earlier age, were formed to protect and safeguard our national existence. This is the sickness for which integration recommends itself as a remedy. The walls dividing the nations of western Europe must

disappear, for they no longer serve the true interests of our citizens. A free flow of men, capital, and services throughout the area must be made possible (Nord, 1957, pp. 216–17).

However, what has been missing in the federalist approach is a realistic analysis of current affairs and the formulation of a viable programme through which a federal Europe could be constructed. The EDC treaty represented the federalists' preferred way of proceeding, and when it was defeated the pendulum swung back to the functionalists, who emphasised a sector-by-sector approach rather than the multisector and political-institution-building stance assumed by the federalists. European federalism has been significantly absent from mainstream academic debate on European integration. Federalism is conceived by the literature as more of a utopia than an appropriate paradigm to analyse the current state of European affairs. The reason for this is that, in the past, federalists have placed politics and political goals in front of economics, but the track record of the EU demonstrates the opposite trend: economics have led politics. Where political integration has been achieved it has been because of the logic of the market and the exigencies of producers (Pinder, 1993).

If federalism represents a possible scenario for the future institutional structure of the EU, it is generally agreed that it must be achieved in a gradual, piecemeal fashion (Wistrich, 1989). The basic federalising institutions in Europe are the European Court of Justice and the European Parliament. The ECJ's purpose is to ensure that integration is based on a definable and enforceable legal structure, and not simply on intergovernmental agreements. Parliament, on the other hand, reflects the unity of the European people and the ability to represent their interests on a direct basis.

The functions of the EU can, in turn, be federalised through two different strategies. The first is to introduce a constitutional separation of powers among European, national and subnational institutions. The second is to absorb the Commission into the Parliament, so that it becomes an elected body with direct links to the organ of citizen representation rather than one appointed by the governments of Europe. The concept of subsidiarity represents in many ways the opening round in defining a federal differentiation of responsibilities for decision making and implementation in the EU (Weiler, 1994). In addition, the introduction of subsidiarity does not at all assume that the appropriate sub-EU level to which policies can and should be allocated is necessarily the national level. In fact the regionalisation of policies in service delivery and economic production suggests that the regions and cities have assumed an important de facto role in these areas. Thus the logic of adequate policy areas and efficiency in implementation would lead to an increased emphasis on solutions that are focused on a division of labour between different levels in the federalising institutional structure.

In a parallel fashion to federalism, the functionalist approach has not been supported by the reality of European integration (Mitrany, 1975). The creation of functional regimes to handle individual policy sectors made its appearance at the beginning of the postwar period through a combination of economic and political international regimes: the European Payments Union, the OEEC, the Council of Europe and, to a certain extent, the European Coal and Steel Community. Mitrany, for one, welcomed the creation of the ECSC as a functional authority but was a severe critic of the results of the 1955 Messina conference and the creation of the EEC.

What disappointed functionalists in the operation of the EEC was that (1) from the beginning the construction of governance mechanisms in Europe have been multisectoral in nature, and (2) the setting-up of economic governance institutions has always been accompanied by the creation of a parallel system of political organisations, whose scope and authority has been broader than the confines of current economic policies.

The ECJ, for instance, was created as a European-level institution by the ECSC, and the concept of community law in providing the legal foundation for the operation of European level institutions found its origin in the 1951 treaty. The representative EU branches (the European Assembly and the European Parliament) went beyond the specific necessities of functional regimes. Instead they found their raison d'être in representing the constituent citizens of the EU and providing a democratic political base for decision making at the supranational level (Dinan, 1994).

The current version of the functional approach to international organisation – international regime theory – also has difficulty in taking into account the significance and impact of the ECJ and the European Parliament as motors driving European integration. These two institutions place the EU in a significantly different position vis-à-vis international regimes. As James Rosenau (1992) has observed, international regimes represent only one part of a broader spectrum of international governance arrangements. Governance can be supplied by government but it is not limited to government or intergovernmental arrangements. Governance is a broader concept in which activities are backed by shared goals and values. In some cases these goals and values remain informal in nature, while in others they become increasingly formalised. Institutional and legal formalisation can proceed to the point where a constitution is recognised to exist and serves as the basis for defining the goals and values of the new political structure, as agreed to by the constituent elements, be they states or ordinary citizens.

According to the definition of governance advanced by Rosenau, the EU could be seen as having undergone an evolution that began when a series of policy areas (that is, international regimes) were moulded together and solidified by the cement of politics, law and supranational institutions, thereby providing the basis for an alternative state system. Supranational systems thereby become one potential means of solving the problems of international governance. Supranational systems are more complex and politically more unified than single-sector regimes or free-trade areas, which lack supranational political frameworks and objectives.

Thus reducing the EU to the status of a generic international regime does no service to the complexity of the European experiment. Nor does it help us to develop theories of international governance that are capable of distinguishing among different types of governance mechanisms and able to predict, given local or temporal circumstances, which kind of governance mechanism will emerge. Such an approach also runs the risk of losing the richness and diversity that neofunctionalists were able to capture in their original work on European integration.

THE DEMISE OF NEOFUNCTIONALISM

Neofunctionalism committed intellectual suicide in 1975 when its founder, Ernst B. Haas, decreed the obsolescence of regionalist theory. In *The Obsolescence of Regionalist Theory*, Haas acknowledged that neofunctionalism had not been able to account for the evolution of the EC. In addition, the expectation that the process of integration would manifest itself in other parts of the world was shattered by the course of world events during the late 1960s and early 1970s. Regional organisations in Africa, Latin America and Asia were disintegrating rather then integrating. Since 1975 there has been no new attempt to revitalise the neofunctionalist approach to integration through further theoretical formulation or empirical studies.

Before drawing the curtain on neofunctionalism, it is useful to identify the major contributions it made to the study of European integration. First of all, neofunctionalists were the first to attempt to place European unification into a wider international context by highlighting the increased interdependence of states in the postwar period, the internationalisation of economic activities, the advantages of collective action among member states through the formulation of common policies to common problems, the role of alternative forces within the nation-state in the determination of policy choices and outcomes, the realisation of economies of scale in putting together multisectoral responses to functional problems within a single institutional context, and the limits of the nation-state in responding to current crises (Haas, 1958; 1964).[2] However the contribution of the neofunctionalists went beyond merely identifying problems arising in the study of supranational institutions; they also pointed to ways in which they could be studied in an empirical manner.

Neofunctionalism supplemented its theoretical formulations with specific concepts for the study of the changes taking place within European-level institutions and the nation-state. Before 1975 the neofunctionalists had begun to make significant inroads into dissecting the content and processes by which decisions were being made and implemented at the European level, and the impact these changes were having on the functioning of the nation-states. Theoretical considerations were placed into empirical categories and tested and analysed over an extended period of time in order to identify the longitudinal changes that were taking place.

A particularly important contribution to the transformation of neofunctionalism from a theoretical projection of the future Western European state system to an empirically based longitudinal testing of hypotheses was made by Leon Lindberg and Stuart Scheingold in 1970. In *Europe's Would-Be Polity*, the authors broke down the scope of the EC system into four main functions: external relations, political–constitutional, social–cultural and economic. These functions were, in turn, disaggregated into empirical categories that were quantified and compared over four time periods (1950, 1957, 1968 and 1970). Each category was then classified according to a five-point scale that covered a spectrum of decision-making foci, ranging from one where all decision-making initiatives were national to one where the initiatives were 'all-Community' (Lindberg and Scheingold, 1970, pp. 75–6). The analysis showed that whereas in 1950 decision making in all twenty-two categories was 'all national', by 1970 only five categories remained as such whilst twelve (predominantly those with social and economic functions) had witnessed a growing sharing of responsibilities between national and EC organs.

If the twenty-two categories of EC action used by Lindberg and Scheingold were to be updated, one would find more and more policy areas being included in the intermediate categories of greater supranational involvement, as illustrated in Table 10.1. Neofunctionalists demonstrated how governmental functions do not remain irrevocably imbedded at one level of the institutional structure. They migrate to other levels and that migration might have political ramifications on the dynamics of political representation and interest-group activity. Neofunctionalists did not assume away, as was to be the case with intergovernmentalists, their definition of the functions of the state, the content of national interest and the powers allocated to supranational institutions. Rather they subjected policy making and implementation at both levels to a process of empirical verification.

This line of research was endowed with considerable theoretical power because it was based on a breakdown of both European-level and national institutions according to a series

Table 10.1 The shift in nation-state and European Union locis of decision for policy areas, 1950–1994

	1950	1957	1968	1970	1994
External relations functions					
1. Military security	1	1	1	1	2
2. Diplomatic influence and participation in world affairs	1	1	2	2	3
3. Economic and military aid to other polities	1	1	2	2	3
4. Commercial relations with other polities	1	1	3	4	5
Political–constitutional functions					
5. Public health and safety and maintenance of order	1	1	2	2	3
6. Political participation	1	1	1	1	2
7. Access to legal-normative system (civic authority)	1	2	3	3	4
Social–cultural functions					
8. Cultural and recreational affairs	1	1	1	1	2
9. Education and research	1	1	3	3	3
10. Social welfare policies	1	2	2	3	3

Economic functions

11. Counter-cyclical policy	1	2	3	3	4
12. Regulation of economic competition and other government controls on prices and investments	1	2	3	4	4
13. Agricultural protection	1	2	3	3	4
14. Economic development and planning	1	1	4	4	4
15. Exploitation and protection of natural resources	1	2	2	3	4
16. Regulation and support of transportation	1	2	2	2	3
17. Regulation and support of mass media of communication	1	2	2	3	4
18. Labour–management relations	1	1	1	1	2
19. Fiscal policy	1	1	1	3	3
20. Balance-of-payments stability	1	1	3	4	4
21. Domestic monetary policy	1	1	2	2	4
22. Movement of goods, services and other factors of production	1	2	4	4	5

Key: Locus of decision: 1 = all national; 2 = low presence of Union; 3 = both, national predominates; 4 = both, EU predominates; 5 = all EU.

Source: List of policy areas and 1950–70 figures from Lindberg and Scheingold, (1970, p. 71). 1994 figures author's own calculations.

of parameters (for example goals, processes and outcomes) as well as on quantification of the component parts of each institutional level (for example executives, bureaucracies, interest groups, individual personalities, courts and so on). Thus changes in one part of the governmental system could be analysed with regard to its impact on other parts of the institutional structure and on civil society. To their credit, the neofunctionalists did not begin with the assumption that institutions operate in a unitary manner and on the basis of one constant set of defined interests. In addition they did not shy away from difficult theoretical problems, such as defining institutional interests and analysing the coherency of actions. Instead they operationalised them and compared them over time and at different levels.

That the results often did not come up to the expectations of the original theoretical formulations was generally acknowledged. The goal of the neofunctionalists was not to certify the demise of the nation-state nor to herald the supremacy of supranational state systems. Rather it was to study how the functions of states were changing in the post-Second-World-War context and how new supranational institutions were increasingly being allocated functional roles *by* the nation-states within a logic of collective action and a policy of economies of scale that were radically different from the logic followed by nation-states during the interwar period.

When the goals of European integration were reaffirmed in the mid-1980s and the EC undertook significant steps toward ever closer union, the neofunctionalists were no longer capable of continuing their research and verifing their initial hypotheses with new data; the school had been disbanded.

REALISTS AND INTERGOVERNMENTALISTS

The void left by the neofunctionalists was only in part filled by alternative schools of thought. During the 1980s intergovernmentalists reaffirmed the role of the state in the international arena and the fundamental role played by the pursuit of state interests in motivating state actions and decisions.[3] Paul Taylor (1983, 1993) has argued that the members of the EU have not lost or compromised their sovereignty by becoming involved in the process of collective decision making that characterises the Council. Rather, sovereignty has been pooled, and it can be recaptured whenever the state desires. For Taylor (1993, p. 104) the freedom of action of a state is 'conventionally defined' and sovereignty is therefore 'the right to act within those limits'. Taylor's approach to sovereignty is relativitic, to the point that 'its perceived aspects change over time'. Sovereignty is what governments perceive it to be 'at that particular time'.

The basis for Taylor's conception of sovereignty is that an institutional structure such as the EU is fundamentally a voluntary association, and governments can at any time withdraw from the entangling alliance. From this perspective, the primacy of EU law over the content of British Acts of Parliament is tolerated because the British Parliament has given (and continues to give) its support to the substance and obligations of the 1972 Community Act. If it were to pass an ordinary piece of legislation abrogating the Act, British courts would no longer have to abide by ECJ rulings (Taylor, 1993, p. 95). Thus the voluntary nature of adherence to the outputs of the European policy-making process suggests for Taylor that state sovereignty and the pursuit of state interests have not been compromised by European integration or increased the power of European bodies (for example the ECJ and the EP) not strictly controlled by national governments.

In support of this, Taylor and other proponents of the intergovernmental approach to explaining European decision making and bargaining have contributed detailed descriptions of salient moments in the history of the EU. However the contributions made by the intergovernmentalists have come at the expense of empirically defined concepts and the inclusion of variables relevant to the integration process, the disaggregation of collective actors such as the 'state' into their component parts (individual leaders, dynamics within the executive, executive–legislative relationships, the role of political parties and factions and so on), and specification of what exactly lies behind such broad concepts as 'state interest' and 'sovereignty'.

Intergovernmentalists have introduced an important new realism into the analysis of EU activities, but they have done so at the expense of empirically verifying some of their basic axioms. All sensitivity to differences within institutions and across time have been lost by emphasising the state as a unitary actor.

A case in point is offered by analyses of the bargaining over the Single European Act (Taylor, 1993; Moravcsik, 1991). In an initial account of the origins of the Single Market, Sandholtz and Zysman (1989) emphasised the role of the business community (Roundtable of European Industrialists) and European-level institutions (Parliament and Commission). Taylor and Moravcsik shifted the emphasis to the Council of Ministers of the European Council, and the role played by nation-states and their leaders in the negotiations and conflicts that characterised the difficult birth of the SEA.

While it is easy to accept the criticism that the emphasis on European-level institutions and international business groups does not represent a complete explanation of the birth and passage of the Single European Act, in a parallel fashion the intergovernmentalists do not provide us with a satisfactory explanation of the dynamic of the decision.[4] First of all, they do not explain how the idea of the single market was born and nurtured in the European debate. We may not accept the explanation that the Commission, the European Parliament or the businessmen's Roundtable exclusively or even decisively placed the goal of the single market at the top of the political agenda at the Milan summit in 1985, but it is difficult not to give them credit for keeping the issue alive and setting about creating the coalition of domestic and international interests that pushed first the Commission and then the Council into taking action. The question is not who played the predominant role, but how the decision was made through the interaction of a variety of individual and institutional actors over what proved to be a relatively short period of time.

Secondly, the intergovernmentalists seem not to have noticed the ECJ's existence and contribution to European integration, nor the fundamental role played by the ECJ in establishing the theoretical basis for the single market by its 1979 Cassis de Dijon ruling. An account of the role of the ECJ was also missing in the neofunctionalists' analysis of the dynamic of European integration. While it is possible to understand the benign neglect under which the court operated in the 1960s and 1970s, it is more difficult to do so in the late 1980s when the impact of EC law generated a significant literature (Weiler, 1994).

Thirdly, the reasons for the switch in French Socialist Party attitudes away from nationalisation and autarky in the early 1980s are not at all explained by the intergovernmentalists in terms of the difficulties incurred in implementing the nationalisation policies and being able to control domestic interest groups and international economic forces. Despite the emphasis placed by intergovernmentalists on the importance of the dynamics of domestic politics, for them the changes in national attitudes toward nationalisation, the integration of European markets, institutional reforms and so on seem to have sprung forth, like Athena from the head of Zeus, fully grown from the minds of European leaders.

Fourthly, the zig zags of Margaret Thatcher on the SEA and ERM and the dramatic about-faces undertaken by Conservative Party leaders on the issues of enlargement and majority voting cannot be explained in a satisfactory manner on the basis of state interest and collective state actors. Rather, Taylor's relativistic approach to sovereignty suggests that once nation-states are prevented from implementing their own definitions of sovereignty they set about changing their definition of sovereignty. The same also applies to the state as a collective actor. The attitudes and strategies on European integration assumed by the Conservative Party have been characterised by a significant level of intraparty conflict (Conservatives do not have a single definition of sovereignty, nor of national interest), contrasting signals from important interest groups (for example the CBI has consistently supported European integration while parts of the 'popular press' have been strongly hostile), and even differing abilities to learn and draw conclusions from ongoing national, European and world events: The entry of the UK into the ERM and the events that led to the fall of Thatcher are illustrative of the widely different conclusions drawn by cabinet members of the impact of international trends on the viability of the attempt to formulate an independent national approach to monetary, industrial and fiscal policies.

Fifth, why should intergovernmentalists' considerations of interstate bargaining over the SEA, the Maastricht Treaty, EMS, ERM or other aspects of European integration be constantly limited to Germany, France and the UK? Has the UK really been part of a trilateral relationship that has dominated decision making in the EU? Accounts of European summit meetings in the 1980s and 1990s have shown the UK to be the odd man out in Europe rather than being at the heart of decision making. Intergovernmentalist accounts pay very little attention to the role played by the other two large states – Italy and Spain – or to that played by the smaller states.

The historical record shows that the Italian government played a very important role in managing the discussions on the single market at the Milan (1985) summit and in undermining Thatcher's domestic stance at the October 1990 Rome summit (Hine, 1992). In a similar fashion, the Spanish government played a prominent part in the Edinburgh summit (1992) and in the entry negotiations with the four EFTA countries. Greece is another country whose role has been important in terms of changing the approach and content of the EU's regional and foreign policies. On closer scrutiny, we could come up with similar considerations for other governments in a variety of other summits. The role of smaller states in the EU decision-making process has not been negligible. According to the decision-making rules adopted with the passage of the Single European Act, the 'minor' governments could have blocked the realisation of the goals of the 'big three' had they wished to do so, or if they had been dissatisfied with the 'side payments' offered to them. Intergovernmentalists' empirical accounts of EU decision making have little to do with reality – they are not faithful accounts of events and they ignore an important component of joint decision making that is a fundamental part of the integration process.

With the end of the Cold War the larger states are painfully waking up to the reality that smaller states cannot be so easily subjugated. The cases of Somalia, Rwanda, Bosnia, Haiti and Israel are indicative of the relative autonomy of local forces and the ability of small states to resist the policy preferences of larger states. In addition, the difficulty larger states have in taking into account the wishes and exigencies of the smaller states reflects their inability to understand the fundamental changes introduced into interstate relations with the creation of international regimes. Adherence to international regimes reflects in part the desire of smaller states to overcome the shortcomings of international economic exchange and power relationships defined by traditional interstate relations and big-power relations as well as the growing difficulty of larger states in controlling small state behaviour. As argued by Paul Taylor (1993, p. 105), the creation and consolidation of European institutions allows smaller states to gain leverage over the hegemony of larger states in the field of monetary (Bundesbank), military (NATO), commercial (GATT) and foreign (EPC) policies, which would have been unthinkable in a system in which nation-states operated on their own behalf and in pursuit of their individual interests.

Integration has in this context fundamentally changed the structure and dynamic of interstate relations in Europe. On the one hand it has reined in the interests of the larger states, and on the other it has permitted societal interests to escape from the domination of national governments. As we have seen above, the strategy of networking has allowed subnational governments as well as interest groups to find alternative ways of obtaining resources and influencing decision making at the European level, where the size of their budget and their discretionary role in allocating resources places European institutions in an important position to reward those groups that have mounted a strategy to influence European-level institutions.

In addition to these specific failings in the intergovernmentalist approach, there is a fundamental failing that is more structural in nature. It is tied to their definition (or lack thereof) of 'state interest'. Analyses, of course, of European integration by intergovernmentalists do not begin with a definition of the state or of state interest. Without a clear definition of the state and its interests it is difficult to proceed with an analysis of how this interest has been protected, furthered and enhanced as a result of interstate bargaining.

In 1989 James Rosenau argued that the study of the role of the state in decision making and international relations is 'plagued with methodological difficulties'. Everywhere the concept is evoked to explain outcomes, but nowhere is it defined. More commonly, the concept of the state been used as an 'all-purpose residual category for analysing those macroprocesses that cannot be readily explained through the observation and cumulation of microphenomenon' (Rosenau, 1989, p. 24).

The same problem is inherent in defining state interest.

Alan Milward and Vibeke Sorensen (1993) argue that the interests of European nation-states led to some (Belgium, France and Germany) banding together to form the European Coal and Steel Community in 1951, while in the UK the definition of state interest as interpreted by both Labour and Conservative governments and the steel and coal industries led to exactly the opposite conclusion.

In Italy the interests of the private and public steel sectors to protect themselves against external competition were counterbalanced by the government's interest in facilitating emigration and easing the social pressure created by land reform and high levels of unemployment. In 1951 the De Gasperi government did not hesitate to adherc to the ECSC, and the logic was repeated in 1957 with the EEC Treaty. By the end of the 1960s and 1970s the gains derived from European integration proved to be much greater than any Italian politician had expected or dreamed of during the dawn of European integration (Romero, 1993; Francioni, 1992).

As Linda Cornett and James Caporaso (1992, pp. 240–1) have observed, one of the fundamental contributions of the neofunctionalists was to conceive of state interactions within the confines of European integration as a means of redefining individual state interests. The national interest cannot be assumed to be a static concept; detailed accounts of European-level bargaining show that it undergoes change and redefinition as leaders learn from interaction and seek to adapt to extra-national events and trends.

The lack of a precise definition of state interest leads to the other weakness of intergovernmentalist analysis. State interest is whatever the existing government defines it as being. Thus we have the phenomenon of a rolling definition of state interest that changes over time and from one political leader to another. This approach does not provide the basis for building theory or dissecting the changes and impacts of policies on existing national attitudes, concepts and structures in response to the forces of integration.

Rosenau has attributed the emergence of an empirically rolling definition of state interest to the 'cascading interdependence' of nation-states, which has narrowed the scope for individual state decision making and action, thereby increasing its dependence on international components and cooperation in resolving internal problems. In other words, to be effective at home nation-states have to become members of international governance mechanisms and institutions (Rosenau, 1992, pp. 3–4). It is understandable why national governments have come up with a variety of mechanisms to justify their participation in international and supranational organisations, their loss of sovereignty, the broadening of national and state interests, and collective action. But it is surprising that scholars assume that all of these changes have not led to a redefinition of national interest, the workings of the nation-state, or relations of citizens toward political institutions and policy choices. Rather than being assumed, they need to be studied on the basis of empirical evidence and relevant conceptualisations of state and interstate behaviour.

THE CONVERGENCE APPROACH TO EUROPEAN INTEGRATION

The need to supplement the insights provided by intergovernmentalism with more empirically oriented research into integration has been present since the demise of neofunctionalism. The frontiers of research must be pushed beyond current disciplinary lines to incorporate the contributions made by economists (Nevin, 1990; Molle, 1990; McDonald and Dearden, 1992), students of EU law (Cappelletti, Weiler and Secombe, 1986; Burley and Mattli, 1993; MacCormick, 1993; Mancini, 1994) and the multitude of political scientists, economic and diplomatic historians, social-policy analysts, regional scientists and students of international relations who have been working on the origins and dynamics of integration. The study of the EU can no longer be restricted or contained within disciplinary boundaries, policy areas or institutional levels. To understand what is happening in the evolution of European domestic and international politics we must adopt multidisciplinary, multilevel, comparative and longitudinal approaches. Considerations of the EU are not limited to supranational decisions and affairs. They also emerge in the analysis of national and local politics. The complexity and multiplicity of the impacts of European-level decisions also require the adoption of a comparative and longitudinal approach that is capable of delving into the various facets of institutional behaviour.

An example of how these disciplines can be brought together to advance the study of the dynamics of European integration is provided by the convergence model presented in Chapter 6. Even though intergovernmentalists have recognised that convergence is taking place in economic models and public policies (Biersteker, 1992), they have not sought to study the causes of these pressures but only their institutional consequences. As a result they have not been able to link the causes of convergence with their consequences, and have therefore been restricted to studying the various differences reflected in regimes throughout the world.

Convergence suggests that we should be studying both parts of the equation: the causes of convergence and the responses to convergence devised by existing institutions. Without studying both sides of the cause and effect relationship (if that is what exists) we cannot start to build theoretical constructs to predict future developments or adequately explain what has taken place in the past. This represents the future challenge for students of European integration.

NOTES

1. For the federalists, the common interest of Europe was not adequately reflected in the summation of different national interests. Rather it must exist 'on its own level and in its own right' (Nord, 1957, p. 219). However it was clear to the federalists that the nation-state could not be abolished overnight. Adequate institutional structures at the supranational level had to be created to fill the institutional and political vacuum, and that the process would take a long time.
2. On the economics of integration see, among others, Nevin, 1990.
3. International regime theory emerged from the writings of Keohane (1984) and Krasner (1983). The continued importance of the state in the pursuit of the national interest and the limits of European integration have been forcefully argued by Taylor (1983), Milward (1984, 1992, 1993), Moravcsik (1991), Hoffmann (1974) and Keohane and Hoffmann (1991).

4.   For a more balanced account of the origins, negotiations and implications of the SEA, see Cameron, 1992.
5.   See the discussion in Weiler (1993).

REFERENCES

Biersteker, T. (1992) 'The "triumph" of neoclassical economics in the developing world: policy convergence and bases of governance in the international economic order', in J. Rosenau and E. Czempiel (eds), *Governance without Government: Order and Change in World Politics* (Cambridge: Cambridge University Press), pp. 102–31.

Burgess, M. (1989) *Federalism and European Union* (London: Routledge).

Burley, A. and W. Mattli (1993) 'Europe Before the Court: A Political Theory of Legal Integration', *International Organization*, vol. 47, no. 1, pp. 41–76.

Cameron, D. R. (1992) 'The 1992 Initiative: Causes and Consequences', in A. Sbragia (ed.), *Euro-Politics* (Washington, DC: The Brookings Institution), pp. 23–74.

Cappelletti, M., J. Weiler and M. Secommbe (1986) (eds) *Integration through Law* (Berlin: deGruyter).

Cornett, L. and J. Caporaso (1992) '"And still it moves!" State interests and social forces in the European Community', in J. Rosenau and E. Czempiel (eds), *Governance without Government: Order and Change in World Politics* (Cambridge: Cambridge University Press), pp. 219–49.

Dutheil de la Rochere, J. (1992) 'Toward a Federal Europe', in B. Nelson, D. Roberts and W. Veit (eds), *The European Community in the 1990s* (Oxford: Berg), pp. 3–16.

Francioni, F. (ed.) (1992) *Italy and EC Membership Evaluated* (London: Pinter).

Haas, E. B. (1958) *The Uniting of Europe* (Stanford: Stanford University Press).

Haas, E. B. (1964) *Beyond the Nation-State* (Stanford: Stanford University Press).

Haas, E. B. (1975) *The Obsolescence of Regionalist Theory* (Berkeley: Institute of International Affairs).

Hine, D. (1992) 'Italy and Europe: the Italian presidency and the domestic management of European Community affairs' in R. Leonardi and F. Anderlini (eds), *Italian Politics: A Review*, vol. 6 (London: Pinter), pp. 50–68.

Hoffmann, S. (1974) 'Obstinate or Obsolete? France, European Integration and the Fate of the Nation-State', in S. Hoffmann *et al.* (eds), *Decline or Renewal? France Since the 1930s* (New York: Viking Press), pp. 363–399.

Keohane, R. O. (1984) *After Hegemony: Cooperation and Discord in the World Political Economy* (Princeton: Princeton University Press).

Keohane, R. O. and S. Hoffmann (1991) 'Institutional Change in Europe in the 1980s', in R. O. Keohane and S. Hoffmann (eds), *The New European Community: Decisionmaking and Institutional Change* (Boulder: Westview Press), pp. 1–40.

Krasner, S. (ed.) (1983) *International Regimes* (Cornell: Cornell University Press).

Lindberg, L. and S. Scheingold (1970) *Europe's Would-Be Polity* (Englewood Cliffs, NJ: Prentice-Hall).

MacCormick, N. (1993) 'Beyond the Sovereign State', *Modern Law Review*, vol. 56, no. 1, pp. 1–18.

Mancini, F. (1994) 'Democracy and the European Court of Justice', *Modern Law Review*, vol. 57, no. 2, pp. 175–190.

McDonald, R. and S. Dearden (1992) *European Economic Integration* (London: Longman).

Milward, A. S. (1984) *The Reconstruction of Western Europe, 1945–51* (London: Meuthen).

Milward, A. S. (1992) *The European Rescue of the Nation-State* (London: Routledge).

Milward, A. S. *et al.* (1993) *The Frontier of National Sovereignty: History and Theory, 1945–92* (London: Routledge).

Milward, A. S. and V. Sorensen (1993) 'Interdependence or integration? A national choice', in A. Milward *et al.*, *The Frontier of National Sovereignty: History and Theory, 1945–92* (London: Routledge), pp. 1–32.

Mitrany, D. (1975) *The Functional Theory of Politics* (New York: St. Martin's Press).

Molle, W. T. M (1990) *The Economics of European Integration: Theory, Practice, Policy* (Aldershot: Dartmouth).

Moravcsik, A. (1991) 'Negotiating the Single European Act', in R. Keohane and S. Hoffmann (eds), *The New European Community* (Boulder: Westview Press), pp. 41–84.

Moravcsik, A. (1994) 'Preferences and Power in the European Community: A Liberal Intergovernmentalist Approach', in S. Bulmer and A. Scott (eds), *Economic and Political Integration in Europe* (Oxford: Blackwell), pp. 29–80.

Nevin, E. (1990) *The Economics of Europe* (New York: St. Martin's Press).

Nord, H. (1957) 'In Search of a Political Framework for an Integrated Europe', in C. G. Haines (ed.), *European Integration* (Baltimore: Johns Hopkins University Press), pp. 215–30.

Pinder, J. (1993) 'The Single Market: a step toward union', in J. Lodge (ed.), *The European Community and the Challenge of the Future*, 2nd edition (London: Pinter), pp. 51–68.

Riechenberg, K. (1994) 'Comments on the Ruling of the German Constitutional Court on the Maastricht Treaty', *ECSA Newsletter* (Winter), pp. 16–17.

Romero, F. (1993) 'Migration as an issue in European interdependence and integration: the case of Italy' in A. S. Milward *et al.*, *The Frontier of National Sovereignty: History and Theory, 1945–92* (London: Routledge), pp. 33–58.

Rosenau, J. (1992) 'Governance, order, and change in world politics', in J. Rosenau and E. Czempiel (eds), *Governance without Government: Order and Change in World Politics* (Cambridge: Cambridge University Press), pp. 1–29.

Rosenau, J. (1989) 'The State in an Era of Cascading Politics: Wavering Concept, Widening Competence, Withering Colossus, or Weathering Change?', in J. Caporaso (ed.), *The Elusive State* (London: Sage), pp. 17–48.

Sandholtz, W. and J. Zysman (1989) '1992: Recasting the European Bargain', *World Politics*, vol. 42 (October), pp. 95–128.

Spinelli, A. (1957) 'The Growth of the European Movement since World War II', in C. G. Haines (ed.), *European Integration* (Baltimore: Johns Hopkins University Press), pp. 37–63.

Taylor, P. (1983) *The Limits of European Integration* (London: Croom Helm).

Taylor, P. (1993) *International Organization in the Modern World* (London: Pinter).

Weiler, J. (1994) 'Journey to an Unknown Destination: A Retrospective and Prospective of the European Court of Justice in the Arena of Political Integration', in S. Bulmer and A. Scott (eds), *Economic and Political Integration in Europe* (Oxford: Blackwell), pp. 131–60.

Wistrich, E. (1989) *After 1992, The United States of Europe* (London: Routledge).

Index